A WAR OF CHAOS AND FURY - PART I

THE LEVANTHRIA SERIES
BOOK FIVE

A.P BESWICK

A.P BESWICK PUBLICATIONS

ISBN

Hardback - 978-1-916671-30-0

Paperback - 978-1-916671-31-7

Editing - Quinn Nichols - Quill and Bone Editing

Cover Design - Rafido Designs

THE MERRY MEN.... AND WOMEN

Seth (The Little) Alexander
Joshua (The Scarlett) Gray
Daniel (The Friar) Dorman
Robin (The Hood) Hill

The Legendary Pieces Of Eight

Seth (Blackbeard) Alexander
Z (The Sparrow)

THE DRAGON

Louis Jay Dombroski
Jen Smith
Zaakir (The Archer) Patel
Sunny Side Up
Señor Neo
Jacob Salm
Rhonda K Koenning
Brandon H Beers
Jeremiah Silva
Seth Alexander
Christopher Simard
Matthew Schaaff
Armin Enjoyer of Well Written Books
Damien Troutman
Meredith Carstens
Tanya Hagel
Michael William
Alexander Gonser

THE DRAGON

Andrew Sheridan
Ian White
Geoff Seutter
R. S. Howell
Brian R Knoblich
Kevin Camps
Benjamin Powell
Oliver Stegmann
Lauren O'Connor
Travis Hawkins
Joshua Gray
Troy Hauck, RN
Kat Holder
Christian Mays
Dominic Jones
Charlotte Lotte de Reuver Valerie Wiechmann and Shane
Libihoul

LEGENDS OF LEVANTHRIA

NeonPixxius
Trevor "TJ" Meeds
Heather Dangerfield
Louis Dombroski
Oleg
Samuel Bellis
Joe Wright
Samuel Silveira
Steven Hessing
Nathanial Landreville
Johnathon VandenHeuvel
Brandon Beers
Philip J. Harley
Alexander Edwards
Brandon Blayney
Bonnielee Radford

Forest of Opiya

Pendaren Hills

Eltera

Gondoron Pass

T

M

Askela

Osar

och Bragoa

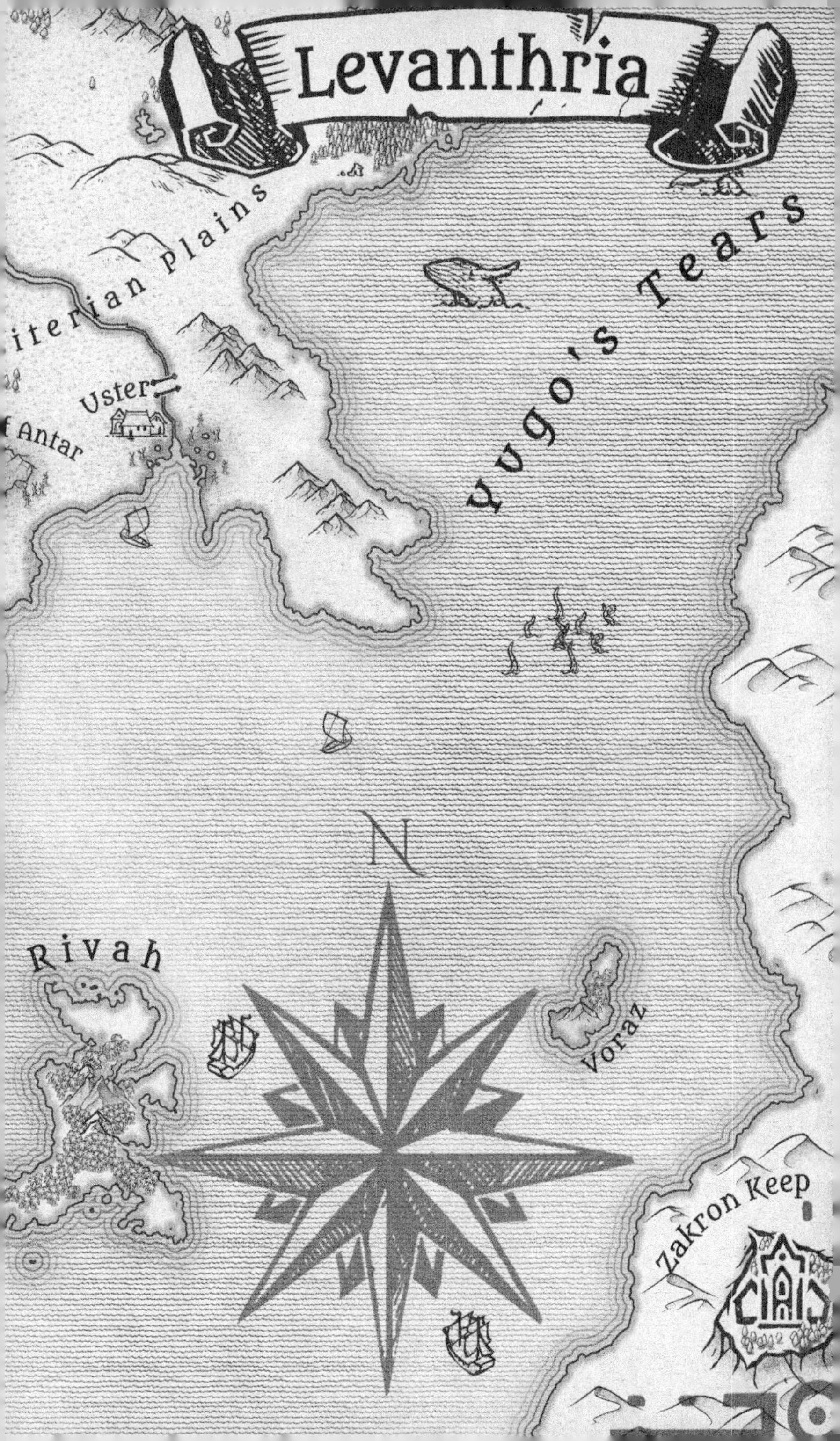
Levanthria
iterian Plains
Uster
f Antar
Yugo's Tears
N
Rivah
Voraz
Zakron Keep

BOOK FIVE OF
THE LEVANTHRIA SERIES

A WAR OF CHAOS AND FURY

PART 1

A.P BESWICK

FOREWORD

Part one in this final story in The Levanthria Series is the culmination of years of work. Please be aware that I have tried to organise chapters to the best of my ability to follow the correct timeline.

I

RHAGOR

To the north east of Uster, it is said that a green-toothed hag haunts the riverbanks, luring children to their doom with enchanted trinkets and honeyed words. The elders warn the young ones to stay away from the river's edge when the mists rise and the moon is low, for that is when the crone hunts for innocent souls to trap within her rotting grasp.

-Gregor Yerald, Journal Entry , 116 KR

I let out a deep, unforgiving sigh of frustration as I stare deeply at the town that sits just ahead of me. The haunting, purple haze of dawn hangs in the morning sky. If I was a poet, I would say it is a beautiful sight to behold, but I am not, and I hate everything about this world.

When I breathe in, the air feels tinged, tainted, corrupted. For others it would taste crisp and refreshing, the morning dew helping to wash away one's sins, but for me it is a reminder of the wretched place I find myself tethered to. Still, it is better than being bound to a stone prison for two millennia.

"My lord," Codrin's deep voice draws me from my thoughts, but it does not distract me from my ire. He pulls up next to me atop his grey horse, clad in black leathers as he takes in the view of Hora. At least, that is what they call this village now. It had a different name a thousand years ago, but I am certain that it is here.

I turn my head to address Codrin. "Report," I say.

Codrin's Elven heritage is the only reason that I keep him on my council. That, and his desire for power and his usual brutal efficiency when it comes to the people of the land that he governs. He is cruel, angry, torturous, all of the things that I find myself drawn to.

Even his appearance is harsh, sharp, with his hulking mass, broad shoulders, and a face and skin cracked with scars from battles, some from before I arrived, but most since. One of his pointed ears has a bit missing as if something has taken a bite out of him, and a golden plate is clipped to the outer edge.

"My scouts have been here for most of the last year searching, but so far they have been unsuccessful," Codrin informs me, stony-faced. "They have searched through every brick of the old temple, checking underground passageways. They have not found it."

"Then you have failed me," I growl. I take in another deep inhale of breath before exhaling, my anger rising from the pits of my stomach. A rage that I feel from the second that I wake to the moment that I sleep. How I hate being bound by the rules of living in a human body.

"If it is here, then we will find it," Codrin assures me. "My men have been searching, they have been extracting information from elders. I have mages and believers in the old gods trawling through any literature we have. It is only a matter of time." He speaks as though he is convincing himself. "If they fail then, they will have to deal with me," he says with a growl, wrapping his fingers around the spiked, coiled whip that he keeps at his side. The weapon groans under his grip and it brings a smile to my face. He is just waiting for an excuse to use it on somebody, and that is what I like about him. Knowing that people like him exist has made this pitiful existence bearable since I was released from stone.

"But my lord, are you sure that this is the right place?" he asks.

My eyes widen as I stare at him, and he shrinks into himself. "Do you dare to question a god?" I ask. My voice is cold, like frost. "Do you forget why it is that you still draw breath? It is because I will it. If I find that I am not in need of your assistance, you can be assured that your meagre life will be snuffed out as easily as the flame of a candle."

"My lord, I did not mean to offend." Codrin lowers his head, but he is unable to hide the anger in his voice.

"How many people do you think live here?" I ask, changing the subject, my attention falling back on the village. A fence sits around it, about my height, drawing all the way around and mapping out the boundaries where it sits. Rows and rows of houses with thatched roofs line narrow streets.

"The last census has the population just over three thousand," Codrin says with confusion. I am impressed that he has clearly done his own research to know the answer so freely. "They produce good livestock. Good farming villages are in short supply, and some of Askela's finest meats are sourced from the farmers here."

"Yet, I find them in my way," I say as I drop down from

my horse. "Tell me, how many men and women do you have searching right now?"

"Around fifty," he says, still confused by the questions that I ask.

"So there are a little over three thousand souls in this remote farming village, plus those you have tasked with searching and failing me?" I take in another view of the village, which is coming to life as the rising sun breathes in new life for the day. I can see the farmers setting about their fields, working hard before first light, tending to their livestock.

But they are nothing more to me than a means to an end, and unfortunately they have found themselves standing in my way.

"My mum used to tell my sister and I stories when we were little," I say as I draw my sword from my waist and press it to the ground lightly. It is heavy, but that is how I like my blades. I grip the hilt with both hands as I stand before it, my eyes studying the farmers as they set to work. "You see, the stories we were told as children of the gods are far different from the ones you will have been told." I give Codrin a wry look. "That is, if you were even told stories as a babe." It wouldn't surprise me if the brute was born through cruelty. I certainly cannot imagine him growing up having loving parents. Maybe he just appeared one day fully formed, as I see him now.

I chuckle to myself at the thought before continuing. "As children, my mother told us about the responsibilities and the burdens that are placed upon them as gods, about the strict rules that they must abide by. Sculpting land, how oceans are formed, how the wind and sun are managed. It is exhausting," I sigh, shaking my head.

"It was exactly what I found weak in my mother and my

sister. She created the forest, she was vain enough to influence man to name it after herself. The Forest of Opiya," I say. "See, she had all that power. She created a forest where her power, her energy, runs deep underneath the very soil it sits on. Yet she still needed man to tell stories about it to feel a sense of purpose. I questioned this. If we were as all-powerful as she said, why was it she behaved in this way? Why was it that some gods only seemed to exist to push back against their own rules, influencing man, giving out curses, tricking people into deals? She couldn't answer. It was something I didn't figure out until I was older. Do you know what it was, Codrin?"

Codrin shakes his head. "No, my lord."

"It was boredom. What is the use of being all-powerful, all-seeing, if you cannot influence and control the very world that you have created? Just what is the point of it all, of being bound by rules that prevented us from walking these lands, from talking directly with people, even though we were gods?"

Codrin shifts uncomfortably in his saddle, watching me with uncertainty.

"But where do you think the temples came from?" I continue. "The statues, how do you think people learned to create the temples, how to worship us? Where the very magic that runs through the blood of Elves comes from? We did it, we found ways to bend the rules that bound us, and with it, life became that little bit more interesting. That's where the curses come from, that is where life itself is drawn. We helped shape this world, yet it is a world where we are forbidden to walk freely."

I look down at myself, at the body that I now possess. "Rules do not bind me. I found a way to walk the land. Do you think this is the first body that I have possessed? How is it do you think that I was able to instruct this very village to be built? What I search for cannot be found so easily. In fact, it is clear to me you are searching in the wrong place. You see, the village here sits far higher than the village I helped build when I first visited here."

I take in another breath and find myself squeezing the hilt of my blade so tightly that my knuckles crack. I pull the blade up from the ground and slam it back down to the earth, my power coursing through me and my trusted weapon. When the tip of the sword makes contact with the earth, the ground rumbles around us as if an earthquake has hit.

Ahead of us, cracks in the ground form in the direction of the village, and I hear the screams and cries of the people that live there. The confusion, the chaos, it is all so appealing to me. Houses begin to crack and sway as they collapse on themselves as the cries turn to shrieks of horror. People run screaming from their homes like confused ants, unaware what is happening to them. The ground shaking around me centres me, and I find that it surpasses the anger that threatens to erupt and I am a picture of calmness as I channel the power of my sword.

"This should make the search easier," I say as I raise my sword once again and slam it back down. The ground shakes even more violently. Birds escape the trees where they sit, scattering in the purple sky. The fence surrounding the village topples, showing precisely how useless it was in the first place. Livestock make a run for safety, away from the centre of the earthquake. The hilt of my sword glows brightly as I continue to channel my power. In this body, I do have my limitations, and I can already feel the strain on drawing on it so freely, but I will do what I must.

I have to find it. It is the only way that my plan will work, I am sure of it.

I let out a roar, part in pain, part in anger as wave after wave of pulsating energy ripples through my body as I become a conduit for the sword. A storm whips up around me until I feel the connection to the power that I crave so badly. The moment I do, I twist my sword in the ground as if I am turning a key, and a wall of fire pushes out from me. There is a fierceness to it, wild and untamed as it immediately scorches the land in front of me, leaving nothing but shattered remnants of what was once there.

The heat is incredible and I am amazed that I myself do not burst into flames as I wield my godly power. It eviscerates the village in a matter of seconds. What was once there, gone in a moment as if it never existed, and in that moment, the screams, the anguish, the pain, they all disappear in an instant. Like a forgotten whisper on the wind, all their pathetic lives gone. What have they contributed in their time on this plane, what have they achieved? Nothing, nothing but a life of misery. If anything, I offer them a kindness by releasing them from this world. No longer bound by the rules. I wonder if Quiron will be able to deal with this amount of souls being sent to the afterlife at once. Still, it is not my problem to deal with.

I twist my sword once again and the flames draw back towards me until they reach my blade and vanish. When I re-sheathe it, it is with shaking hands. The pain is agonising, but I do not wish to show this to Codrin, or anyone else for that matter.

I inhale a deep breath of air as I take in what remains in front of me. Suddenly the air tastes clearer. Singed embers hang in the air and a thick blanket of smoke has replaced the morning dew. Some of the stone has survived from the blast, but the majority has been turned to ash.

"That's better," I say as I sample the air like a connoisseur tasting the finest of wines, allowing the singed taste to sit on the back of my tongue. Then I turn and smile at Codrin. "I suggest you start digging."

I turn and hop onto my steed, grabbing hold of the reins as I balance myself and take in the scintillating view once again. All that life gone, in a moment, but in the charred remnants of this once vibrant farming village is the answer that I am looking for. "Have word sent to me as soon as you find it."

I have never seen Codrin look so wide-eyed and shocked as I see him now. Sweat beads on his bald head, and it is clear to see that he is shaken. Of all the power I have displayed in my time here, of all the time that I have wielded my blade in front of others, this has been the most ferocious display of what it is capable of, what I am capable of.

"Imagine the stories that will be told," I quip as I heel my horse and leave Codrin to delve through the ruins.

He has to find it. Otherwise all of this will have been for nothing.

2

VIREO

"Are you sure this is the place, old friend?" Killian asks. We're standing at the bow of a ship, looking across the lands that surround Zakron's Keep. Killian's greying red hair is almost as thick and matted as the wild beard that he carries, a beard in which I am certain wildlife could find a home. We could both do with a proper bath.

We will soon disembark, having managed safe passage across the ocean between here and the waters that lead to Loch Bragoa.

"That I am certain," I tell him. "Our scouts said that Jordell has been spotted on these shores. We must find him, Killian. He is key to our success." My throat is dry, so I reach for my flask and take a large drink to quench my thirst. It is warm here, warmer than what I am used to. The hot, dry air seems to burn my throat. The land ahead of us is filled with barren lands and scorched shrubs – the complete opposite of the Forest of Opiya.

"Why?" Killian asks, letting out a sigh. "Why would

anyone choose to exile themselves to this place? It will be a miracle if we don't simply find his weathered bones."

The gangplank is lowered, and Killian leads the way, stepping across the walkway with confidence. I, however, struggle with my balance as the height of the ship and the distance to the ground causes my stomach to churn.

I pass the ship's captain a coin purse before beginning my descent to solid ground. He is an older captain, one that has seen plenty of the world, with a thin greying beard and balding head. His wears a long, tattered overcoat that has been devoured by moths. He holds his hat to his chest and offers me a polite nod and a yellow, toothy smile, years of decay and scurvy apparent.

When I reach the bottom, I let out a sigh of relief as my feet hit solid ground. The journey was short, but two days on the open ocean is enough for me. There is a reason why I never joined the King's Fleet; the thought of sailing the seas brings thoughts fresh from nightmares.

"You okay, Vireo?" Killian laughs. "You look a paler shade than you usually do." He slaps me on the back as he makes his way off the jetty.

"I'm fine," I mutter. As I take a step forward, the land beneath me seems to rock as though I am still sailing, and a wave of internal heat flushes over me. "Then again . . ." I rush to the side and heave into the calm waters beside us, almost bending in half. Luckily my stomach is relatively empty, so it is mainly bile that I bring up, the retching noise about as dignified as you could expect.

Killian laughs again at my expense before setting off. When I am done retching, I fetch another sip of water, then hurry to catch him up.

What I can only assume used to be a vibrant port is now

nothing more than decrepit wooden walkways and hollow stone remains of the town that used to be here.

"Do you not find it strange that no one knows what happened here?" Killian asks as he pokes his head into the crumbling remains of a building, eyeing up the stonework.

"It is clear the gods do not favour these lands. I am surprised that they still fall within the boundaries of Levanthria. There is nothing here in these secluded parts," I say as I draw my hood over my head to give me a brief reprieve from the harsh sun above. "The question is, if Jordell is here, what is it that he has been doing all this time?"

"That is something I would like to know, too. I don't like being away from the forest, especially when there is a bounty on our heads." Killian cuts a concerned figure as he continues to examine the blackened stone. Rubbing his fingers over the surface, he turns his hand to reveal soot. "Fire," he grumbles. "What could do this level of damage? Do you know of any volcanoes in these parts?"

Curious, I trace my own fingers over the surface of the hot stone. Killian is right, the rocks are scorched in a manner that the sun would not cause. "As far as I know, there are no volcanoes in these parts, brother. Perhaps it was something worse."

"What could be worse than a volcano?" Killian asks.

"I don't know. A dragon, perhaps," I tease.

Killian gives me a stern look, then bursts into laughter.

I give him a dry smile. "What? Stranger things have happened. We live in an age now where gods walk the lands." But the thought quickly dampens my mood.

It has been eight years since the Battle of Opiya, when Laith found that blasted sword and unleashed Rhagor on our lands. Eight years since that bastard god took control of Laith's body and the kingdom. If we thought the reign under King Athos Almerion was reckless, Rhagor has proved himself to be a far worse king.

My attention moves towards the deckhand who is walking towards us from the ship with our horses, a set of reins in each hand. Clad in nothing but a pair of baggy pants, he is a gangly man with barely a scrap of meat to his bones. His skin is coated in a dark, oily grime, and his hair is darkened and shaggy as if it has not been washed for months.

"Here you go, sirs," he says nervously, passing us the reins. "It takes either a brave man or a foolish one to wander these parts."

"Thank you – " I pause for a moment, realising I do not know the man's name.

"Grimm," he says. "The name is Grimm."

"An apt name," Killian whispers under his breath to me.

"Thank you, Grimm," I say. "Please pass on my thanks to your captain. The remainder of the coin will be paid on our return from our task. I pray that your captain's ship is still here when we return." I would be foolish to give all my coin, especially to pirates. Still, it is the only way we could have reached these shores, and I am grateful for the safe passage to this point. We were lucky that the crew seemed unaware of the bounty on our heads, and I can only hope it stays that way.

How the rest of the journey will fare is another question.

Large birds circle above us as if waiting for our demise already, their shadows dancing around us as we both mount our steeds.

"Come, Killian. The ruins of Zakron's Keep lie south of here. We must make haste."

"Here's hoping he is actually here this time." Killian rolls his eyes at me.

"I must admit, we have been away from the forest for far longer than I would have liked, but at this stage, what option do we have?" With that, I heel my horse forward and we set off towards the barren hills where I have been told Zakron lies. "Rhagor does not care about our people. The world is in even more of a dire state than when King Athos ruled. You know how important it is for us to find Jordell."

"At least no one will dare invade Levanthria as long as Rhagor is on the throne," Killian fires back. His tone surprises me. Does he in fact root for this self-proclaimed god?

"King Athos Almerion was an egotistical man, driven by the desire for land and power," I reply. "But Rhagor is cruel. He is a monster."

Killian shakes his head and offers me a short laugh. "A monster you seem intent on going to war with. Remind me, Vireo, is it vanity or valour that drives you?"

A surge of emotion rises up inside of me, and in this moment, it is anger and grief that burn in my core, the embers of that battle still charring my soul. "It has been eight years, my friend, eight years. I will do what I must."

"Do you think Laith's soul will be intact?" Killian asks. It is a question I have asked myself many times. "Would he even want saving if he was to know the things he has done since Rhagor possessed him? It would destroy him. If we can even save him at all."

"*When* we save him, I can only hope that he will remember nothing. After all, it is not he who carries out these unspeakable acts." Letting out a long sigh, I look out at the terrain. There is no sign of life.

"You told me you believe Jordell's staff can aid us

against Rhagor because it was forged from the Elder Tree. But even if we do find Jordell, who's to say he still has the staff?" Killian asks. "Vireo, we have been searching for Jordell for so long – " he hesitates as if considering his words carefully. "Do you not think this has become a fool's errand? Are we not better served aiding our people at home, in the forest?"

"Our community has the means and the skills to run sufficiently without me. Our path, our mission, has become much bigger than ourselves."

Ahead of us, the vast, rocky terrain leads towards a crack in the mountains where a stone tower that I did not notice before protrudes from the back of the mountainside. I smile. "The keep is here. Which means our scouts may be right."

Excitement overcomes me and I heel my horse into a gallop. We race towards the mountainside at speed, but my thoughts race even faster. I have not seen my friend for so many years, just the knowledge that he is alive and well would bring me solace. Rhagor's possession of Laith's body hit Jordell the hardest. How could it not? The boy was like a son to Jordell, the two of them having travelled Levanthria together for so long.

The weather here is harsh, and as fast as we ride, I feel little breeze to cool my skin as my horse navigates the rocky terrain. By the time we reach the foot of the mountain, it is clear that we must continue our journey on foot from this point.

"Come, we can leave the horses here," I say, dismounting and wrapping the reins around a nearby rock.

"Hopefully they will be here when we return," Killian says sceptically as he does the same.

I can't help but feel that Killian is growing frustrated

with me. "You can always turn back if you do not wish to join me, Killian. If you want to return to the forest, I am more than happy to make the rest of the journey myself. Do not feel like you are tied to this quest."

"What, and leave you to have all the fun?" Killian grins. "Besides, you wouldn't last two minutes on your own. You are too brash, too brazen. Come, the sooner we find the mage, the sooner we can return."

I put my hand out in front of Killian and stop him in his tracks. His frame rivals that of Lek when he was at his most powerful. "Remember, he prefers the term wizard. He does not use his magic to cause harm to others."

"I'll worry about what to call him when we find him," Killian says, taking the lead over the rocks.

It is hard to tell how much time passes as the sun seems to set slower here than in the forest. It continues to cast down a harsh, dry heat that only serves to make this walk even more arduous than it needs to be. My hands are calloused and sore from climbing, but we have kept a steady pace, making it to the top of this pass. I turn to look out over the land we have covered since our ascent and the vast ocean that separates us from the rest of Levanthria. The sight is breathtaking. I do not think I have ever been this high up, and I take the moment to appreciate how little everything appears from up here.

"Can you believe the lives that have been lost over the years, just for this land?" I say. "Imagine how much has been lost over the wider world." My eyes trace the darkened clouds that sit over Levanthria.

"Feeling philosophical, are we?" Killian asks, slapping

me on the back before taking a drink from his flask. His tunic is wet with sweat and his breath is heavy.

"Does it not make you think why it is we do all this? Why we choose to push back against a god, rather than step in line?"

"Careful," Killian says, "you sound a little like the Vireo of old. You have worked hard to redeem yourself. Do not fall into the trap of thinking that there is an easier path. People follow you, people trust you to do the right thing, no matter the burden. It is why I still follow you."

Killian is right, although for me, redemption is not the right word. I do not seek redemption. I seek to only repent for the sins that I committed out of selfish greed. It was only when I truly lost everything that I became free, that it opened my eyes to the world.

I turn and continue our trek towards Zakron's Keep. The sea breeze catches on my torn green cloak and in a brief, startling moment, I swear I smell the faintest scent of Allana. It brings me a welcome comfort in this time of restlessness.

Maybe when all this is over, I can finally rest.

3

ZERINA

It is believed that the ancient Fae were the first to wield magic in the realm of Levanthria. Their innate connection to the arcane arts was both revered and feared by the other races. As time passed, the Fae intermingled with humans, giving rise to the Elven lineage – a people blessed with an attenuated yet still potent magical heritage.

-Lydra Silverbough, The Fae Progeny, 187 KR

T he winds howl a deafening roar as the force of the sea threatens to rip our ship apart. The fury of the ocean knows no bounds, and she is far from happy. Much like myself. For years we have sailed these waters heading from one bounty to the next, for so long have I endeavoured to keep Esara safe, just as I promised Ulrik all those years ago. Never did I realise when making such a promise that the most difficult thing would be keeping her safe from herself.

I strap myself to the mast of *Esara's Revenge* and watch through strained eyes as Esara, under the glamour of their brother, Ulrik, steers the ship through these rough waters.

Rain lashes against my skin, causing a sharp, stinging sensation as water laps up the sides of the ship with every wave that we crash into. The boat rumbles as she strains against the powerful force that the ocean brings.

As I watch Esara, I swear I see her – him – smiling, a dark look in their eyes that catches the reflection of the moon above. I have often wondered how Esara would look in her own form, but it is not one she has worn for so long now that I have no clue how she would appear in adulthood. I have known her for far longer as Ulrik, the now most feared pirate the world has seen. The fear that they project to those who dare cross them, their anger knowing no limits, their beard as black as their heart of stone. It is something that saddens me greatly, for they never got to experience a childhood, forced to make decisions no child should, burdened by taking the lives of others at such a young age.

My vow is what keeps me going, keeps me from leaving them. After all, when a child has experienced what they have, it is no wonder they have grown into such a cold, ruthless adult. It is something that I do not shy away from. I have played my part in their story. It was my visions that took us to Treventine, it was a vision that would steal this very ship and turn its crew to piracy, all with the vow of thwarting those who wish us harm.

Even with my unlocked magic granted by the Elves themselves, I was unable to save Ulrik all those years ago. A failure that triggered Esara to take her brother's form and vow revenge on King Almerion and his fleet that hunted us like dogs. I helped Esara. I agreed to go into Zarubian territories and I aided her to do just that. Through our actions, we brought chaos to the lands of Levanthria. When they succeeded in assassinating the king, I thought it would bring all this to an end, that I would be able to greet Esara as themself once more, but I did not. All I found was someone too young to be burdened with the title of Kingslayer, someone who stepped into adulthood sooner than they should have. Now they are of age, and even having achieved what we set out to do, I find their heart only growing darker, their determination to find new treasures far greater than their need to kill the king ever was.

True, the booty we've plundered has enabled us to continue to develop our ship, been able to ensure we can continue to recruit men and woman to join us on our foolish treasure hunts. Somehow we are still here, somehow we are alive. If you can call this living.

They insist on me calling them Ulrik. It is as though Esara no longer exists as she continues to channel her magic to maintain her glamour, aided by the ancient Elven waters that can reverse the effects of the magic we use.

As I continue to watch Ulrik steering to keep control of the ship, a wave crashes over them and they let out a roar of laughter. Something is different about Ulrik on this night. They are often stony-faced and only seem to light up when in the midst of a battle or – like tonight – when in the eye of a storm created by the gods. I know not what treasure it is that we search for on this occasion, and if I am honest, I am not entirely sure that Ulrik does, either.

The ship groans loudly and creaks as the wood of the hull strains. I fear that it may break and see us plummet to our deaths, never to be seen again. I wonder if this would be a gift to the world, for I no longer know what goodness we bring to it.

"What is it that has you in such a fine mood?" I call to Ulrik over the sound of the storm, a salty taste in my mouth from the sea. Rain lashes my face like small daggers.

"We are nearly there," Ulrik growls. They are unmoved, their gaze fixed on the blackened waters that surround us. Waves as big as I have ever seen, rising and falling around us.

"Nearly where, Ulrik?" I shout, a rasp in my voice that stings the back of my throat. It is one thing to hold a conversation with someone at a distance. It is another to do so when every word you speak threatens to be carried off in the winds that whirl around us.

"You will see, Zerina. In time, you will see," they say, an almost maniacal look in their eyes. "I know all too well what would happen if I told you."

"That I would stop you? That I would not allow you to put our lives and those of the crew at risk?" I roar, my frustration rising faster than the changing tides.

"Exactly." They grin without any sign of remorse for their actions, as though the impact their decisions have on myself and the crew means nothing to them.

I would be lying if I did not say it breaks my heart to see them this way, to see them so angry with the world, hurting in such a way that the only thing they show to anyone else is cruelty. A far cry from the loving, loyal, fierce child that I first met when we escaped from Eltera.

"Do you seek to bring us to our deaths?" I call out.

"I do this so that we can do the exact opposite," they snarl, their words wrapped in spikes and barbs. "You will see soon enough. We are exactly where we are meant to be." With this, Ulrik lets go of the ship's wheel, raising their hands away and into the air, their eyes widening in awe.

"What are you doing?" I cry in utter disbelief. "Ulrik, this is madness."

"Our lives are in the hands of the gods. If we make it through this, then I will know that they will it, that they want me to find the treasure that I hunt." Ulrik lets out a maddened laugh once again and seeks to keep themself balanced as their body pulls against the rope that binds them to the column under the helm. "The gods will guide us, Zerina."

The wheel spins so fast that I can no longer see the spokes, only a blurred circle. There is only so much strain that the ship can take and I fear that we are on the edge of our ship's limits. The ship shakes and groans louder than the thunderclouds above us, the rain becoming even heavier than before. The ship turns quickly one way, then the next, each movement jarring, snapping my head from one way to the other. My heart pounds heavily as my nerves reach a point I have never faced before. This is it, this is the moment that I have feared for so long. Ulrik has steered us into uncharted waters that will see the end of all of us. At least in death I could be reunited with my sisters. I have so many stories to tell them. How I long to hear their voices, to see the smiles on their faces in the afterlife.

"Zerina! The ship is near breaking!" Darmour's voice reaches me as he fights against the howling winds to peer up from below deck. "We are retaining too much water!" Then his eyes land on our crazed captain. "Shit!" he curses as he realises that Ulrik has let go of the helm and the ship is being guided by the storm and currents of the ocean. "What madness has overcome them?" he yells.

Darmour is the only other person on this ship that knows Ulrik's true form, the last survivor of our initial crew that took us to the island of Treventine. He has helped us ever since as a fiercely loyal first mate, to Ulrik and to myself, as I gave my heart to him.

Darmour loses his balance and threatens to slide back down the steps to the crew's quarters. He slams the hook that is fixed in place where his hand once was and the sharpened tip buries into the ship's wood, stopping him from falling.

"Captain, where is it we sail!" he calls from below, garnering Ulrik's attention. "You know I will follow you to the ends of this world, but even I know we need to set course on a chartered destination."

When Ulrik looks down, their smile is sinister, the lines on their rain-soaked face creasing. "Darmour, that is it, don't you see?" They beam. "Where we are going cannot be found by the rules of a normal map, by the rules that so often bind us. For where we sail, there is treasure that has not been hidden by man, but by the gods."

"Aye, Captain," Darmour bellows, his resolve and commitment to Ulrik remaining unwavering, even in these conditions.

Unlike mine.

Darmour's dedication to being the first mate of the ship often leads me to question: if he were tasked with a decision between choosing me or Ulrik, where would he stand? Not that I would ever put him in a position where he would need to choose; it is his resolve, the loyalty he shows us both that is what attracts me to him.

Rain and seawater pour over Darmour and his tensed arms as he holds on to his position as best he can.

"Darmour, get below deck," I demand, my worry for him at the forefront of my mind.

"Trust me when I say, there is less water up here than there is below deck!" He grins, "I'll take my chances here." Then he hollers into the air in a crazed cheer as if he is enjoying the storm nearly as much as Ulrik is. Is this how pirates think, how they feel? Never truly alive unless battling the forces of the ocean? If so, it should be a feeling that I echo, having spent nearly all of my adult life at sea.

But it is not.

I hate the ocean, I hate these troubled, cursed waters and the foreign lands they take us to. I despise the treasures that we seek, I hate the greed they bring out from men, even though it is what has got us by all these years. Our plunder has brought us more riches than I could ever imagine, but at what cost?

The ship shudders again, jarring me from my thoughts, then turns harshly to the right, causing me to lose my footing and come crashing to the floor. Pain erupts in my knees and my right elbow as I slam down with force and slide towards the edge of the deck. The ship is turning at such a steep angle that I fear we are about to capsize.

"Zerina!" Darmour calls as I continue sliding, only stopping when the rope around my waist pulls against the mast. My torso burns as the rope digs into me, jolting me so harshly that I fear my body will snap in two from the force. I lift off from the deck of the ship and am suspended in the air as the ship continues to turn and tip. All I see below me are darkened waters.

For the first time, I see the depths of something more black that Ulrik's heart.

4

JORDELL

Sitting by a ramshackle table, I find myself getting lost in the journal that I scribble my notes down in. My desk is laden with varying ingredients, torn, charred, and chopped in no semblance of order. The rest of the crumbling room also draws comparisons with my mind, chaotic and fractured. I mumble to myself as I trace over the ingredients again in my mind, hovering my hand over the table and stopping to grab them as I need them. "Heru mushroom, belera seed, narvin root," I say. "Or was it lyvar root?" I pause for a moment, flicking back through my notes. My journal rivals my spell tome, although the scribing inside is less intricate, a mere reflection of my mind and my findings since being in this self-imposed exile.

Hastily, I continue to flick through the pages, all the while muttering to myself as I feel my own frustration continue to rise up within me.

"I did, I used it before, I tried this before," I say as I stop on a page and read through my notes from three years and seventy-five days ago.

A chill creeps up on me and I instinctively turn to look at the doorway, my senses telling me that someone is present. Or is it just my mind playing tricks on me again? After so long on my own, I have seen things that only a fractured mind could create.

A scurrying noise in front of me catches my attention and I slam my hand onto the table, causing the ingredients that sit on top of it to bounce up in the air.

"Got you," I say as I look down to see my hand flat against the tail of the mouse. It struggles to free itself, and I smile and let it go, then pick up one of the mushrooms and pass it to him. "Here you go." It is a game that we have played on an almost daily basis for so long now that I do not remember how we actually got to this point.

The mouse takes the mushroom from my fingertips and turns to leave, disappearing into the shadows by the edges of the walls. I trace the shadows towards the window that looks out at the rocky cliffs. This tower, one of the few intact parts of these ruins, has proved to be all the shelter I need.

The weather here is harsh and unforgiving, similar to the Biterian Plains, but my research leads me to believe that it has not always been this way, that magic once coursed through the very veins of the rocks that this keep sits on. Why else would there be such a ruined castle here? Why else would there be such large grooves carved through the side of the mountain where rivers once flowed? The real question is, what caused the water to dry up, the weather to change, and life to no longer flourish here?

My research over these years has led me to many possible conclusions but nothing that I could evidence. It seems that only the gods themselves would have had the power, and given that I know that gods can walk this land, it is more a question of which one.

My research here is all I can do to occupy my mind, to keep me distracted from the self-loathing that consumes me.

Standing from my desk, I arch my back and click my neck. My body aches as it should for someone of my age. I cross the room to the stone window and take a slow, deep breath, placing my trembling, weary hands on the window ledge.

"One day," I whisper into the wind.

I close my eyes and imagine that Laith is here with me. I imagine the conversations we would have and the laughter that we would share, but these comforting thoughts are quickly replaced with the images of the Battle of Opiya. Men and women being laid to waste on both sides of the fight as we desperately tried to stand our ground against Lek and the King's Guard. Fight we did, drenching the earth with our blood.

All the while I foolishly clung on in desperation, staring into the trees whilst the battle unfolded, praying that Queen Zariah would not leave us overwhelmed and outnumbered. That she would send her fae to aid us in our hour of need, making way for a new alliance between us.

Instead, more bodies fell and as the grass turned red, my faith was left diminished, a useless whisper in a storm, lost and broken. The fae did not come. They left us there to die. Even with the power of the Elder Staff that Zariah had gifted me, we were losing. It was in this desperation that Laith turned to the sword, the one that I was sure would bring an end to the Great War before it began, the sword we spent so long searching for.

But I was wrong, and it is a mistake that will haunt me

for the rest of my days in this world, for the moment the sword was released, I lost Laith. The son I never had, the warrior who was meant to lead us into battle. His body became nothing but a vessel for Rhagor, the sword seemingly freeing the banished god from whatever plane he was being held in.

It is why I retreated to this abandoned place, it is why I stay here out of the way of the rest of the world. I cannot stand by and watch as a god parades around in Laith's body. I can't bear to be face to face with the fae people who abandoned us in our hour of need. As a priest in the Great Temple, I always sought to serve the gods. Now I wish that each and every one of them would suffer like I suffer.

"Jordell," a voice says.

I shake my head and ignore it, willing the hallucination to leave me alone. My mind must be playing tricks on me again. It would not be the first time. The voice is one that I recall, one of a friend. A friend that should not be here.

"Old friend, it is I," the voice speaks again, but I still refuse to look.

"Go away," I say. "Why must you torment me?" I place my hands on either side of my ears in an attempt to drown out the unwelcome noise.

Something grips my shoulder and I spin around.

"Why would I simply leave without saying a word when I have travelled so far just to find you?" It is Vireo. His usual torn green cloak is draped over his shoulders even after all these years. He lowers his hood to reveal his darkened eyes, stubbled jawline, and long, messy hair.

I slam my eyes shut. "Go away! I know you are not real!" The gods tortured me with a false vision for years. I will not be deceived by them again.

"Jordell, it is me." Vireo grips my shoulders and shakes

27

me lightly. When I open my eyes, there is a look of concern etched into his furrowed brow. Behind him stands an equally perturbed Killian. He stands taller than I remember, and his once red hair is now grey. He has a thick beard, and his arms are folded in front of him as he studies me.

I stare into Vireo's deep eyes and see his pain, the anguish he has lived through, the lines of battle etched into the wrinkles that form around his eyes.

"Vireo," I murmur. My voice is hoarse and gravel-like, as if the words I try to form are lodged in my throat, suffocating me.

"Yes, Jordell, it is I," he reaffirms, his look of concern turning into a welcoming smile. He pats my arms and then embraces me. It is a hug that threatens to break my fragile bones.

"Vireo," I say louder, and this time I smile at the realisation that he is actually present. "But how, how did you find me?" No one should have been able to find me in this place. It is why I am here, I did not want finding.

Vireo steps back from me and looks at me with happiness, and for a moment, it seems as if he has become teary. "I am so glad to see you, my friend, it has been far too long," he says with a smile. "I have been searching for so long for you. I had all but given up."

As good as it is to see a familiar face, my face draws into a frown as I look into those eyes of his with suspicion. "What is it that brings you here, Vireo?" I say, stepping away from him. "What is it you want from me that would pull you away from the Forest of Opiya, from your people?"

Vireo becomes solemn in his demeanour, but he quickly puffs up his shoulders and gives me another smile. "Well, I was hoping we would have some food and catch up before getting straight into things," he says, rubbing the back of his head.

Vireo is a confident man, so why is it that he is suddenly nervous around me?

"Vireo," I repeat wearily. My voice is husky and aged as I speak. Not having a conversation with another person for nearly a decade will do that to you. My throat stings when I speak as if I have swallowed glass.

"If you insist, but know I did not wish to burden you as soon as I landed on your camp." He looks around at the crumbling ruins that I inhabit. "Your home," he corrects himself. "Jordell, Levanthria is in disarray. Rhagor is a tyrant. He is a cruel king, crueller than you could even begin to imagine."

His words send an icy chill down my spine that causes me to shudder, the hairs on my arms standing on end. "Do not speak his name," I stutter, my mind descending into darkness at the mere mention of Rhagor.

"Jordell, the man is a monster," Vireo protests.

"Except he is not a man, is he? He is a god. One we didn't know about, one hidden from our tomes and our history books. What did you expect from him when the gods themselves tried to hide him?" I need to escape, I can't bear to discuss him any further. A knot forms in the pits of my stomach that threaten to cause me to retch. Taking my leave without warning, I shuffle to the door, but my aching bones slow me and I do not move as quickly as I would like.

"Jordell, as much as it pains you, you must listen to me," Vireo calls after me.

I make my exit by ducking under a fallen stone plinth that lies at an angle, bracing the crumbling stone walls beside it. "Leave," I demand, waving my hand above my head flippantly. "I have no time for this."

"Then what do you have time for?" Vireo's tone changes to that of frustration. "Why is it you exile yourself in such a way? What is it that you do here?" His voice bounces off the stone like a pebble skimming across the surface of a lake, and I can't escape it.

I hear their footsteps as they follow me, and when I reach a dead end in the ruins, I spin on the spot and mutter to myself before pushing past them and walking in the opposite direction.

"Jordell, you must listen to me, I need you to listen to me." Vireo leans into me as I push past, my legs wobbling underneath me. "I will protest as long as I need to, at least listen to what I have to say."

"If I do, will you leave?" I snap as I reach my bedroom. It is a sorry sight, and when Vireo and Killian catch up with me, I see them look at the squalor I live in.

"At least hear me out." Vireo leans against the doorway and I give him a sceptical look before he steps inside the room, leaving me space to leave if I wish.

I exhale deeply. The man is persistent at best, and I know that he will follow me for as long as it takes. "Very well, but tell me, Vireo, how is it that you want to take on a god?" Vireo tilts his head at me as if struggling to understand what I say, so I repeat myself. "How do you fight a god?"

Vireo exchanges a look with Killian before turning back to me. "I want to form a band of men and women," he says. "A group of those who have proven that they are the strongest and most powerful across Levanthria. Men and women whose combined powers will match that of Rhagor and his blasted sword."

"It is not possible," I say. All I can do is shake my head. "No, no, no no no," I repeat over and over again, becoming more and more frustrated each time I say the word. "This is madness. You cannot take on a god with such foolish ambition. To do so would lead to certain death for everyone." This isn't the real reason I protest, however, but I cannot tell him that.

"Calm, friend." Vireo's eyes widen with concern as he raises his hands to try and reassure me.

I pace up and down in my room, tracing my hand against the stone, mimicking runes that I have carved into it.

"I have heard so many stories of valiant feats, displays of power that just a decade ago I would have never believed," Vireo continues. "But the world is changing, and I believe that with those who these legends surround, we have a fighting chance."

"It is a fool's errand, one I cannot be part of." I shake my head again. It is not Vireo's mission that I fear. It is what will happen to Laith if they do by some miracle find a way to defeat Rhagor. Would he perish with him? Is he already dead, or is he trapped in a void similar to what the god was held in? I have too many questions, and there are too many unknowns for my liking. I cannot let Vireo take on Rhagor. I cannot risk losing Laith forever.

"Jordell, I believe that you are a vital piece of the group that I want to form. You with your spell tome is a force to reckon with. But with your staff, too . . . I believe your power would be integral to us succeeding on our quest."

The word 'quest' is what tips me over the edge. It was my own foolish quest to find that blasted sword that created this whole mess in the first place. If I had not been so stubborn in my search in believing that my vision was a gift from the gods, then maybe, just maybe, Rhagor would not have been unleashed on us all. And Laith . . .

I freeze to the spot as a single teardrop falls from my eye, splashing the dry dust and dirt beneath my feet. Laith is gone and it is all because of me.

"I can't," I say. "You should leave." I turn away from Vireo. All I want in this moment is to be left alone to my exile. "You can't possibly succeed," I snap. "You cannot even protect the people closest to you. First Gillam, and then Laith. What makes you think you can take on something like this?"

"Gillam made her own decisions," Vireo snaps, his cheeks reddening.

"And Allana?" I snipe back. "What about her?"

For a second, I think Vireo might strike me. A dreadful sense of guilt forms in my stomach as I watch a flurry of emotions flash across his face, but I stand my ground.

"Very well," he says finally, turning to leave.

I can tell by the way Vireo breathes that he is defeated.

He pauses at the doorway, but does not look back. "I wasn't going to tell you, but do with this information what you will," he says, his voice like ice. "There is a child. She is eight years old. Her mother named her Gillam." Vireo's defeated tone changes to one of hope. "She is the daughter of Yaelor, and the one true heir to the throne. After all, it is her father who sits on it, even if it is only his body. They are safe, hidden in the town of Osar."

And then he walks out, leaving me alone with this news.

Could it be?

Could it be that Laith has a child?

5

MORGANA

The Sages of the Emerald Tower maintain that all those capable of wielding magic must surely carry some measure of Fae blood in their veins. Whether through distant ancestry or more recent intermingling, the touch of the Fae is said to be the key that unlocks the potential for magical prowess.

-Eiric Thornwood, Lineages of Power, 221 KR

There is a knock at the door of my chambers that stirs me from my thoughts. "Come in," I say with a sigh.

My chambermaid approaches with a letter in hand.

"Did anyone see you?" I ask.

She gives a shake of her head and passes it to me. She is a beautiful thing, with long, flowing brown hair, hazel eyes, and a figure that even I could be envious of. She has been with me for some time now, and she is one of the only people that I can trust.

This is not the life I expected with being Queen of the

Realm, a power that I have desired and worked towards for so long. A power that I have craved since the gods first started taunting me with my visions. So why is it that I feel more lonely than ever before? Why is it that even with the power I now possess, I find my life so mundane? It is everything I have ever dreamt of, yet the walls that surround me feel more like a prison than a palace. I can feel the irony in being bound to a place of stone just as Rhagor once was, the very god responsible for my visions.

"Thank you, Vaya," I say with a polite nod, and she hastily walks towards me and passes me the letter. "I will be out shortly, please have breakfast prepared."

"Right away, my queen," she says, offering me a polite curtsy before making her leave and shutting the door behind her.

I pause for a moment, then open up the letter and read through its contents. As I take in the words, I find a soft smile pulling at the corners of my mouth and a solitary tear runs down my cheek. When I am done reading, I hold the letter over a candle that flickers beside me and burn it until nothing but wisps of smoke rise up into the air. These updates of my sister's wellbeing and that of my niece are all that keep me motivated.

I reach up and grasp my necklace, finding myself lost in thought. Closing my eyes, I imagine what my life could have been like. What it should have been like, had the Barbaraqs not taken everything I hold dear away from me, had not sent me on the darkened path that I now walk. How different everything could have been if my papa had not perished on that day, if my sister had not been taken from me.

Knowing that I cannot let people see me like this, I wipe away my tear before looking at myself in the ornate mirror that sits at the centre of my vanity table. Flowing red hair drapes down over my shoulders, and my skin is soft, pale, and unblemished. The gown I wear is black as if I am in mourning, with gold embroidered flowers adorning it. It sits tight against me, almost suffocating me, leaving the tops of my shoulders uncovered. It is a face I see cast back at me each and every morning that I stare into this mirror, so why does it feel as though a stranger is staring back at me? I smile at myself with the news that I have received, and I push my chair back and make my way down to the great hall.

After eating breakfast, a ghastly pale man approaches me, his features reminding me of the snivelling coward Breyton.

"Gorton," I snort in acknowledgement of him as he bows to me.

Vaya stands beside me, her hands crossed in front of her as I take a drink of water that she has prepared for me.

"My queen," he says, bowing his head to me as I wonder what I have in store for me today.

"The king has still not returned. Today we have the Lords and Ladies of Levanthria attending for council. You will need to address them in the king's absence."

I feel a skip in my heart at the news, but I mask the smile. "Tell me, Gorton, do you think I do not know this?" I say callously. "When was the last time that the king attended a council meeting? Who do you think it is that keeps order across Levanthria, my husband or me?" My stare threatens to ignite Gorton on the spot. I cannot stand the man.

"No, my queen." He bows again. "I did not mean to cause you any offence, I merely wished to make you aware."

"Consider me aware," I say and I wave my hand at him

to leave. He backs towards the door slowly before turning away, his polished shoes echoing loudly down the hallway. Even his footsteps irk me.

"Tell me, Vaya, are you aware of which lords and ladies will be in attendance?" I ask as I finish my drink.

"I am, my queen," she says with a smile, her beautiful eyes telling me everything that I need to hear. I do not ask directly. After all, these walls can be thin and I do not wish for people to hear us. It is why we have learned to speak cryptically. It is why I trust her. She is loyal and obedient, both traits that I admire.

"Then we must ready ourselves for council," I reply. "It seems as though the day has got that little bit more interesting."

It feels like an age passes as I find myself pacing up and down the meeting chamber like a wild animal. Why is it I resort to this state whenever he comes, whenever he visits this kingdom?

In the meeting room, the walls are made from darkened stone with rows of benches and chairs carved into wood that has been fitted perfectly around the outer edge. There are twelve seats in total. The largest seat sits in the north, the king's seat, and to its right is where I sit. Each chair is carved differently, denoting the animal or crest associated with each family. Odd, given that over time, the families who hold the power change. As far as I know, these carvings have remained the same for well over a hundred years. There are windows higher up, casting a contrasting light into the room, and candles are lit throughout so we are not sitting in darkness.

Gathering myself, I take a seat in my chair, the fabric of which is soft and comfortable. And it needs to be; these meetings can take the better part of the day. They are boring and laborious, and the only positive thing about the king's eventual return will be that he can take these meetings in my place. Still, Rhagor would likely insist on me attending. He has not the time for such trivial things.

A large oak door stands at the end of the narrow room, and it is pulled open before Gorton makes an appearance. His white hair is slicked back and tied, making it look like it is stretching the skin on his face.

"My queen, the Lords and Ladies of Levanthria are here," he says without making eye contact as he bows his head.

My heart rate rises. "Very well, let them in."

Gorton stands tall and places one hand behind his back, raising his head as though greeted by a bad smell. "May I welcome Lady Isolde Greymont."

A well-dressed woman enters wearing a long emerald-green dress, the neck of which has yellow stitching. She is a portly woman with a reddened face, mainly around her nose, a sign that she likes a drink.

"Lady Greymont." I nod my head towards her as she offers me a curtsy. "It is lovely to see you here in Askela. Tell me, how is your husband?"

"Still old," she sighs before taking her family chair to my left. Her two aids follow closely behind her, her twin daughters. They are not as rotund as Lady Greymont but their skin is just as unblemished, their teeth vast as they offer me polite smiles.

"Lord Galadon Hartfield," Gorton announces shrilly before Lord Hartfield makes his entrance. He is an older man, his hair short and grey, thinning in the centre. He is not a man who trades wealth, choosing to wear a simple white and red tunic. As old as he is, he is wise and knows the rules of the land, the systems and processes that need to be followed.

"My queen," he says as he nods. His voice is like a whisper, as if he threatens to draw his last breath. He is followed by a younger aid who helps him to his chair at the end of the room opposite the main door.

"Welcome, Lord Hartfield," I say politely before Gorton coughs and announces, "Lord Draven Whitestone."

Lord Whitestone enters, a young lord on the opposite side of the spectrum to Lord Hartfield. He barely looks like he has reached adolescence. His face is full of pock marks, and he has a long, rat-like nose. His long, dark greasy hair is slicked back. Lord Whitestone only recently came into power when his father took ill out of the blue. He was an ox of a man in his prime, and it took us by surprise when we learned of his passing. No doubt something to do with his snivelling son.

He bows and heads for his chair without saying a word. His arrogance will be his own undoing. Lord Hartfield does not seem to appreciate this and offers a tut in dissatisfaction. The slimy lord is followed by his mother Thora Whitestone. Now there is a calculating woman. If her son had nothing to do with her husband's sudden illness, I could be sure that she had.

"My queen," she says calmly and politely before following her son to sit beside him.

Gorton continues to announce the lords and ladies who continue to take their seats around the room. The process is slow and painful, and all the while I wait for the name that I am truly waiting to hear.

"Lady Vivara Everwood."

"Lord Illyrian Vailcroft."

"Lord Haldor Everbrook."

"Lady Cecilia Dunhaven."

"Lord Elandor Blackford."

"Lord Alaric Brierly."

One by one, Gorton reads their names out and they each pompously enter, and I continue to feign pleasantries. I am not interested in any of them; only in that of the name yet to be read out.

Gorton looks just as fed up as I feel as he arches his back and raises his head one last time to announce the final lord, and my heart quickens.

"Lord Orjan Varega – of Rashouya," he adds, clearly not happy that someone not from these lands has the title of Lord. It is the least Orjan deserves for helping liberate the people of Eltera.

The room falls silent. It always does when Orjan enters. That said, you would think these lords and ladies would be used to attending these meetings in the presence of a lizard man by now. It is a term that I know Orjan hates, but it is the best way to describe his scaled appearance.

I sit up straight in my seat as I anticipate his attendance, my eyes fixed on the door. There is a pause, and I wonder if he intends to enter at all. In this moment, I find myself holding my breath.

Then he walks in, chin raised proudly. He stops in front of me and bows his head. "My queen," he rasps, avoiding my eye contact.

"Lord Varega," I reply as he takes the final seat in the chamber, three away from me to my right where the pompous arse Lord Wistler would have once sat before a foreign warrior took his place by my side. Orjan wears the yellow of Rashouya in his tunic instead of the colours of Eltera. I like this in him. His ward follows him closely, a young man with short black hair. He does wear the blue tunic of Eltera as he takes a seat by Orjan's side. He is handsome, his jaw rugged with dark stubble lining his face.

"Thank you, Gorton," I say, and Gorton returns with another bow before leaving the chamber and shutting the large oak door behind him. With a click, I am left on my own with all the powers of Levanthria.

"Thank you for coming," I say before we get the council meeting underway.

It takes many hours to get the reports from each of the lords and ladies, each offering updates for the lands where they are stationed and how they aim to contribute to the construction of Levanthria. Something I want to see improve, not that my beloved husband would care. That's why he leaves these matters to me, whilst he is off doing whatever it is that gods do with their time.

There is nothing particularly of interest that is discussed, and I find my eyes falling heavy from time to time and need to suppress many a yawn as we make our way around the chamber. As much as I do not like the majority of these lords and ladies, they have helped to ensure compliance from the people of Levanthria for over the last decade, long before I was crowned queen.

The room finally reaches Orjan, and I eagerly await his address to the chamber. When it gets to him, he stands impressively tall, his shoulders straight, his eyes unmoved in his focus straight ahead of him, avoiding eye contact with me. His hood is raised, hiding the scales that cover his head, but his haunting yellow eyes remain to be seen by everyone. As I focus on him, I see that no one else in the room is looking at him, choosing to look at the ground or different parts of the room as he addresses us.

"My queen, I am pleased to say that Eltera continues to

grow since the days of its former lord. People are returning to the kingdom, produce is up, and so is the gold in taxes."

"Thank you, Orj – Lord Varega," I correct myself. "I appreciate your efforts in the name of the crown."

As I look at him I remember the day that I used my magic to momentarily peel away the scales that form on his face, revealing his dark eyes and olive skin, so soft to the touch. I made a vow to him that day, one that I have not been able to keep so far. Not for lack of trying. The curse that plagues him is a powerful one, one that I have been unable to free him from. Despite this, he has remained true to his word. He has watched over Eltera and brought it to a point where it is prosperous once again.

"I think that concludes our business for the day," I say, "unless there is anything else that someone wishes to share." I look around the room. Normally by this stage, everyone is just as fed up as I am and ready to leave.

"Gorton," I call, and the large oak door opens once more and a refreshing breeze enters the room. The air has been stuffy and the room is hot, so it is a welcome reprieve, especially given how tight my bodice is.

Gorton enters, his face even paler than usual. "I have a message for Lord Varega," he says. Curious, the room watches in silence as Orjan's ward stands to collects the message before returning to Orjan.

"Thank you, Rior," Orjan says, unrolling the letter. As his eyes scan the letter, his body language changes. He scrunches up the letter in his hand, his fingers forming tight fists.

"What is it, Lord Varega?" I ask, concerned for what would affect him in this way.

"I suppose you best speak to your dear husband," he hisses as he steps from his chair. "It would appear he has cleansed the town of Hora, land that falls too close to the boundaries of my ward." There is a venom on his tongue, an anger.

"What is it?" I ask. "What do you mean, cleansed?"

"It is no more," he growls, hatred in his voice. For the first time, he turns his gaze to meet my own and I see nothing but disdain and animosity in his deep, yellow eyes. "He has wiped an entire farming village from the plains of Levanthria and every single person who lived there."

There are gasps throughout the room as the lords and ladies begin muttering to one another. Before I have a chance to say anything else, Orjan storms out of the chamber, leaving me in the presence of the hushed conversations that surround me. Many have believed that my methodology, my necromancy magic was bad, that the power that I wield is unnatural. But this . . . if this is true, if what Rhagor is said to have done is true, it will only solidify what these lords and ladies already think: Rhagor is a monster.

A monster even worse than I am.

6

ULRIK

My eyes strain as light forces its way through my closed eyelids. A heat kisses my skin as the still, calm air washes over me, a contrast to the stormy weathers we faced before I fell unconscious.

My eyes flutter open and I take in a gulp of air as if I have been holding my breath underwater.

I am alive. We survived the storm. It seems my instincts to allow the currents to guide our path paid off. After all, how else are you meant to find a treasure hidden by the gods?

I sit up and pat myself down, checking for injuries. Aside from some mild bruises, I find myself relatively unscathed.

Pulling out my dagger, I hack at the rope that binds me to the ship's wheel, the knot too tight for me to untie. The damp rope frays until the dagger finally cuts through and I breathe a sigh of relief at the freedom from its constraints.

The gods clearly favour my quest, but I have pushed my ship and my crew to their limits. The waters that surround us are translucent and green, exotic. We are in the shallows, a short distance away from the bright sands of an island. I can see the sand beneath the waters where fish of varying colours dart around, swimming under our ship to kiss the hull. Examining what strange object has taken over their waters.

A rush of blood courses through my veins and I cannot help but muster a dry laugh, for I feel certain that we have finally found the Island of Averaza – the very island I have spent so long searching for in my desperate quest for a treasure never found. One that will change everything.

Beyond the inviting white sands of the nearby beach, rows of palm trees, coconut trees, and a bed of woodlands promise plenty of opportunity to hunt for food. It matters to me not how long it will take us to move my ship, or even if we can. All I care about is finding what I came for.

By the end of the ship, Zerina is removing the rope from her waist. When her gaze meets my own, she bears a look of anger that I know I will soon face, an anger that will be fiercer than any storm I have sailed us into and rougher than the very seas we navigate.

"ULRIK!" she growls as I make my way down the stairs to the lower deck, a wry smile on my face.

"It worked, we have found the island," I say, raising my hands up in the air in mock surrender.

Zerina slams her hands into my shoulders, forcing me backwards. "You fucking fuck!" she says, anger in her eyes that I have seen before, just not aimed at me. "You could have killed us!" She pushes me backwards again. "When will you learn that this is not a game that we play? We have a crew whose lives we are responsible for."

"They know the risks," I say coldly, looking out at the sands of the beach that continue to invite me.

Zerina's nostrils flare and a flash of intense heat greets my face as her arm ignites into flames.

For a second, I think she may in fact use her magic against me. My cheeks burn at being in such close proximity, but I stare into her furious eyes and say, "We both know you are not going to harm me." She never has, no matter how hard I have pushed her, no matter the path I have walked. She has remained with me as she promised to my brother in his final moments.

A vein throbs in the side of Zerina's head as she seems to toy with the idea of slamming her white-hot fist into the side of my face. If I was her, I would. "Do not wait for an apology from me," I tell her. "I put my fate in the gods and look where it has landed us. Exactly where I want to be."

"Where you want to be." Zerina's cheeks blush red as she steps towards me, but she stops herself from acting out. "You really don't care do, you?"

"Zerina, all I care about is finding the treasure on that island," I say sternly, raising my arm and unfurling a finger in the direction of the luscious island ahead of us.

"Treasure!" She scowls. "You don't even know where the fuck you are!" And she fights the urge to step at me again with a conflicted look on her face.

This is the hardest I have ever pushed her. The fact that she threatens to use her magic on me tells me this, but I do not fear her. I should. After all, I have seen exactly how powerful she is, how she can wipe out entire armies with a clap of her hands. But to fear her would mean that I would have to fear death, and that is something I am not capable of, not anymore. It is what sets me aside from other pirate captains that inhabit this world. If one can shed the fear of death, one can accomplish anything.

It is why my crew follows me into these unknown

waters. All they care about are the spoils from our conquests and they know that I can deliver. All who survive have all the rewards they need to stay motivated and obedient.

"As I said, the crew knows the risks," I say, lowering my hands as Darmour's head surfaces from below deck.

"Captain," he says. He wears a black bandana wrapped around his head, and beneath it, his one eye darts between myself and Zerina whose gaze remains fixed on me. It is not an argument he would want to get in the middle of, but he walks towards me anyway. My tricorn hat is gripped in his one good hand. "Here you go, Captain," he says, passing it to me.

I take it from him and place it on my head. It is damp and reeks of ocean water, but it will do. It grants me instant reprieve from the harsh sun above, although not from the fierce flames in front of me.

"Darmour, ready the small boats. We are to head for the island as soon as possible," I tell him, my eyes remaining on Zerina who continues to stare into my soul.

"READY THE SMALL BOATS," Darmour roars behind him, and the sound of feet rushing up the stairs to the main deck thunders in the quiet air as a group of bedraggled, exhausted crew members emerge, each of them squinting as the harsh light bursts into their eyes.

"Captain, where is it that we are, exactly?" Darmour asks, looking out at the island and up at the large birds which cast flight in the skies above.

"The Island of Averaza," I say.

Darmour's expression shifts from confusion, to wonder, to worry. "Captain." He makes to leave and join the crew, but before he leaves, Zerina calls after him.

"How many?" she says, her gaze still focused on me.

"Pardon?" Darmour asks as though treading on eggshells in bare feet.

"How many of the crew did not make it?" she asks, an unforgiving tone in her voice.

"Erm, what we need to remember is –"

"I said, how many?" Zerina turns her head to look at Darmour, who freezes in his tracks.

"Four," he mumbles under his breath. "We lost four in the storm. Borah, Surini, Levur and Nuno."

Zerina glares at me once more and her eyes burn into me more fiercely than her magic ever could. Her arm is still engulfed in white-hot, molten flame. "Their deaths are on you, Ulrik. Not me, not Darmour, but you." The flames on her arm burn brighter in a flash before she extinguishes them and turns to leave.

"As I said, they knew the risks," I say calmly, my heart beating fast with excitement.

Zerina spins and throws a clenched fist at me, crashing it into my jaw. A flash of light erupts in my vision but I remain rooted to the spot, my excitement superseded by a burst of rage. Who does she think she is to strike me? If she was any other member of the crew, she would be met with the tip of my blade.

I take my own step forward, my teeth clenched together, ready to grip her around her throat, but I stop myself. I allow her this moment. I give her a smug look and smile as she growls and turns again, shouldering past Darmour who stands wide-eyed in shock at what he has just seen. He knows all too well the fury I can show, the cruelty I can inflict on those who displease me. But he also knows that like him, I care for Zerina, and no matter how much I push her away from me, I would never willingly harm her. Not unless she gives me no choice.

"When you have finished staring at me, go and help the crew ready the small boats. That is, if they survived the storm."

"Aye, Captain," Darmour mutters before turning to help with the pulleys.

I walk towards the edge of the ship and plant my hands on the railings, savouring the breeze as it catches my hair and presses against my face. I close my eyes and think of my brother. This is what motivates me to keep going, to keep searching, and I will not stop until I have found exactly what I am looking for.

I grip the railings tightly as the face of my dying brother comes to the forefront of my mind. Me, kneeling by his side, crying uncontrollably as the feeling of being too powerless to stop his passing consumes me like darkened shadows. It was from that darkness that I rose. Out of those shadows, I became the person I am today. I will not let fear guide me, I will never let it stop me. The darkness where I found solace keeps me safe, keeps me at peace with the decisions that I have to make, the lives that I have had to take.

When I took the shot that killed the king, I hoped it would bring me the peace that I so desperately desired, that it would somehow dampen the flames of hatred that burn so fiercely in my belly.

But it did not.

Now, finding the treasure that I believe is hidden on this island is the only thing that could bring me back from the darkness that I live and breathe. And if I told Zerina what it is that I search for, she would do everything in her power to stop me.

Grabbing hold of one of the pulleys, I hop over the side of the ship and lower myself to one of the small boats.

The six crew members whose eyes meet mine look on in

eager anticipation. In the next small boat across from us, Zerina sits stony-faced, searching out across the tranquil waters.

"Tell me, men, are you ready to find some treasure?" I ask.

7

ORJAN

On the isle of Azuremyst, the legendary Siren's Lyre is rumoured to rest within the submerged ruins of a once-great temple. This enchanted instrument, has the power to control the minds of all who hear its haunting melody. Many treasure hunters have long sought the lyre, hoping to harness its power for their own nefarious purposes.

- Caspian Wavecrest, Tales of the Isles, 231 KR

"Orjan," Rior calls after me as I stomp down the corridor. The sooner I get away from this wretched place, the better. "Is it true?"

He reaches me and pulls on my arm to slow me down. His strength has improved over these years but he is still no match for me. When I face him, he is a picture of worry.

"We must ride to Hora, to truly know for ourselves," I tell him. "But why would our men send word if it was not true?"

I see panic in Rior's eyes as he takes in the gravity of

what I have announced. "But there are so many who live there, people I know."

"Not anymore," I hiss. "Come, we must make haste."

"And do what, Orjan?" Rior tightens his grip on my arm as I make to leave. I understand the boy's concern, his anger, his frustration, for I feel it too, but he should know better than to challenge me in front of others.

"You know I promote autonomy, that I freely accept questions, but do not challenge me in such an open place, Rior. Especially when we are in this vile cesspit." I pull my arm from his grasp and turn to leave. "We ride to Hora. Only there will we learn the truth."

Rior does not say another word as he falls into step behind me.

"Orjan!" Her voice skips down the hallway and stops me in my tracks. It is like I have been caught in a bear trap. I try to ignore her, but I can't. I have things I need to say, regardless of the consequences.

Rior stops too, but I wave him on. "Go, I will catch you up."

"Orjan, wait," Morgana says, and for a moment I consider simply turning away and following Rior. Why am I giving her a chance to explain herself to me when time and time again, she only seems to prove everyone else right about her? That she is not a good woman, that she serves only her own needs and not those of others. How else did she end up as queen, tethered to a false king parading around as a god in the body of my former squire?

She was someone I once held so close, following the battle of Eltera where we fought off the Wyvern and Barbaraq onslaught together to liberate the people. I thought I knew who she was, but now I could not feel further away from her. Now she is just the woman behind the stories that shroud her in darkness.

Her face is a picture of concern as she hitches her dark dress up and moves towards me.

"What is it you want?" I ask coldly. "It would appear that your husband, or should I say master, has been busy taking more innocent lives. And what for?"

"You have to believe me when I say I did not know," she protests. Her cheeks are reddened and she looks flustered. "I do not know what it is that Rhagor is looking for, why he does the things that he does. I cannot control him. You of all people should understand that."

"Yet you choose to stand by his side, all for the power that you have always desired. Tell me, Morgana, what is it like to lie with a god?" Vitriol spills from my mouth in my fury.

At my words, she strikes me across the face. In truth, I more than likely deserved that for my outburst. Besides, it doesn't hurt; my scaled skin is too thick, and the blow feels dampened as her open hand connects with my face.

Her flustered look turns to one of anger. "You have no right. You know that it is not like that. Of all the people across Levanthria, I thought you would understand. Orjan, we were friends. After Eltera, you became part of my trusted envoy. I have told you things that no one else in this world knows about me. Every time you visit for the council meetings, I wait in anticipation of speaking with you, but every time you avoid me as best you can. What happened to us? Why do you refuse to speak openly with me as we used to?"

"You made your bed," I say, my voice deep and commanding. "Your choices are what has defined this moment, the consequences you will have to live with for the rest of your miserable existence."

I hate how I speak to her, but I must. It was her betrayal that led to all of this. The guilt I feel for Rhagor being here, for him being able to commit these atrocities without any fear of reprisal for his actions . . . It is all my fault. Had I not given Laith's location to Morgana, she would not have sent that brute Lek to the Forest Of Opiya. That battle would not have happened, and that fucking sword would not have released Rhagor into the world.

I thought I was doing the right thing. Now I can see that my feelings and argument with Laith are what led me to this rationale. If I could go back and stop this from ever happening, I would. Perhaps then Laith would be here as a free man, with his own life to live. Instead I find myself at Rhagor's disposal, remaining in the position of steward over Eltera so I can ensure the people's safety. But given the situation in Hora, I realise that not even this can be guaranteed. I feel as though I am waiting for Rhagor to snap his fingers and destroy all of Levanthria, everything I hold dear. That I used to hold dear.

"I had no choice, Orjan," Morgana protests as she seeks to raise her hand to my cheek, gently this time.

I grab her wrist and push it away. "As I said, you must live with the consequences of your choices. As must I."

"I did not know about Hora. You must believe the words that I speak."

"Why would I believe you now, Morgana, after all this time? After everything that has passed between us? Need I remind you of the promise you once made me, or was that just a lie to get me to do your bidding?" There is a coldness in my voice. Up until now, I thought I had cut off all emotion when it came to Morgana, but that itself was lie, for all that rises up from me in this moment is anger. So much hurt, so much pain, so many lives lost.

"I have tried, Orjan, more than you will ever know. This curse, I do not know how to break it. I do not know how to free you." Her voice cracks as she speaks, as if she is truly sorry, but I cannot bring myself to believe her. Not anymore.

"Perhaps it is something your husband will know." My reply is harsh, like I breathe ice.

"You know as well as I do that if I asked this of him, he would know that we are close. It's not worth the risk."

"As I said, we have both made our choices." I turn my back on her and start to walk down the corridor. "Now I need to go and see how best to support the people of my land to deal with Rhagor's latest display of power. That is, if Eltera still remains when I return," I snap.

I leave her standing behind me, and she does not follow, but I hear her heavy breathing as she sobs where she stands. I will not fall for this feigned emotion. I fell for it once and now my heart is coated in stone. It is the only way I can protect myself in this cruel world. To think I once believed that I was falling for the sorceress, against my better judgement, despite the stories that people spread, despite the atrocities I knew her capable of. I will not make that mistake again.

By the time I reach Rior in the courtyard, he is already mounted on his steed, holding the reins of my own.

"Took your time," he says sarcastically. I merely growl from the pits of my throat. He knows not to test me. To do so when I am in this mood would be foolish.

I climb onto my steed, a large brown mare that stands a good few heads taller than Rior's. Given my larger size in my cursed form, it is only natural to assume that I need a bigger horse.

The courtyard is busy with guards patrolling the outer edge of the walls, making sure there are no breaches in security. Do they think I do not notice their eyes fixed on me? Not only am I a Rashouyan, but I am also a monster, scaled and cursed. They would fire their bows at me without hesitation given the chance. I simply stare back in challenge at the ones foolish enough to keep their gazes fixed on me.

"Come, Rior," I say, "I have had enough of this place." And we leave the courtyard, making our way through the streets of Askela. "We ride through the night. We have no time to stop and rest."

"I understand," he says. He is loyal and has come a long way since I first started training him as my squire. He has become adept with his weapons in his own right, although his weakness is his thirst for ladies, and men by all accounts. I wouldn't let him know it, but I do not think he is too far off being able to best me in combat.

The streets are in better condition than they once were. Houses are still boarded up as we pass them, but there are signs that the city's repairs are well underway. Stonemasons are busy getting to work, laying the lower foundations for new houses, and the markets appear to be busy and thriving.

To the east I see where the Great Temple once sat, a sign of this once prosperous city. Before Jareb committed his atrocities, I think of all the men and women that were locked inside and left to starve, and it stirs up a fresh wave of frustration. If I had my way, this whole wretched kingdom would be dragged to the ground and rebuilt, stone by stone. It is the only way you can truly forget everything that has happened.

In the temple's place now stands an egregious white stone statue of Rhagor, his sword pressed to the ground in front of him, as if he protects these people. To my surprise, there are a group of people crowded around the statue, leaving offerings as if he will hear them. It is enough to make me snap, and I swerve off course towards them.

"Orjan!" Rior calls after me, but his words fall on deaf ears.

When I reach them, I let my horse run close enough to push them back before my steed rises up on its hind legs.

"What are you doing?" I ask, exasperated at what I see with my very own eyes, such mindless stupidity.

"Rhagor keeps us safe. We give offerings so that we can prosper," someone says. They are like a mindless horde as they continue what they are doing.

"Rhagor is a false god, he serves only himself." I spit on the ground. "You are all fools to believe that he is here to keep you safe."

Boos and jeers start echoing from the crowd, and stones are launched at me, bouncing off my chest.

"Heresy!"

"Fuck off."

"Lizard scum!"

The words are no worse than what I have become accustomed to, but that does not mean I am not disappointed. Surely word must reach them of the horrible things that Rhagor does, the lives he takes without warning? I tell myself that they must worship him only out of fear. It seems to be the only logical explanation.

"Come, Orjan," Rior urges, "I fear we are drawing unwanted attention from the guards."

I circle my horse on the spot and face the people who jeer at me and throw stones as well as insults. "Know that what has happened in Hora can just as easily happen to you," I announce for all to hear, but my words are to no avail, and I look at the large statue once again, a sign of the vanity that surrounds Rhagor. No doubt he feels that he is indestructible. That no one can beat him.

But by the gods, I swear I will avenge the lost souls of Hora if it is the last thing I do.

8

YAELOR

In the heart of Osar, I stand amidst the sweltering heat of the forge, hammering away at the steel blade that I'm shaping. The rhythmic clang of metal against anvil rings through the air, a testament to the skill I've honed since leaving my life as a Barbaraq behind. My long auburn hair, tied into one thick plait, falls far down my back, whilst the sides of my head are shaved.

As I work, the intense heat of the furnace surrounds me, a welcome reminder of my purpose here in the place that has brought me solace, the village that helps keep me hidden from the world. With each strike of my hammer, sweat pours down my ash-covered face.

Through my craft, I have found a sense of belonging in this bustling village. My days are filled with the satisfaction of creating something with my own hands, bringing to life the visions of those who seek my expertise. My work as a blacksmith has earned me the respect and admiration of my fellow citizens, a far cry from the life I left behind, when my people left me tethered to a post, to die alone and in shame.

I hammer the blade with one final blow, the glowing steel red-hot as it is manipulated into shape. Satisfied, I place my hammer beside the anvil and pick up the sword by its hilt and submerge it into the bucket of water beside me. The heat is intense and the water bubbles instantly as the blade cools, finalising the sword's shape. I still need to sharpen and polish the metal before finishing the detail on the pommel, but I am hopeful by the end of this day this weapon will be finished.

"Yaelor," a deep voice beckons me from my concentration.

Raising my head, I see the familiar form of Trivor standing in the entranceway to my smithstore. "Trivor," I greet him with a smile, "what brings you here this time? The hammer I made you didn't break on you already, did it?"

"Oh, definitely not. Your work always holds up better than that."

"One moment," I reply, pulling the sword out from the bucket to cast over it a perfectionist's eye before resubmerging it in the bubbling water.

As I step away from the forge and make my way into the front section of my smithy, I catch Trivor eyeing up my wares as he pulls a tree felling axe from the wall and looks it over.

"Such a finely crafted weapon," he smiles through his thick red beard. His hair is slicked back with oil and his beard seems better tended to than usual. He is a large, thickset muscular man, and he checks his reflection in the steel head of the axe before placing it back on the plinth, below the other axes that I have crafted.

"That is not a weapon," I laugh. "That axe is used for

felling trees. I am just waiting for Gretia to come and collect it, after she broke her last one."

"It has a sharpened edge, does it not?" Trivor protests with a twinkle in his eye. "Therefore, it is a weapon."

"Whatever you say," I laugh again. "What is it that brings you here this morning? Have you not got farm land to be managing?"

Trivor is a good man, from what I know of him, anyway, but he does not understand the struggles of everyday life like the rest of us. His parents were given these lands by the king in exchange for their allegiance to him. His parents have allowed Osar to flourish, with Trivor even stepping in to help the running of the farmlands, which this area is mainly known for.

Farmers always need new tools, and when I travelled through here years ago and learned that the old blacksmith had passed on to the afterlife, I decided it was the perfect place to set up shop. When the villagers here made me feel at home and did not judge me, my decision to settle here was solidified.

My mind can't help but drift to the past I left behind, and I am awash with shame for the life I once led as a Barbaraq. One filled with chaos and bloodshed, one where I did things that I'm not proud of. I can still see the fear in the eyes of those I crossed, the sound of steel clashing against steel, and the screams of the fallen echoing in my ears. I shudder at the thought of those I hurt, the lives I took, and the suffering I caused.

Now, in the bustling village of Osar, I've managed to find solace and acceptance. The villagers treat me kindly, admiring my skill as a blacksmith and welcoming me as one of their own. But I can't help but wonder, would they still look upon me so kindly if they knew the truth of my past? Would they still trust me to shape the metal that forms the backbone of their lives if they knew the hands that now create had once destroyed?

I wrestle with these thoughts, the guilt and regret weighing heavily on my heart. I've tried to bury my past, to build a new life free from the shadows that once defined me. But there are moments when the memories resurface, threatening to pull me back into the darkness. It's during these times that I fear the villagers will see me for who I once was, rather than the person I've become.

Yet, as I stand before Trivor, sweat beading on my brow after a solid morning's hard work, it reminds me that I am no longer that person. I have traded the chaos of battle for the steady rhythm of hammer and anvil, and with each piece I forge, I strive to atone for the sins of my past. Perhaps one day, I'll find forgiveness within myself, and the fear of discovery and my past will no longer haunt me.

"I just wanted to stop by and check when the scythes will be ready?" Trivor says. "The crops are almost ready for harvesting and I am sure the workers will appreciate being able to use newly forged, steel scythes rather than the blunted ones they are used to."

"I suppose you'll be joining your farmers in the fields, then? You know, most nobles sit in the comfort of their own homes whilst their workers toil in the fields," I say playfully.

Trivor grins. "You know me better than that."

The door bursts open and I am greeted with the panicked face of Orpa, one of the children of the woodcutters here in Osar. "Yaelor, Yaelor," she pants, her face red from running as she attempts to gather her breath, her light hair clinging to her face.

"What is it, child?" I ask, but I know what the problem will be before she utters a word.

"She's gotten into a fight," Orpa says hurriedly. "Come quickly."

The gods will have to hold me back for what I will do when I get my hands on her. A sigh escapes my lips and I shake my head. "Trivor, can I ask you to watch over the smithy for me for a moment?"

"Of course," he says, "anything I can do to help."

"Take me to her," I demand. Orpa sets off back into the street and I follow her at a fast walk. Outside, the weather is overcast, the sky still darkened by the storm that has since passed. The ground is sodden, and the mud-lined streets are relatively quiet with most people having sheltered indoors to wait out the rain. One man struggles with his cart that he tries to push through the thickened mud. He curses to himself before asking me to lend him a hand, but I ignore him, barely noticing his request for help as my blood simmers.

Orpa is further ahead of me but stops at a crossroads in town by the silk weavers and points frantically down the street. "Down here," she says, "she is down here."

Picking up the pace, I set off at a steady jog, almost slipping as I catch up with Orpa. My frustration rises as I see a group of children tussling in the street, and I wonder why no adults have broken up the fight. As I approach, a group of four or five children writhe around in the mud. Ahead of them, two more roll around on top of each other. A girl with a thick braided plait straddles another child, her usual blond hair barely recognisable because it is caked with mud. The girl strikes down at the boy beneath her over and over, each time knocking away his flailing hands as he seeks to defend himself.

"Stop!" I bellow, but the girl ignores my words, continuing her assault.

I rush forward and wrap my arm around her, hoisting her up into the air and off the boy. "I said that is enough, Gillam!" I roar as I hold her as tight as I can, her arms and legs flailing wildly as she seeks to land another blow.

"He called me a bastard!" Gillam snarls. She is a wiry one, and thanks to the mud she has bathed in, I struggle to hold her in place. "He said things about you too. Might think better next time." She spits at him as the boy groans whilst his friends help him to his feet. A thin stream of blood trickles from his nose.

"Gillam, STOP!" I roar, a sternness in my voice that I know will garner her attention. As fierce as she can be, she knows how far to push me and she would be ill-advised to push any further.

I lose my footing and land on my arse, a sharp pain shooting up my buttocks. I keep hold of Gillam and simply say, "Breathe," stroking my hand over her filthy head. She pants like she has galloped across the Mouth of Antar, and I shush her gently, cradling her in my arms, subduing her rage.

The group of children clamour to their feet and leave, and the boy she was attacking has a look of fury on his face as he scowls at Gillam. "Wait until I tell my father about this," he sneers before running off with his friends.

Gillam attempts to break free of my grasp and she nearly succeeds, but I hook my arm around her even tighter.

"I'll show him!" she says. "Five of them couldn't beat me. Cowards!"

"Enough!" Keeping a tight hold of her, I pull myself up, then grip the back of her tunic and yank her to her feet.

"Home, now!" I command as I set off at a brisk walk, dragging her along with me.

Eyes burn into me that peek out from the surrounding houses. No doubt the whole village will be talking about this.

Gillam attempts to dig her feet into the ground, but as strong as she is, she is still a child and no match for me. I drag her towards the smithy with Orpa following closely beside me.

Casting my gaze across to her, I say "Thank you." I am thankful that Gillam has a good friend in Orpa, and I appreciate her drawing my attention to Gillam's exploits.

"You shit," Gillam scolds her friend. "Out of all the people to get, why did you have to go running to her?"

"I think it is best you go home, Orpa. Gillam will not be leaving my sight for some time," I say, gripping Gillam's tunic even tighter as we reach the front door of the smithy. "As for you . . ." I kick the door open and toss Gillam inside. She rolls over the floor and Trivor looks on in shock. "Thank you, Trivor, that will be all," I say, my eyes unmoving from Gillam.

"Of course," he says, exiting quickly through the open door behind me.

"By the gods, Gillam, I swear you are trying to get us exiled from this town." I slam the door shut, nearly ripping it from its hinges.

"Well, he shouldn't have insulted me," Gillam says defiantly.

"You need to control that temper of yours. You can't go around thumping everyone who offends you." She is more like her namesake than she knows, her defiance knows no bounds. Was I this difficult for my father?

"The arse called me a bastard, the stupid shit!"

"GILLAM!" I roar, my temper fraying dangerously thin. "You will hold your tongue or so help me."

Startled by the height of my anger, she backs down, her body language submissive.

Her eyes are just like his, full of emotion and fight.

"Go to your room, and if you even think about sneaking out, I swear to the gods you will be polishing swords for the rest of this cycle!"

"But –"

"GO!" I bark, causing her to jump again. I do not like raising my voice to her, but she knows how to test my patience.

She gives me a disapproving glare and sulks off towards her room. "I am sorry, Mother," she says.

I let out a sigh before heading towards my forge and returning to the blade I was working on before. Maybe beating it into shape will help get out my own frustrations.

9

RHAGOR

In the early days of our world, a mortal man named Zephran was blessed with a voice that could enchant all who heard him. His words held such power that the gods themselves took notice, granting him immortality and dominion over echoes and whispers. To this day, it is said that Zephran's voice can be heard on the wind

-Penned by Orion Silverquill, Scribe of the Great Temple, 37 KR

My return to Askela shows me everything that is wrong with this wretched place. I would be forgiven for thinking that this body is in itself a fresh prison, albeit better than being encased in stone.

As I ride towards the castle, people line the streets as though I am some kind of war hero, a triumphant king returning to his people, victorious in battle.

People clap and cheer, it is something I have always insisted on. After all, I am a god, I deserve the adulation, I deserve to be worshipped. I have shown these insects the power that I wield and there is no one in these lands brave or stupid enough to try and challenge me.

My mood is sour, frustrated that Hora has not turned up the secrets that I seek, and as people continue to welcome me back to this petulant city, their faces tell a different story. Some mask it well, but I can smell the fear, I can see the resentment in their eyes, they do not think I am worthy, they do not think I deserve this ceremony on my arrival.

I do not know how long I have been away. I do not see the point in keeping track of something as trivial as time, but I know that it has been a while. In my absence I can see that the central part of the city looks different. New houses have been built, and I spot a tavern that used to be nothing but an empty husk, vibrant with people pouring out from inside to see the returning king, a god amongst men. I ride alone, I do not need an escort, and I look down at these people with disdain as scores of them continue to line the streets, like rats from a sewer.

A group of children push one another, playing, but it draws ire from me that they are not paying attention to me. My lip curls in frustration, but I bite it back down. Then there is a commotion and my horse rears back. I grab hold of my reins, almost losing my seat but just about managing to keep my composure.

"What is the meaning of this!" I demand, a threatening growl in my voice. A child sits in front of me in the muddied street, his hands planted behind him, his eyes wide with shock and fear. It is a boy with short black hair, his eyes purple as if he is sleep deprived. Across from him stands the same group of children, and it appears that one of them has pushed the child. It is not his fault, but he is in the wrong place at the wrong time. These people nearly saw their immortal king fall from his horse and that is not something I can allow to go unpunished.

"Sorry, I didn't mean –"

"Silence," I bellow, my voice commanding an instant silence from the crowd. They know what is coming, they have seen it before. "You think you can address me?" I sneer.

A woman runs out from the crowd and helps the boy up, patting him down before turning to face me. "Oh Great One, I am sorry for my child's behaviour. He is only young."

My eyes widen. The mother has seen it fit to address me, too. Who does she think she is, to address a god?

I dismount my horse and walk towards her, my black armour chiming with every step that I take.

"Do not look at me," I say and the woman bows her head in shame.

"Look at her," I demand, but the child is hesitant. "Look," I bark, startling him, and he looks up at his mother. Both of them are pathetic as they tremble.

"I am sorr –"

I cut her off as I wrap my left hand around her throat and start to squeeze. Naturally she struggles, but I am far stronger as my grip grows tighter and tighter. I turn my head and stare deep into the boy's eyes. They are green, inexperienced, they have not witnessed much.

"Remember this moment, remember that you caused this," I say. With a flick of my wrist and a satisfying crunch, the woman's neck breaks, leaning at an unnatural angle. All the while my eyes remain on the child who can do nothing but wet himself out of fear. It is this fear that brings a wry smile to my face as I let go and allow the woman's body to slump onto the ground.

There are no gasps from the crowd. No one rushes in to help. There is only absolute silence aside from the child that sobs before me.

"Perhaps you will learn from this," I say as I walk back to my horse and grab the reins. I think I will walk on foot the rest of the way. As I look into the crowd, their silence slowly turns into clapping once again, all fearful for what I will do to this kingdom if they do not. After all, I have to keep myself entertained somehow.

When I reach the castle, I head towards the main hall where I expect a lavish feast will await their god's return. I am also curious to see what offerings have been left by the people of the land. As I walk through the stone archway, I am happy to see a long table sitting to the side, adorned with all manner of foods. Every meat you can imagine, waiting to be carved, fruit and grapes, a balance of vibrant colours and the smells, how the smells tantalise my senses. The chefs have really outdone themselves.

I must admit that food is one of the things I have come to enjoy. When I walked these lands in my true form, I only ate for pleasure, I didn't need to. But with this body, I find myself needing to eat to function, something that brings too much of a similarity between myself and all these people that sit beneath me. Still, the food does taste better in this body, a silver lining to my fresh curse.

My footsteps echo in the nearly empty great hall. A single man places the last bit of fruit on the table, avoiding looking at me as he scurries away. I walk to the centre of the room, look up at the large stained-glass window, and growl under my breath.

"Mother," I say as the image of Opiya stares down at me through frosted glass. Then I grab an apple from the table and take a crisp bite, allowing the flavour to explode in my mouth. I close my eyes and enjoy the taste, really savour the moment. Next I pick up a fork and stab at some chicken that is already sliced. I spit it out at once and my mood sours.

"Cold," I say, my frustration spiking. Lukewarm food – someone will pay for this.

"Rhagor!" I recognise Morgana's voice. I do not, however, appreciate her raised tone.

"Yes, dear?" I say, turning and feigning a bow to her as she steps towards me. Her face is one of fury. She wears a navy blue dress, plain yet beautiful all the same. For a moment I wonder if she will strike me. Would she be so foolish?

"Is it true?" she demands of me.

"Is what true?" I say, pleading ignorance at the situation. I turn back to the table and start popping grapes into my mouth.

"Hora," she says, showing a little more restraint. "You levelled an entire farming town."

"More disintegrated," I smile as I correct her, tossing another grape into my mouth. "Don't pretend to be offended, you have done far worse in that dungeon of yours."

"I did what I had to, for the visions that I have as a seer. I am not proud of what I have done, but how many souls were lost in that village? Why, what is it you seek there?" she asks, drawing level with me.

"Ah, those visions of yours," I goad. "Remember, it is your visions that make you valuable to me. It means I still have use for you." I smirk again and toss another grape in my mouth before biting down and releasing a satisfying crunch.

"How am I meant to keep the people of this land happy

and functioning when you keep on doing things to make people doubt you, to make people fearful of you?" she asks, her cheeks reddened. I have never seen her react this way, and I must admit that I am somewhat surprised to be receiving such a scolding from her.

"Because that is how I like things. They need to fear me, to worship me. Every now and again they need to see what I am capable of to remind them of this. That is all the motivation these people need. Just like those little experiments that you used to carry out in the name of research."

"When I became queen –"

I cut her off by stepping into her space and she swallows her breath. I can hear her heart beating faster as I stand in such close proximity. "You are queen because I willed it, because I allowed it."

"As reward for freeing you –"

I smile at her again and raise my hand to cup her face, rubbing her cheek with my thumb. "And out of all the things you could have asked for, you asked for more power. Does that make you better than me?" I tut at her insolence. "Your visions are what keep you alive, but do not think that you are immune from my wrath, Morgana." I lean in to kiss her softly on her cheek, but she turns her head away.

I muster a laugh and step back. "Is that any way to address your husband? Your king? Your god?"

"You are neither of those three to me." There is ice in her voice, which spikes my curiosity.

"I have killed before," I say callously. "It didn't bother you then. Why is it that Hora's destruction bothers you so much?"

She turns from me, she is hiding something from me. "It is consequences that I have to face. To keep these people happy. You cannot be worshipped if there are no people left."

"Then I will just move onto new lands," I say. Levanthria is my land, I have helped mould it from the very beginning, when the landscape was first formed. Besides, I know that moving to other lands would be a surefire way to antagonist the foreign gods, ones who do not abide by the same rules as ours. Perhaps I do have more in common with them after all.

"You will continue to serve your purpose here," I tell her. "You will share any visions that you have with me." This is how I will stay ahead. Having my own limitations within this body means that I no longer have the foresight I once had. It is an interesting concept, being able to see the consequences of your actions before you take them. It makes my plans so much easier.

Morgana freezes to the spot. Her arms stretch out and her back arches backwards as her head tilts until she can see me. Her eyes are completely white and a strange croaking noise leaves her throat, rasping as if she is struggling to breathe. Her arms and legs are taut with tension, and I wonder if her bones are at risk of breaking.

She is having a vision, something that I have never seen firsthand, and I find it fascinating. It only happens for a few moments before she collapses. Her body falls like a puppet being cut free from its strings and she crumples onto the ground. She pants heavily as she comes around. I do not rush to help her up, I just stand and watch, curious what she has seen this time.

She gasps for air and sits bolt upright as her eyes open and she scans the room in a panic, scurrying away from me on the ground.

She looks up at me, a fear in her eyes that I have not

seen before. She is as cold as I am and usually nothing scares her, yet this vision has. I take a step towards her and she pushes herself further away, as if my mere presence terrifies her.

"I see – I see what you have planned," she says.

"I wonder who it is that shares these visions with you, now that it is not me?" I muse, turning to look up at the stained-glass image of my mother who continues to look down on me from above. Those judging eyes. "Was this you?" I ask as if she is in our presence. Perhaps she is somewhere around us hidden in plain sight.

"The amulet," Morgana says.

Her words surprise me. Of all the things I was expecting her to say, that was not one of them. As far as I know, there is only me who knows about it.

"What did you say?" I ask.

"I saw an amulet, carved from flesh and bone."

How is this possible? If she has been made aware of the amulet through her vision, then that means another god knows of it too.

I need to move quickly if I am to put my plan into fruition. "Who is it that speaks to you?" I ask. I want to know which god I am dealing with.

"I do not know," she replies venomously. "Even if I did, I wouldn't tell you."

My temper flares and I slam my fist into the table. The legs give way and it crumples in a heap, a plate beneath my hand shattering into pieces and spraying around me.

I do not know if Morgana is telling the truth – if she truly does not know which god is using her for her visions – and I contemplate snuffing her life out right here, right now. But unfortunately for me, she does have her uses. I can make no mistake; she has seen the amulet, she has described exactly what it is.

"Have you seen what it can do? This amulet," I ask as I step towards her.

She shakes her head. I can sense her heart is beating as fast as I have ever heard it, and I know she is lying.

A drip of blood distracts me from my thoughts. It drops from my cheek and splashes on the hardened oak floor where I stand. I bring my hand up to my cheek and press my fingers against it. When I inspect them, they are coated in fresh blood. The plate must have caught me when I smashed it.

Morgana eyes me as I quickly turn away, hoping that she has not seen.

After all, gods should not bleed.

10
VIREO

The journey back to the mainland is solemn. Jordell has become a shell of his former self, his powerful, commanding presence replaced by a broken, frail man. His body is skinny and gaunt, his muscles diminished almost as much as his mind. Much of the words he spoke to me were incoherent mumbles, it was a miracle I was able to even converse with him. His descent into madness has been his undoing, but I was so sure that his magic would prove key to succeeding with my mission, of uniting a force against Rhagor. It hasn't been a wasted journey, though. At least I have found him and at least he is alive. I can only hope that one day when he recovers his mind, he will see sense and help us.

All I can do now is continue my search. I need to find those behind the legends I hear to lend aid and bring down Rhagor. I hope my news about Laith's daughter will bring Jordell some semblance of comfort.

Only Killian and myself know of the child. We helped Yaelor hide, helped her create a new life for her and the girl. The moment Yaelor told me she was with child, I knew it would be my duty, my mission, to help her. I still remember the pride that consumed me when she brought the child into this world and named her Gillam.

Staring up at the stars above me, I know I cannot rest. When the day breaks, I have had little sleep, my mind unable to rest in this world. There is too much at stake, and we have much to do.

Killian and I find ourselves setting up camp in the woodlands surrounding Loch Bragoa, where bad weather has delayed our progress. This is a place I would not normally dare to stop, but we had little option other than to take shelter and wait out the storm.

My thoughts are disrupted by the sound of Killian snoring. I reckon the noise is enough to scare off any of the creatures fabled to walk these woodlands – or perhaps lure them straight to us. Bandits are rife in these parts, and the thought makes me all too aware of the prices on our heads.

Rolling onto my side, I try to find comfort as I stare into the embers of the fire in front of us, the warmth fading against my cheeks as the fire diminishes.

"Can't sleep?" Killian lets out a lion-like yawn and stretches out his arm before cracking his neck and slapping his lips together. "Not going to lie, that was a shit night's sleep."

I laugh. It is I who has barely slept, and I can attest that Killian has been fast asleep for the majority of it. "You say this like I haven't endured your snores for the entire night."

Killian chuckles, then reaches for his flask and takes a drink. "At least the storm is over," he says cheerfully. "I am starving." He raises the rabbit that he snared last night and takes out a knife before starting to shed it from its skin.

I have given little thought to breakfast, although the

thought of eating rabbit makes my stomach growl with pangs of hunger.

"When do we make for home?" he asks as he adds some more wood to the fire and sets up a spit.

We have been gone for a while, and as much as I wish to continue my search for people to join our cause, I understand Killian's need to return, if only to check on his daughter. "About that," I start. "I will not be coming back with you. Not yet, anyway."

"Vireo," Killian growls, "you cannot travel these lands on your own. We have discussed this. There is too big of a price on your head. Let us head back to the forest, regroup, and come up with a plan. Neither of us could have comprehended the madness that has taken Jordell. His mind is lost, and with it his ability to help you lead the fight against Rhagor." He does not attempt to hide the frustration that is etched deeper into his face than the wrinkles on his forehead.

I can't disagree with him. Jordell is in no shape to fight alongside us, his mind lost to the trauma of that day and living in solitude for the last eight years. "I can't give up," I say. "We may not have Jordell's magic, but there are others out there. Others who can make the difference."

"Jordell was the one we were counting on though. His magic is unrivalled as far as I know. To lose him at the start of our journey, well, it is why I think we need to return to the forest and regroup." Killian adds the rabbit to the spit and it starts sizzling on the fire instantly.

"It is a blow," I agree, "but I cannot return yet. It will cause too much of a delay. Every moment wasted allows Rhagor further time on the throne and only the gods" – I pause as my frustration rises – "only *he* knows what his plan is. I want you to return to the forest, I want you to be united with your daughter. But I must continue my search. I care not how long it takes me. I only know that I cannot sit idly by whilst Rhagor sits on the throne."

"Vireo, this is madness, I can't leave you," Killian protests.

"But you can, and you will. There are dangers everywhere in this world. You cannot protect me from all of them. I will search for just a while longer, and I assure you, I will return to the forest if I have no success."

Killian gives me a grunt of dissatisfaction, but I know he will respect it. He is a good man, as good as I could ask for to fight by my side.

After breakfast, we break down camp and prepare to part ways.

When the time has come, Killian swings himself onto his horse and eyes me wearily. "Are you sure I cannot change your mind?" he asks.

I simply smile and shake my head. He knows me well enough to know that I am a stubborn man. "Be on your way, Killian. Know that you have my thanks for everything you have done for me up until this point."

"You talk like you will not see me again." He holds my gaze for a moment, then rears his horse in the air. "Remember, this is not a suicide mission. I expect you to come home in one piece, you hear me?"

"I will see you soon, friend," I say. With that, I slap the rear of his horse and send him on his way. Once he is out of sight, the realisation dawns on me. This is the first time I have been truly alone since well before my exile from Askela, the events that forged the path I now walk.

Gillam and Lek are gone, and although Killian has proved to be a great friend and ally, no one can fill the void that those two have left behind. We travelled everywhere together, we fought together. Ever since settling in the forest, I have always had someone by my side. Someone for me to share my thoughts with, to offer me counsel and guidance.

Mounting my own horse, I look around the land that surrounds me. The mountains north of Loch Bragoa could be a good place to begin my search, although I have heard stories that warn to keep clear of the loch itself. Apparently the Beast of Bragoa resides there. It is an old wives' tale, but in these days where gods walk the earth in the flesh and strange creatures stalk the forests that I never would have thought possible, I have every reason to believe that this beast could very well be real after all.

"I wouldn't go down there," a gravelled voice says, catching me off guard.

When I turn, I am expecting to see Killian, but it is not him.

Before me stands a thickset man that would have made Lek look small. His hair is long and grey, his beard is thick, and he wears a heavy reddened cloak with a fur-lined hood.

I look up at the sun above us and then at the garments he is wearing. It is a hot day, but this man is dressed as though he is about to lead an expedition through the frozen lands north of Levanthria. He stands at the foot of a sledge led by a herd of yakulas. The peculiar animals are tall and powerful, their swirling horns above their heads every part as impressive as they are formidable. A strange aura surrounds the man as he searches over me and my effects, and I almost wonder if I am dreaming.

"What is it that brings you to these parts?" the stranger asks, his voice husked and stony. "These lands are not safe, especially for someone travelling alone."

"I have my reasons," I say, not wanting to give too much away.

"Unless you are looking for death, I would advise avoiding the path that takes you by the loch and up to the mountains." His wrinkled eyes trace the path that I was just about to set down. "There is a creature in these parts that has sworn vengeance against the king's colours of Askela. Trust me when I say that many men and women have perished travelling along that path."

"I am not of the king's army," I point out. "Old or new, I hold no affinity to Askela, only with the people of these lands who I want to ensure are able to live a free life."

The man combs his fingers through his thick beard as he ponders on his thoughts. "Still, it is not wise to travel this path. Many have fallen victim to the creature's temper and rage."

"So it is true then? The Beast of Bragoa does reside in these parts?"

"She does. I have travelled here to find her." The man climbs down from his sledge and walks towards the yaku-las, stroking them with affection. "There there, you did good, old friends," he murmurs to the animals.

"Why would you want to find her?" I ask with surprise. To me, this sounds like a creature to avoid at all costs.

"I try not to get involved where gods are involved, only where demons are at play. This beast was no doubt cursed by a god. The only question is, which one?"

"How do you know it was a god that cursed her?" I ask. "Better still, how do you know that this creature is real?" I steady my horse, who seems unnerved by the rustling of nearby trees where birds gather on the branches as if they are watching us.

The man looks into my eyes with a serious expression

and it is as if he is looking into my soul. There is something different about this person. I do not know if it is magic or something else, but there is a way in which he carries himself, as if the weight of the world is on his shoulders. Maybe this is why I feel drawn to him, because I too feel this burden.

"Because I have faced her before," he says. "And on that occasion, she got the better of me." He smiles as if recalling a joyous memory, which I find peculiar. "I have the scars to prove it." He walks to the back of his sledge and my eyes widen as he removes a huge broadsword and straps it to his back. The length of the blade must be half my height. The hilt is thick and heavy, yet he moves it as though it weighs no more than parchment.

"That was a long time ago," he explains as he kneels down and picks up some dirt from the ground. He rubs it between his hands and looks up at the sky above, closing his eyes. When he opens them again, he says, "That was when she was in her beast form. In the next few days, her curse allows her to take her human form again, and on this night, she hunts the lands looking for revenge for her lost clan."

"I have been told about this beast since I was but a babe," I say, "but surely it is nothing more than a tale." I am beginning to realise this man might be mad, to believe he has come face to face with this creature before.

"Where do you think these stories come from?" the man asks. "I have long documented my findings. I have hunted more monsters and demons than you have had days on this world. Heed my warnings. Stay away, especially when her curse is momentarily lifted. It will not matter if you fall near to the water's edge. She will find you and she will kill you."

The man is steadfast in his belief. He seems so calm, so sure. "Who are you?" I ask slowly. I am beginning to have an inkling as I study his red cloak and his ginormous broadsword, but it does not seem possible.

"No doubt you have heard stories of me," he says. "My name is Gregor Yerald, and I have spent more than a lifetime hunting these creatures."

"Gregor Yerald? The fabled monster hunter?" I have heard stories about him since I was a babe, too.

Gregor gives me a mock bow. "In the flesh."

This is too much of a coincidence that our paths have crossed on this day. If he is anywhere near as strong as I believe him to be, he could prove perfect for my plan. In that moment, I debate whether I should tell him my name. Would he turn me in for a bounty?

"Gregor," I finally say, offering my hand towards him, "my name is Vireo, Vireo Reinhold, formerly of Askela."

"Reinhold, you say?" Gregor focuses on my surname as if tracing a distant memory.

I hold my breath. If he were to decide to turn me in for the reward, I do not think I would be strong enough to stop him.

"The name rings a bell," he says. When the two of us shake hands, the firmness of his grip is so strong, I worry he might crack the bones in my hand.

"Can I offer any help with this beast?" I say, giving my hand a sly shake and massaging it gently.

"I try to stay away from companions at this stage. I have lost too many over the years," he says without hesitation.

"That I understand." We have lost many over the years, but nothing in my life has ever filled the void left behind from when Gillam was ripped away from this world. "I am, however, free to lend aid, should you need it."

Gregor sighs deeply as if reluctant to accept my offer. "If you wish, but do know that if you slow me down or get in my way, I will leave you behind."

"I wouldn't expect anything else," I say with a smile. "Lead the way."

"Leave your horse here," Gregor says. "We need to travel on foot if we are to capture the beast."

He ties his yakulas to a nearby tree and I do the same with my steed.

The two of us set on the path towards a thicket of trees that will no doubt lead us to the loch.

"Hamish," Gregor says. "Hamish Reinhold. Had an issue with a warlock. Now I remember. You have his eyes."

"Hamish," I repeat with confusion. How can this be? True, Hamish Reinhold is an ancestor of mine. But it simply would not be possible for Gregor to have known him.

He has been dead for near one hundred years.

II

ZERINA

Even the serene, white-sand beach cannot bring me calmness. My blood boils over the ignorance that Ulrik displays like a proud peacock. They certainly are a cock.

When we land ashore, the rest of the crew riding with us skip out of the boat and drop to their knees, planting their hands on solid ground.

The sand sticks to my wet boots as I walk ahead until I am far enough away to grab a moment's solitude.

I watch on as Ulrik climbs out of their small boat and makes their way ashore, pulling an old map out of their pocket. After they search the map for a while, they grin, roll it back up, and point in the direction of the large palm trees that mark the edge of the forest.

My mind casts back to my first time on Voraz, to the hidden cave I had seen in a vision presented to me by my deceased sister. As I remember the skeleton guardians we had to face there, I stare into the trees and wonder what horrors await us – and how many of us will make it back from this fool's errand. Perhaps I've become too paranoid.

Letting out a tut of exasperation at Ulrik's blatant disregard for our lives, I scoop up a handful of sand and let the grains pour through my fingers like the sands of time. Just how long can I go on like this? How long can I watch on as Ulrik grows angrier and angrier, more irrational? If they won't confide in me about their plans, I cannot help them.

When the sand empties from my palm, I close my fist and rub my fingers against the rough coating that remains stuck to my skin, then raise my head and close my eyes, allowing the sun to cast down its soothing warmth on me.

Inhaling deeply, I savour the moment, which calms my frayed mind from its fractured thoughts.

"We will be united again, sisters," I say out loud towards the vast ocean that sits calmly before me with turquoise waters. "I promise to do good with this life, with my powers." I wait for a moment, hoping above anything else for a response, but all I hear is the waves caressing the shoreline. I let out a sigh and fall onto my back. For a few moments, my mind plays tricks on me and I feel as though I am still rocking on *Esara's Revenge,* but the warm sand against my back is far more comforting than my bed on the ship.

"You okay?" Darmour's words interrupt my solace and I open my eyes and give him an unimpressed frown.

"No, I am not," I say curtly, "I just wanted a moment to myself."

"I see. Well, I'll just be getting our effects ready for the excursion." Darmour looks downcast as he turns back towards the others.

"Wait," I say, and Darmour turns back towards me. "I am sorry, I do not mean to take my poor mood out on you. It is just . . . I cannot go on like this, Darmour. I can't continue to follow Ulrik when they are insistent on getting themself killed. I can't go on watching them grow into the cruel person they are becoming."

Darmour drops the satchel he is carrying from his shoulder, his white shirt torn with the V in the neck showing his upper chest. He sits beside me, letting out a groan of comfort as he does so. "I am just about getting too old for this too," he says. "There is only so long that my body will allow me to keep up."

Darmour is fifteen years older than I am, and I have never seen our age difference as a barrier to our relationship. The man is loyal and attentive, as caring as he can be fierce when needed. He has devoted his life to being Ulrik's first mate, but even I can see the rate at which he has been slowing down.

"My body aches for weeks at a time after we finish with these excursions," he says. "But the two things that keep me going are our captain, and you." He lies back in the sand and stretches out his arm, inviting me in.

I oblige and rest my head on his shoulder, breathing in his scent. He smells of endless sea salt but also oak, as if he has absorbed the fragrance of the wood from the ship. I place my hand on his chest as I feel the beat of his heart against my ear. By the boats, Ulrik and the rest of the crew are busy readying for the journey inland.

"I believe all of this is fated," he says, interlocking his fingers between my own. "I am Ulrik's first mate, and as such, it is my responsibility and duty to follow his command, to keep the rest of the crew adequately motivated. To show no fear when called upon, to show loyalty to our captain when others question their motives."

He rubs his thumb up and down the back of my hand gently. "And despite what others may think of them, how they may question their judgement, I believe that it is through Ulrik's lack of fear that we have found such bountiful treasures. It is that lack of fear that has pushed us to the edges of rough waters where few have gone before." He pauses for a moment. "And you, of course. We couldn't have achieved any of this without you. This is what makes us such a good crew, a family."

"Families don't intentionally try to kill members off," I say coldly, removing my hand from Darmour's. I cannot believe that he is actually justifying Ulrik's decisions.

"Remember, I am in the middle of all this. Every time you two have a falling out, it is me who gets grief from the both of you." He reaches across for my hand to comfort me. "And that is okay, because that is my role in all of this."

"Darmour, I meant what I said. I can't continue like this. I can't go on trailing behind them." I raise my eyes and look across the beach at Ulrik who continues to watch on into the trees, a confident smirk adorning their face. "I know I promised Ulrik – the real Ulrik – that I would do everything I could to keep Esara safe, but how was I to know that things would turn out this way?"

"I believe that things happen for a reason." Darmour lets out a heavy sigh, and with my head on his chest, I feel his heart flutter.

"What is it?" I ask, looking into his dark eyes.

Darmour turns his head away from me, avoiding eye contact. "It's nothing."

"No," I say. "We promised not to hide our thoughts from one another." I raise my hand delicately and turn his head to face me again, tracing my fingers down the side of the thick, rough stubble that forms on his face, the dark hair streaked with traces of white.

"It's just . . . Do you ever wonder what would have

happened if he hadn't died? Do you think we would be us, that I would have your heart?"

I sit up and hug my knees into my chest, considering my answer carefully. "There was an unseen attraction between us from the very first moment I met you, when you introduced me to the men and women you had banded together," I say.

"That is not what I asked." Darmour sits up beside me. "Do you think I would have your heart, even if he had survived on that day?"

"How can you ask that?" I say defensively. "Ulrik is no longer here, he gave his life" – I look up at his glamoured form standing on the beach, the form his sister still takes in her grief from his loss. My heart fractures like a broken mirror, leaving only small broken shards that reflect unrecognisable memories.

"Ulrik is gone," I say, my throat burning as I struggle to force back my tears. "That is not him."

The Ulrik I first met was kind, brave, and loyal to those he cared about. He sailed across the seas to keep us safe as we searched for a way to free myself and Esara from the burden of our magic. He gave his life on that very quest. The Ulrik I see now is a fragmentation of his image, the complete opposite of what he stood for. Every time I look into their eyes, it is all I see: the man I was growing to love before the gods ripped him away from us.

"Do you know how hard it is?" I continue. "Every conversation, every disagreement, every argument. Watching them walk around in his form, making choices and decisions that he would never have made. Becoming twisted in anger and hatred."

"You are avoiding my question, and that's okay," Darmour says.

His kindness makes me curse myself for not just answering the question. For not just telling him that he would still have my heart even if Ulrik was still alive, but that would be a lie, and I cannot lie to Darmour. No matter how much it hurts.

"I think you have said all you need to," he says, and with that, he stands and leaves, picking up his satchel from the sand and placing it over his head.

My heart belongs to Darmour and I have given it freely. I love him. But I do not think that he would have my heart, not wholly, if Ulrik was still alive, because when he died, a little piece of me died, too. And the more I see his sister walking down this path, in his form, the more that hole in my chest grows, expanding into a void of grief and sadness, for I dread to imagine what Ulrik would think of the monster that I have allowed his sister to become. He would not approve of the things that I have done to enable her, and I carry that shame with me every day.

With a sigh, I stand up and dust the sand from my clothes, then head back towards the others.

When all this is said and done, I will charter a new path. One which will no longer see me trail behind in Ulrik's shadow.

12

JORDELL

Valthor, once a great warrior, swore an unbreakable oath to protect his king. When the king turned to tyranny, Valthor was forced to choose between his oath and his morals. He broke his oath and struck down the king, becoming the embodiment of broken promises and difficult choices. Warriors and rulers alike offer prayers to Valthor when faced with conflicting loyalties.

-Inscribed by Cyrus Inkshadow, Scribe of the Great Temple, 51 KR

My mind races and I find that I cannot settle. I try to sleep, but my skin itches and my legs are restless. When the sun rises, breathing new life and eery shadows into my chambers, I cannot recall whether I have slept or not. Given the weariness I feel, I think it is the latter. When you stare into the void that magic brings, sometimes it can be hard to differentiate between dreams and reality. I pray for the days where Laith greets me in them and we recall conversations from the past.

Vireo arriving at my camp has unsettled me, disrupted my thoughts, and hindered my routine. The day has only just started, yet it feels like it is already written off.

Letting out a sigh of exasperation, I toss onto my side and sit up. My chance for rest has passed me by.

On the wall, I see all the chalk marks from the etchings and writings I've made since Vireo and Killian visited me. Their visit brought fresh memories, fresh pain. Laith is gone, something that I have never been able to accept. For years I have tried to discover if Rhagor's possession of Laith's body is reversible. I have all but given up hope, lost to the grief that has tormented me in my exile. Over the years, I built up a wall to protect myself like a dam, removing myself from the world, its affairs, and current state.

But news of a child fathered by Laith has let all that emotion come flooding back into me like a river bursting its banks. It is overwhelming, and at times, suffocating, as though a heavy rock has been placed on the centre of my chest. My body aches as my heart aches, and the pain is as sharp and brutal as it was the day that I lost him. The day that I decided that I had to leave, for my own selfish reasons.

In Vireo's time of need, in Levanthria's darkest hour, I abandoned them like a coward. How could I go back to them after that? My magic could have helped Vireo on his quest, perhaps, but instead I chose to push him away, just as I chose to come to this crumbling, long-abandoned keep eight years ago.

Within these walls, I feel traces of magic. Not all the

time, but every now and then, I feel the thumb of power akin to a pulsing vein.

Its sources I have yet to find, but I know that powerful magic lies latent in these grounds and I know within this, there could be a way to rid the world of Rhagor and bring my boy back.

I arch my back and stretch, my muscles aching as my back clicks multiple times, which is to be expected given that I sleep on a bed that offers little comfort. I may as well sleep on a rock face. Smacking my lips together, my throat is dry and I am in need of a drink, so I know I will need to walk to the nearby waterfall to fetch some water. Maybe while I am there, I will take a swim in the infinity pool above the falls. Maybe even bathe, gods knows I likely need it. The fact that I am thinking about swimming or even bathing tells me that Vireo has gotten into my head. Such things have not concerned me for as long as I can remember.

No matter what I do today, it is all a distraction, it all serves to occupy my mind against what it is that unsettles me.

"Gillam," I say hoarsely, almost in a whisper. It feels strange saying the name and knowing it is attached to someone of this world. Laith has a daughter, Yaelor is alive. Perhaps in their child, there does lie a purpose. Perhaps in the knowledge that she is safe, Laith lives on. His legacy need not be wasted at the hands of a fallen god.

"No!" I say, shaking my head. I know full well I need to distance myself from all thoughts of this child. No matter how powerful my instincts, no matter how intense the temptation to find them, to see the child. Would Yaelor even accept me after all this time? She likely discovered she was pregnant shortly after I left without explanation. I would not blame her if she baulked at any attempt of contact, I am not deserving of it. And as such, my mind continues to cycle through this process of self-pity and loathing, each breath I take feeling as though the very air I breathe is tainted. I do not deserve to be here, it should have been me that was lost that day, not Laith.

"Over here," a voice stirs me from my manic thoughts, and for a second, I think that Vireo has returned to my home. Did he and Killian wish to once again try and convince me to join their ill-conceived quest? I, for one, am done with quests. Especially as it is my fault that Rhagor is now free from his prison.

"It smells like piss," another voice says. It is a younger voice, spoken with a commoner's accent, which tells me that it's not Killian or Vireo.

"Rhagor wants us to tear this place upside down," a second voice growls.

I am surprised to find that this one is familiar, but I cannot place it. It has been too long since I have spoken with others, and suddenly I feel like I am in a cell full of swarming rats.

"This way," the deep, commanding voice demands. "We need to find the staff."

The staff, why would they travel all this way just for the staff? In an instant, I know I must do all in my power not to let this happen. My staff isn't in this room, however, it is in my study, and judging by how close the voices sound, I do not have much time. I dart from my room and cross the hall to the chamber on the left. There is no roof here, but there is enough of a wall for me to hide behind. I get there just in time as a soldier walks past wearing the black and gold of Askela. My heart races like it hasn't for a long time, and I keep myself hidden as the soldier glances in over the crumbled wall. He does not see me.

With a frustrated grunt, he says, "There is nothing up here." He peers into my bedroom. "Smells like an animal has been living here."

"The mage must be around somewhere," the familiar voice calls from below. "Keep looking."

A mage, a bloody mage. I feel my blood simmering at the insult. I am no mere mage. When will the world realise that I am in fact a wizard, and that there is a distinct difference between the two?

As I lean forward, I dislodge a stone, and it is enough to send mortar spraying onto the floor.

"Over here," the soldier says, and his footsteps quicken as he sets off towards me.

When he enters the room, I step out in front of him, and with a groan, I channel magic through my palms and slam them into his chest. The force sends the soldier hurtling through the air and slamming into the stone bricks behind him before he lands in a heap on the floor with a laboured groan.

"Up there, go!" the leader commands again, and I ready myself. They are downstairs, which is where I need to be to get my effects. There is no way I am leaving here without my tome or my staff. I skip down the stairs, my arms already heavy with magic use. The pain is jarring, and the dull ache sinks deep into my bones as if they have been replaced with ice.

Two more soldiers make their way up towards me.

"The mage is here," one of them calls, and he swings his sword at me without a moment's hesitation.

I draw on my magic to conjure a barrier that deflects his blow, then push past the soldier, knocking him into the other. With momentum on my side, I send them tumbling backwards down the steps, but in the process I lose my own footing, rolling on top of them before skidding across the dirt.

My skin stings as my arms and legs are grazed, but I gather myself and climb to my feet as fast as I can, getting my bearings and running towards my study.

"Get him!" the leader bellows, his frustration growing as his grainy voice sends a chill down my spine.

When I reach the study, I am short of breath, gasping and panting for air, a slight wheeze rattling in my chest. My tome lies open on a table, the defensive spell I cast to protect it doing its job. I know its presence because I know its location. I grab the tome and place it into my satchel on the far side of the room before frantically looking for the staff. Where in the blazes did I put it? I do not have time to be delicate, so I quickly grab my journal and some scraps of parchment with some of my findings as I start tracing my steps. I have not used the staff for so long, it has become part of the fixtures and fittings in this place.

"Table, chairs, walls, window, waterfall, tree." My gargled words spill off my tongue as I frantically try to remember. For someone with ill intentions to get their hands on the staff would be disastrous. I must find it.

"Think, think, think," I say aloud as the footsteps grow closer. "Fire, fire!" I remember, and I spin towards the fireplace. Buried under a pile of firewood in the corner sits my staff. I dive towards it and start pulling logs away to unbury the staff from its hiding place. In a moment I see the top of the staff and my eyes light up. The wood is tarnished and covered in cobwebs, but it is still here.

Grabbing hold of it with two hands, I grip it tightly, and the icy surge that is corrupting my arms fades as I let the staff's power wash over me as though I have a blessing from the gods.

"Jordell!" the voice growls from the doorway, and I raise my head to see the Elven brute Codrin standing in front of me. I should have known.

His face is thick with anger and he has his hand clasped around the hilt of his sword at his waist. On the opposite side, I see the spiked whip he no doubt used on Laith in a time since forgotten, coiled up and ready to be used. The sight of it brings an anger from me that I am not expecting.

How much flesh has been torn from bone by this weapon, by the monster who wields it?

"Codrin," I say, standing defiantly. I slam the foot of my staff into the stone floor, standing more prominently than I have in a long time.

"It has been some time, mage. You have done well to remain hidden all this time, but I knew it was only matter of time before Vireo came looking for you. All it took was a tip-off from the ship's captain that fetched him here."

That blasted fool. Had Vireo not come here in the first place, I would not be in this situation. "Bastard pirates," I sneer, "can't be trusted."

Codrin smirks at me as he starts to raise his sword from his belt. "I tend to find that with the right motivation, they can be." He removes his sword fully now and his gaze travels from mine to the staff that I grip in my hand.

"Just hand me that staff, mage, and we will be on our way. There does not need to be any bloodshed."

"Tell me, is that what you said to those poor souls in Askela, the ones you trapped in the Great Temple to simply perish?" The wood of the staff groans as I squeeze it.

"That was a long time ago, Jordell."

It may be to him, but I will never be able to unsee the atrocities that took place when we consecrated the bodies. So many lives taken, so needlessly, all overseen by this charlatan.

"Mark my words, Codrin, your time will come."

"Not on this day!" Codrin lunges forward with his sword outstretched towards me. His speed is impressive, but I parry his blade with my staff, then flick out the bottom and press it into his side, pushing him past me. With a snarl, he quickly turns and tries to detach my head from my body with a back-handed swipe.

I duck the blow, then jump backwards and channel my magic as a protective barrier forms in front of me once again. The more power I channel, the more the tip of the staff glows, feeding my magic without it having any effect on my body. Codrin swings his sword again and this time it hits the barrier. My spell splinters like that of fracturing glass, but it is able to hold off his attack. I strain to keep the barrier up. It has been so long since I have channelled this power, and I am out of practice.

Codrin slams down another blow and another, each time the barrier spell fracturing that little more, his face snarling with anger and rage.

By the third blow, the barrier gives way, and I swing my staff towards him, clattering him in the side of the head with every ounce of strength that I have. But in my weakened, dishevelled state, it is not anywhere near enough force to cause any injury to such a brute.

My staff bounces off his head with a thud and it only serves to make him angrier as he dives towards me, slamming his shoulder into me and sending me tumbling backwards in a heap. It is a solid blow, one that knocks all air from my chest, and I heave as I roll onto my side, gasping for air. I panic under the suffocation and try to crawl away towards the doorway.

"No you don't," Codrin says, and I feel the cloth of my tunic stretch from my back before I am launched into the wall on the opposite side of the doorway. The force is tremendous and enough to send me through the stone and land on a pile of rubble, broken and buried. Agonising pain tears through me as I push myself back to my feet, blood pooling in my mouth which I spit onto the floor.

"That strength," I stammer, "it is not natural." I point towards Codrin. "Rhagor, he – he has done something to you."

Codrin doesn't answer. He simply tilts his head as if he doesn't understand what I say. I point my staff towards him and call upon more magic, firing a blast of raw energy at him. It rips into his shoulder and knocks him back, albeit only slightly. It is enough to cause him to drop his blade, but he seems undeterred; he simply reaches for his spiked whip and lets it uncoil onto the ground.

"Oh, I am going to enjoy tearing your skin from your bone," he sneers, demonstrating the whip's power with a flick of his wrist. It cracks against the rubble that sits between us.

I draw on my staff as he launches the whip at me, and our blows hit each other at the same time. I knock Codrin even further backwards as his whip slices against my upper shoulder, ripping my tunic and tearing into my flesh as he promised. The pain is immense, and I draw on my staff to summon some healing properties. My body does not grow weak from magic, but from the frailty of my skin and bones as I become older.

Then I notice my satchel on the ground, the strap torn from the whip's strike. As I lean down, another crack of the whip hits me, this time just by my hand. The skin slices and I pull my hand back as the pain throbs all the way up my arm. Before I have time to do anything, Codrin waves his whip around above him and unfurls another crack, this time hitting me in the upper thigh. The pain is enough to cause my leg to buckle.

He has the upper hand and my body is failing. I back up to the edge of the room, the wall crumbled with nothing but a sheer cliff face behind me.

"Give me that staff," he demands.

I look down at the satchel on the floor that contains my spell tome before looking up at Codrin as he raises his whip once more. I can't get to it in time, I know I can't. If only I wasn't as frail as I am now. I look back over my shoulder. I must not let this staff fall into Rhagor's hands, but there is nowhere to run.

I am left with only one option.

I let myself fall backwards down the cliff face. The last thing I see before I disappear over the edge is Codrin's whip cracking just above me, barely missing my head.

I fall fast and hard. A few moments feel like a lifetime, and I embrace my fate, hoping to be reunited with Laith soon. Maybe he will greet me in the afterlife.

Then everything falls black as I crash into the waters of the river that flows beneath the keep.

13

YAELOR

A forceful knock at the door tells me that this next encounter is not going to be a pleasant one.

"Open this fucking door," the voice demands, low and aggressive. I know who it will be, the father of the boy that I saw Gillam beating in the street. We need to keep as low a profile as possible, so things like this serve to be a major inconvenience. The best I can do is keep the peace. Hopefully this will go no further.

It is dark outside, but I can see the light of a torch lighting up the area immediately outside our house. I have been working on a dagger and when I finish hammering it, I dip it into the bucket of water beside my anvil. A loud hiss comes from the water as it bubbles up fiercely.

"I said open, this fucking door!"

"I'm coming, I'm coming," I say, my apprehension growing. I grab hold of the door to be greeted by a large man whose name I do not know. He is far taller than me and twice as wide, his broad shoulders threatening to fill the frame of the door. "What can I do for you?" I sigh. I know where this is going already.

"That fucking bastard daughter of yours has made a mess out of my son's face."

"I appreciate that my daughter has done wrong," I tell him sternly. "She has been dealt with, but please, she is just a child. Remember this when you talk about her like this."

"Done wrong?" the man fumes. "It will be a miracle if my son is not left with any scars."

"I am sorry for what she has done. I have disciplined her and she will be over to apologise in the morning."

The man puffs up his chest, a move I do not take kindly to, but I continue to bite my tongue.

"I beg you to go home," I say, "this doesn't need to escalate any more than it already has."

The man grips the inside of the doorframe as he attempts to step into our home. "I want you to fetch her here so I can give her a good hiding myself, maybe then the runt will learn."

"No," I say, "she is my daughter to punish, not yours."

"Is everything okay here?" I recognise Trivor's voice straight away and I am grateful for his intervention.

"No, it isn't," the man snarls. "My boy's face is a right mess. All because this whore doesn't know how to keep that bastard in fucking tow. Fucking scum."

Against my better judgement, I can't help but react. He can call me what he wants but I will not have someone speak about Gillam in this way.

"Perhaps you should have taught your son better manners," I snap.

"What did you say, you cheeky bitch?" he demands.

It is not the first time I have made a man angry simply for being a woman willing to stand up to him. I let out a sigh and continue, "Gillam tells me that your son was not being very kind. In fact, she said that your son insulted her." I eye him up. "I can see where he must get that from. Perhaps you should train your son how to fight better."

The man's face turns bright red as he steps through the doorframe despite Trivor's attempts to calm the situation down. He swings a punch at me, but I duck it easily before shoving him with both of my hands back towards the door.

"This is your last chance to get out of my house. You know the laws. I can use whatever force necessary." I have taken down bigger warriors than this arse in my life. He does not scare me nor will I allow him to think he can intimidate me.

Hands wrap around him from behind as he is hoisted back out through the front door by Trivor.

"I said that is enough!" Trivor orders.

The man holds his hands up in the air in mock surrender. "You haven't heard the fucking last of me. Foreign scum," he seethes.

If only he knew the irony in his words. I am more Levanthrian than he is, the ignorant prick.

"Just because you are screwing the leader of our town doesn't make you above us all." And then he storms out of my shop, cursing under his breath as he barges past Trivor.

"Are you okay?" Trivor asks, looking bashful from the man's false accusation about our relationship.

I smile and nod. "I've dealt with arses before. It isn't the first time or the last."

"You didn't need to goad him," Trivor scolds me, his tone worried. "Dronsar is not one to get on the wrong side of. Hopefully he will see this all as a misunderstanding. I'll speak to him in the morning once he has cooled off. This is just kids being kids."

"Thank you," I say sincerely. I appreciate Trivor intervening when he did. If Dronsar had not left, then I would not have hesitated to use one of my hatchets on him.

"Goodnight, Yaelor." Trivor smiles and makes his leave.

"Goodnight, Trivor." I shut the door behind him. I just want to go to bed so that this day can be over. "Fucking children," I sigh to myself.

I pretend not to notice the prying eyes of Gillam peering through the crack in the wall.

It is the dead of night when a creaking floorboard startles me awake. Without hesitating, I am up from my bed and reaching for my hatchets. I press my ear to my bedroom door and listen carefully. Another creak.

Is it Gillam sneaking around the house? It isn't like her, but these days I never quite know what to expect from her acts of rebellion. I pull my door open slowly. Gillam's room is opposite mine, and her door is shut. I step across the hall as lightly as I can and push her door open just a crack. It is pitch-black inside. Holding my breath, I listen to see if she is awake. She murmurs in her sleep and rolls over in bed.

Then I hear another creak of floorboards. Someone is in the house. I walk down the hall on my tiptoes, one with the shadows, all my instincts, all my training returning to me in an instant. On high alert, I make my way to the smithy that joins onto the side of the house, thinking that they are in there. Likely someone wanting to rob me of my wares. It would not be the first time.

Out of nowhere, hulking arms grab me from behind, and a thick, odious hand wraps around my mouth to keep me quiet.

I drop my hatchets and flail as I attempt to wriggle out of the vice-like grip that threatens to crush my ribs.

"Keep still, you little bitch!"

I recognise the voice in an instant. It is Dronsar, his snarls almost as repulsive as his odour. He strikes me in the side of the head and I see a flash of white in my vision before he slams me to the floor. "I'll show you," he sneers as he starts to unbuckle his pants.

It takes a coward to break into a house where a woman lives alone with her child. But it takes a foolish one to do it to a woman with the skills that I possess. I feign being groggy from the blow, and when he reaches me, I kick out, hitting him in the groin and causing him to howl in pain. I jump to my feet as he swings his fist, making contact with the side of my head. Another flash of white erupts in my vision. Perhaps I am a little rusty, and I curse myself for not blocking the blow.

I aim a punch back, but he grabs hold of my arm, holding it in place before striking me again and again. I am dazed, my face throbs, and I can hear the splatter of my own blood as it drips onto the floorboards.

He lunges forward, grabbing me around the throat, and we fall backwards into the door to the smithy. Luckily, the door swings open and it puts us both off balance. As I fall backwards, his body presses against mine. I use the momentum to hoist him over the top of me and he lands on the ground in the centre of the smithy.

Dronsar grunts and growls as he climbs back to his feet. Through the glow of the remaining embers in my forge, I see him remove a blade from his side.

"I am going to cut you up," he says.

Weapons are not in short supply, and I reach by the anvil, pulling out the dagger I was working on earlier. The two of us start circling one another. With my dagger gripped tightly in front of me, I wait for him to make his move. He swings wildly at me with his blade, and I knock his arm away before ramming my dagger into his shoulder. I am surprised at how much bulk greets me as the blade embeds in his flesh down to the hilt. He howls again, but he grabs me and pulls me towards him. I manage to turn in time so I am facing away from him as he pulls his free hand towards me, dagger ready to strike. I slam my hand against him and cry out in pain as his weapon rips through my hand, but I use all my strength to stop him from pressing the blade into my chest. I struggle against him as my arms shake from the force, grimacing at the pain that has erupted in my hand.

"Scum!" he says, his breath kissing the back of my neck.

I throw my head back into his face and hear an audible crunch that fills me with satisfaction as he stumbles backwards. He loosens his grip and I am able to get some distance between him and myself. He falls against the forge and embers spill out. Grinning like a maniac, he reaches for a poker and hits the embers, spraying them across the room.

Before I know it, smoke is filling the room as a fire starts. The flames light up his face, illuminating his maniacal smile.

"I told you I would be back!" he yells. "You don't fuck with me or my boys."

As he steps towards me again, I take the initiative this time and lung forward, diving into him with a roar of anger. We roll on the ground as one of us desperately tries to get the upper hand. He is stronger than me, but I am more agile, and as he tries to pin me down, I grab the hot poker out of the forge and press it against his skin. He cries out in agony, and as he does, I pull back the poker and shove it into his open mouth. His scream is masked by the singeing noise as the poker burns his flesh. I feel the poker force its way out of the back of his head. He falls forward limply and I use what strength I have left to push him off of me. Unfortunately for him, that results with his head landing in the forge, where he remains as the embers lick up his body, igniting his clothes. Panic overcomes me as flames rise high in the smithy.

"Gillam," I shout, the smoke choking a cough from my lungs. The smoke is thick and heavy, suffocating as I feel my way around the smithy to get my bearings. Flames kiss up the walls around me, the intensity of the heat stinging my skin as my eyes weep, making it even harder to keep them open.

"Gillam!" I call out once again.

"Mama!" I hear her cry. I keep low to the ground, crawling until I see the doorway back into the house. The smoke has billowed in here, too, quickly filling up the hallway. My hand slips and an intense pain grips me. Blood pulses out of the open wound, making it harder to crawl, but I push on. I need to get to my daughter.

"Gillam, I am coming," I groan as I continue to crawl, and then I hear her cries.

"Mama!" she screams, and I can hear the fear in her voice.

"Gillam, get by the window!"

Above us, the ceiling begins to groan as the flames rip through our home in its entirety. We don't have long.

I grab hold of her bedroom door and push it open. Smoke billows in, but I waste no time as I rush towards Gillam. The sound of the flames is intense behind me, louder than I could have imagined. Gillam's terrified face is lit up by the growing flames that rake down my back like a clawed hand. The ceiling is creaking even more, it is about to give way.

I dive at Gillam, reaching out and pulling her towards me whilst using my momentum to turn my back. We slam through the window and into the street. I hear Gillam yelp as I land on the dirt outside, just as the roof collapses in on itself.

Gillam lands on top of me, sobbing. I rub my hands over her face, checking her for injuries. She is okay, but she is coughing like I am. My lungs hurt with every breath I take, but the clean air is a welcome reprieve from the smoke.

"Mama," she whimpers as she squeezes me tightly and I hug her back.

My breathing is heavy and laboured, but at least Gillam is okay. She is all that matters to me, in this life and the next.

14

ORJAN

Deep within the shadowy depths of the Erlking's Wood, a monstrous black dog with glowing red eyes stalks the ancient paths. This demon hound is said to be an omen of death, its chilling howl a sign that death is closer than you would like.

-Thorne Eldridge, Beasts of the Erlking's Wood, 241 KR

The lingering smell of ash still tinges the air distastefully. All around me, I see nothing but scorched land, houses turned to rubble and ruin, charred husks left sprawled on the ground where the once vibrant and prosperous farming village of Hora once stood. My blood runs cold as I take it all in. I cannot see how anyone could survive such a power.

It has been at least a week since the attack took place, yet the ground still smoulders as if we stand on the ground of an active volcano. A blanket of smoke sits close to the ground, a sinister fog tinged with death and torment. I can only hope that the lives lost here were taken quickly and there wasn't any suffering.

A knot forms in my throat, part from grief and part from anger as I take in the ruins. My breath trembles with the rage I feel building inside of me.

"Why would King Rhagor do this?" Rior asks. He is knelt by the charred remains of a woman. She is lying on her side, an arm reaching across her face as if she seeks to shield herself from something. Nothing remains but a blackened cocoon, preserving her body, eternally frozen in one horrendous moment in time. Rior continues to inspect the remains, shaking his head at what he sees.

"Rhagor is no king," I growl, my throat rattling as I speak. "No king, no man, would inflict this on his own people." Similar husks litter the streets, collapsed bodies frozen in their final moments. The rest turned to ash in the blink of an eye. "The magic that Rhagor used must have been tremendous." There have been stories of his power and the sword that he wields, although the sources of these stories remain unknown. Rhagor seldom leaves any survivors.

"This is not the first time that he has wiped a village from the face of this world, without warning or reason." I continue to inspect our surroundings, the putrid stench stinging my nostrils. "I do not think we will ever know his reasoning."

That does not mean I do not wish to find out. Why would he level an entire village in such a way? Why would he be so angry, so cruel as to punish all of these people?

"You are a brave man to question his reign," Rior says, looking over the woman one final time before standing up.

"It is a good job I am cursed already. What is he going to do, smite me? Come, let's see if there are any survivors." I know the chances are slim to none, but I still hope that someone has somehow survived this.

Around us, semi-collapsed buildings remain in place, fractured walls embedded into the black, burnt ground like giant tombstones. If I knew the names of these people, I would etch every one into the stone.

"When we return to Eltera, we will send Petra to consecrate the grounds. Perhaps then their poor souls will rest." It is the least that we can do, it is the least these people deserve. "Keep searching what remains of the buildings, look for any survivors."

"Orjan," Rior protests, "how do you expect anyone to have survived Rhagor's power here?"

"With hope," I say. It is the only thing that keeps me going. A test of will and character. "I know that there is little chance of survivors, Rior, but if we do not search and there are, their hope is lost, as is ours. Without hope, what do we have?"

In the distance I can hear voices. These are not the cries of people asking for help, of people that are trapped. The sound of tools against stone tells me that people are at work.

Confused, I speed up through the town. The ground feels strange with each step I take, crispy on the surface yet softening with each step as if I walk in marshlands. Every few steps, my feet sink into the ground. The earth is warmer under the surface, causing me to wonder if the terrain could ignite into flames at any moment.

"What is it?" Rior asks, clearly not hearing what I hear; my reptilian curse allows me enhanced hearing compared to others.

"I hear something," I say, moving at haste.

I have visited Hora a few times in my time as steward of Eltera, but I am not familiar enough to know where everything is. I know towards the centre there was a temple, one that now lies in ruin. Its walls have crumbled to the floor as if they were made of sand, what stone work remaining dismantled by the men and women I see digging where it has stood for so long. Pickaxes chip away at the stone and winches are in place, moving the large rocks into a growing pile.

"What are they doing?" Rior asks as he catches up with me.

"Digging." I point to the side of the land where the temple used to sit. There are steps down beside the footings that lead into a dug-out tunnel. Wooden plinths and stone arches prevent the earth from falling in on them as multiple people emerge from the opening, pushing carts filled with dirt which they tip out into a pile before returning to the tunnel.

"What's going on here?" I say, my voice echoing over the dig site.

"Is this wise, Orjan?" Rior asks as the group ahead of us stop what they are doing.

They will know who I am. After all, how many lizard men walk Levanthria? How many lizard men serve as steward of the land they are desecrating?

"I advise caution, Orjan, we do not know if they are hostile."

With the mood I am in, I hope they are. Someone needs to pay for everything that has happened here.

"What are you doing?" I demand once again. Their faces are filled with dirt, but they remain quiet and stony-faced. Most choose to stare into the ground rather than meet my furious gaze. Marching forward, I reach for the collar of a gangly, gaunt-faced man, and his eyes grow wide with fear as I yank him close to me.

"Do not make me repeat myself," I seethe, my jaw clenched tightly. "Or am I to assume that you are raiders?" My grip tightens around the cloth of his tunic and the man gulps.

"No – no, my lord," he stammers. "We are just doing as instructed by the king."

My eyes burn into him so much so that he turns his head to avoid my gaze. "Stop this right now! These grounds have not been consecrated. Have you no respect for the dead? Where is your honour?"

"Please, my lord, we are merely doing as we have been commanded," he says with a quiver. I toss him to the ground and it takes every ounce of my inner strength not to remove my morning star and stove his head in.

"I did not have you down as a cleric, Orjan," a deep, gravelly voice looms from the shadows of the tunnel as the speaker begins to emerge.

I already know who it is before I see him. His is a voice I have come to despise over the years.

"Codrin," I hiss as the Elven man's hulking frame steps outside from the tunnel. He claps his hands together, brushing the dust free. Like he has done a hard day's work in the tunnels. But he wouldn't know a thing about hard labour. His only skill is inflicting pain and suffering on others, and what is worse, he enjoys it.

He gives me a smug grin and raises his hand to the spiked whip that sits coiled to his belt. "To what do I owe the pleasure?"

"This land falls under my stewardship. I demand to know why these people have been slaughtered."

There is a moment's silence, one that feels as though it

lasts an eternity, as if the only people present in this moment are him and me.

"Because the king wills it," Codrin's voice fills the void between us as he continues his walk towards me. "I wouldn't say it was a slaughter though, do you see any blood? It all happened very quickly."

I step towards Codrin, incensed by his callous words, but Rior grips the inside of my arm tightly.

"As I said, perhaps caution is the better path here, Orjan." Rior's voice is calm and collected. He has the situation measured, and I heed his warning, taking in our surroundings. I can see at least a dozen men and women, likely guards from Askela. Some will be skilled in combat, but others look less so. There are at least three more in the tunnel as we saw them re-enter just a few moments before.

"Why did Rhagor do this? What did these people do?" There is a rawness in my voice. I am angry but my manner is better controlled than it was prior to Rior's intervention.

"I think you should go back to Eltera, Orjan. This has nothing to do with you." Codrin's voice lowers and he speaks slowly, in a threatening tone.

"I do not take kindly to being told what to do," I growl, my throat rattling as I speak. My body tenses, my frustration rising even further.

"Yet you obey every command like the animal that you are," Codrin says with an infuriating smile. The ignorance of the oaf, he literally does everything that he is commanded to by Rhagor and Morgana, never questioning his orders.

"I do what I have to, to keep the people I am responsible for safe."

Codrin laughs, his shoulders rising as he tightens his

grip around his whip. He looks around at the ruins that we stand in. "How's that treating you?"

A rage flows up from the pits of my stomach, and in this moment, I feel as though I am ready to breathe fire on all of them, ready to show them the dragon that I am. If only such a power existed, then I could make these wretched fools pay for everything that they've done.

"Do not bite, Orjan," Rior says. "He merely seeks to goad you."

"And he is succeeding," I growl under my breath. I lower my hand to the hilt of my morning star and squeeze it tightly, my knuckles cracking under the strain.

"Orjan, do not let him get the rise from you that he seeks. Look around us. There are too many of them. You may not have a care for your life, but I happen to."

Rior is right; to start a fight under these circumstances would be foolish of me. Codrin has been goading me since the day that Morgana asked me to watch over Eltera and its surrounding towns and villages. All the times I have visited Askela and he has looked down his crooked nose at me, as if he was better than me somehow . . . Codrin is without doubt one of the vilest people I have ever had the displeasure of coming across.

I have seen him do unspeakable things and all the while I have needed to stand by idly, rendering myself complicit in his cruel, sick acts. If I am a monster, I've yet to come across a name to put on this vile creature.

I take a deep breath and gather myself, knowing I cannot risk Rior's life.

If Rior was not present with me, I could not promise to restrain myself. After all, I like to fight just as much as Codrin. The difference is, I like fighting and defeating people like Codrin, people like Grush. Monsters that prey on the vulnerable and get a kick out of showcasing their power.

What I would give to go one-on-one with Codrin right now. He may not have wielded the magic that caused this chaos, but he certainly played his part. In his death, at least, there would be some form of justice. Unfortunately, it will not be this day. Rior has been through too much, and I feel he is destined for greater things than falling foul of a blade in the ruins of Hora.

"Come, Rior," I say, turning my back on Codrin.

Rior sets off with me. "That was a wise move," he says under his breath. "I am in shock that you actually listened to me."

"That's right, Orjan, turn your back. Walk away," Codrin roars, and a few petulant laughs erupt from his guards. My jaw tightens and it takes every ounce of my resolve to not spin on my heels and charge into him.

"Keep walking, Orjan," Rior says as if he can read my thoughts.

"I intend to," I say through frustrated breath as we walk through the desolate village. "We will wait for nightfall, then we will return."

"What is it you have in mind?"

"Rhagor is looking for something. Something important enough to level this entire village. When we return, we will enter the tunnel. We will find what they are looking for before they do, and then we leave."

Rior sighs deeply. "You make it sound easy," he says. "How can we find something that we do not know the appearance of? We have no clue what it is that King Rhagor is searching for. Besides, what do you plan on doing once we have found it? If you go directly against the king's wishes, he'll have you stripped of your title, if he doesn't just outright kill you. Not even Morgana would be able to protect you."

"I never had Morgana's protection," I snarl. "Only her lies. She has made that much clear. Besides, he is not my king."

My mood saddens when I see another husk, crouched by a crumbled wall, as if they sought shelter from the blast. The wall offered them nothing. From the size of the body, I think it is a child, and my heart sinks.

The best thing I can hope for us to do in this moment is cause as much disruption to Rhagor's plans that we can. It is not much, but it is the least I can do to honour the lives of those that have fallen here.

15

ULRIK

The Great Library of Askela has ancient tomes that speak of the Fae as beings of pure magic, their very essence tied to the ebb and flow of arcane energies. It is said that the Fae could manipulate the elements, shape the very fabric of reality, and even bend the wills of lesser creatures to their whims. As their descendants, the Elves are said to have inherited a fraction of this immense power.

-Isindril Morvor, Tomes of the Ancients, 103 KR

Zerina continues to follow from the rear, sulking like a child, ignoring me since our spat on *Esara's Revenge.* What does she want me to do? We are pirates, after all. Wanted for the crimes that we have committed. I am the Kingslayer, and as such, I can never set foot on Levanthrian soil again. My path is chosen, marked out in the sands in front of me by the gods.

The greenery of the exotic trees here reminds me of Voraz. I was a lot smaller then, less developed, less able. It was I who trailed from the rear that day, nervous with anticipation of what we were about to discover. The fact that we ended that day being chased by Elven skeletons is something that drives the excitement I now feel when hunting for ancient, lost treasure.

This time is different, however. What we search for is more valuable than any gemstone. You cannot put a price on what I seek, what I long for.

I press further inland, searching for any signs of the lagoon that is said to hold the entranceway.

"Captain, I fear we do not have much light of day left," Darmour says as he pulls up beside me. He is red-faced and sweat beads on his head. Even under the canopy of the leaves, there is a humidity in the air which has made this hike through the sands of this island harder than it needs to be.

"Do you not feel it best to let the crew rest?" he asks, keeping his voice quiet so no one can hear him questioning me.

"We can rest when we find it," I growl.

"Captain, as far as I can see, there is no one else on this island. What is it that has you rushing to get there? If you would just tell me what it is that we search for, it might help me keep the crew motivated." There is a sense of frustration in Darmour's voice as he looks back at the group that falls behind us.

"Tell me, Darmour, is it the crew you want this answer for, or Zerina?"

Darmour sighs as he hacks some thick overgrowth away, clearing a path for us to walk through. Our movement disturbs some birds above, and they squawk and flutter their wings disapprovingly as they take flight. "She is tired, Captain. She has followed you around the world, as have I. I worry that she grows tired of hunting for treasure."

"Has she told you that?" I glance over my shoulder at Zerina, who looks up at the blanket of trees above us. "I did not ask her to follow me."

"Captain, you know all too well who did. She made a vow."

"Well, let her be free of it. She owes no debt to me, and she clearly is not happy with my ways." I am still angered by her drawing her magic on me. There was a moment where I saw a hatred in her eyes and I thought she might even use it.

"Just talk to her. If not myself and the crew, just tell her what it is we are searching this island for. Maybe then she will understand."

"Understand?" My nostrils flare as a rush of anger rises in me. "What is there to understand? I am the captain, I set the course, you all follow me. That is how this works." I know in my blackened heart that she would not understand. She already grows apart from me because of my choices, because of the things I have done in my brother's name. The distance between us has never been greater, a far cry from when I used to look at her big blue eyes and long for her to be my sister. I cannot allow her to figure out what I am looking to find on this cursed island, or the dangers that we must overcome if we are to succeed. It will all be worthwhile, no matter the cost to myself or my crew.

Whatever the price is, I am willing to pay it.

"Do not come to me on behalf of Zerina," I continue. "If she wishes to speak to me about her concerns, she can do it herself. Although I cannot promise that I will not react if she threatens me with her magic again."

"Aye, Captain," Darmour says as we continue to hack

and slash our way forward through the increasingly dense trees. Though I do not want to admit it, the heat is getting to me and my body is telling me to stop and rest just as Darmour suggested, but I know we must press on.

I stop for a moment and listen to our surroundings. Behind me I can hear the huffing and panting of the crew as they push through the trees into the opening where we stand. Different wild calls from the vast and varying animals of the island echo in the trees, calling to one another. If this island was one created by the gods, then I know all too well the kind of dangers that will await us as we travel deeper inside.

Reaching into my jacket, I pull out the ancient map once more. Its edges are frayed and torn, but it is drawn onto thick parchment, the main body of which remains relatively sturdy given its age.

The diagram indicates that a lagoon should sit beyond a cluster of trees. Looking at the bearings on the map, I feel certain that we should have travelled through the trees by now. For how long we have been walking, we should have made it through to the other side. There is an ancient language at the top of the parchment that I have been unable to translate, despite having scoured pages and pages of ancient books. Asking Zerina for assistance with the translation would have drawn too much scrutiny from her, something that I could not afford.

"Does it tell you where we are?" her voice startles me from behind.

"I have already said we are on the Isle of Averaza," I reply coldly, rolling up the map.

Without word or warning, Zerina shoots forward and grabs the map from my hand. Panic overcomes me as I fear what she may uncover from it.

"Zerina, give me the map," I growl.

She scowls at me, rolling the map out in her hands whilst looking at me with hostility.

My anger rises further and without hesitation, I draw my cutlass and raise it to her. "I said, give me the map."

Zerina's eyes drift from mine to the open map, then to my sword.

The crew gasp in surprise and alarm, freezing in place, unsure which line in the sand they need to stand on. As their captain, I find this infuriating.

"I will not ask again." My arm is steady and my mind clear. It is my turn to make the threats.

"All it says is 'To find a treasure hidden by the gods, you need to be lost in order to find what you are looking for'," she reads aloud before tossing the map to me forcefully. "Well, consider us lost." She turns her back on the edge of my sword as if she wouldn't care if I drove it through her. "The fact that you would draw your sword on me tells me all I need to know. That there is something you are purposefully hiding from me. So tell me, Ulrik, what exactly is it that you are not telling me?"

I glare at her, sword still drawn.

"Have it your way." Zerina flicks her fingers and a spark ignites from their tips. In an instant the map ignites, disintegrating into nothing but wisps of ash that dance in the air around her.

"What have you done!" I rage, my head feeling as though it will explode with anger.

"This map makes no sense, Ulrik. You are making no sense. Have you descended into madness? You are going to get us all killed!"

Gripping my cutlass, my hand trembles as I grind my teeth together. I have often fallen out with Zerina over the years. We disagree with each other on a regular basis, but this is the first time that I have had to fight the temptation to strike her down. I swallow down on my darkened thoughts, shame pushing its way to the forefront of my mind.

"You have no idea what you have done! I need that map to find it."

"To find what, Ulrik? Be honest with me for once! I can't help you unless I know what your intentions are. Tell me we are not running some fool's errand for a treasure that does not exist."

"Even after all this time, you do not trust me." My temper frays like a twisted rope, hanging on by mere threads. I will not strike her; I know that my poisoned words can cause more injury to her than any blade. "Tell me, Zerina, is this how you were with your sisters?" I stare deeply into her deep, blue eyes as a fire ignites inside them.

The crew members are hesitant to act. I stare at one who stands as if he is about to piss himself. He is trembling, his eyes darting from me to Zerina.

"Fuck you!" Zerina says, her right hand erupting into a blinding heat, surrounded by molten fire.

"Let's take a moment to calm down!" Darmour finally interjects, stepping in between us. He uses the palm of his hand to push away the cutlass that I still have pointed at her.

I do not take kindly to her threats.

"Sooner or later, Darmour, you are going to have to pick a side," I warn under my compressed jaw. "I needed that map."

"Why?" Zerina asks. "All it stated was that we needed to be lost. And I believe that is exactly what you are, Ulrik." Her voice cracks as she speaks the words.

"Fuck you!" I return. "I have no time for your riddles or your counsel. If I am that deplorable, if I am that much of a lost cause, then you are free from the promise you made him. I don't need you." Venom pours from my mouth as from a coiled viper. In this heated moment, I want to hurt her. I want her to feel a semblance of the torture I experience every single day.

"I am beginning to agree with you there." She exhales in exasperation. The rest of the crew seem to be doing their best to not be drawn into the spectacle.

Zerina turns to leave, heading back through the tracks we have formed. She shakes the flames from her arm as light speckles of molten flame spray onto the ground, melting the sandy earth underfoot.

"I'd think it wise not to turn your back on me, Zerina," I snarl, spit leaving my mouth as my eyes burn into her back.

She raises her hand nonchalantly and gives me the finger as she continues to walk away from me.

Darmour emits a great sigh of frustration himself as he stands beside me.

"Tell me, Darmour, how does it feel to be the lapdog for two people?" I hiss. "I suggest you follow her and stop her from doing anything stupid. If she has her way, I will be returning to a smouldering ship and no way off this godforsaken island."

"Aye, Captain," he says before following her as she makes her way back into the thicket of trees.

"What are you looking at!" I roar at the crew member who is unfortunate enough to be looking in my direction. He was clearly a portly man once, judging by the sagging skin on his stomach. His olive skin is darkened by sweat and grime. He does not speak, he simply evades his gaze whilst the rest of the crew stand around idly, unsure what it is they should be doing now that we are lost.

Without that map, I do not know where to go. I close my eyes and centre my thoughts. The sound of the leaves rustling in the light breeze, the birds singing, it is not enough to calm me from Zerina's disobedience.

Then, through the rustling leaves, critters scurrying around and calls of wildlife, the sound of rushing water catches my attention, and my face erupts into a smile.

Without a word, I turn on my heel and head towards an area of even denser trees, towards where the sound of tumbling water comes from. Is this it? Has the entranceway revealed itself? Has Zerina burning the map rendered us truly lost as the gods desired, making it possible for us to gain access?

I continue to rush forward, my heart racing like a herd of wild horses thundering across the Biterian Plains. Once I enter the trees, it is as if all the white noise around me disappears. The chattering of my crew behind me fades, the sounds of wildlife disappears.

My eyes beam widely at the gushing water that falls over the brow of the hillside. The cascading water is snow-like in appearance as it crashes into the turquoise-blue pool below. A manic grin pulls the corners of my cheeks wide.

The lost cave of Averaza. And inside it, a treasure more valuable than any coin or jewel lies hidden.

All I have to do now is find it.

16

MORGANA

I slam the door to my chamber, and the bang echoes through the room. One of my ornate vases rocks, then falls from its stand and smashes on the floor by my feet. It makes me jump, and I curse. That was one of my favourites.

My body aches tremendously and I feel exhausted. That was the first time I have had a vision whilst awake. Normally they appear in my dreams.

Something is different, something is off.

My chest burns as I breathe and the bile at the back of my throat stings, leaving me on the edge of nausea. The room rocks around me as if I am on a ship in a stormy ocean.

I close my eyes and I see flashes of blood and screams, flames cast out as wide as eyes can see. A river of death, bodies strewn around, burnt and charred. I can't un-see my vision, it feels so real, it is a though I am there. I can smell the burning flesh, I can hear the people's cries of agony as clearly as if they are right in front of me. I can feel the air against my skin and I reach out my hand but feel nothing, and it grounds me. I open my eyes with a gasp as another wave of nausea overcomes me, a hot flash rising up my body and into my cheeks. Is this what I must endure every time that I close my eyes now?

The amulet is what is at the forefront of my mind. It is carved from what looks to be bone, bound together by flesh as though it is a living, breathing thing. A red jewel is carved into its centre, the sinew that surrounds it stretched as if the jewel is trying to escape. Opposite forces in contention with one another, like water and fire.

I swear I felt it pulsate as if it breathed life itself in my vision. It was around my neck and I was walking through a chaotic battlefield, a new power awakened from deep within me. I felt unbreakable, I felt immortal, like nothing could defeat me. But something felt off in my form. I was a passenger as I always am in my visions, but still, something felt different from usual.

The pulsating feeling intensifies, as does the knot in my stomach. When I can't take it anymore, I run as fast as I can to my bathroom and vomit into the bath. I keep vomiting until I retch and nothing comes up. Is it the vision or what I have seen that has affected me this way?

As far as I know, the visions I had previously were manipulated by Rhagor. They were his way of influencing the world so that he could be released from his personal prison. So he says anyway, but I cannot be sure. As a seer, I know that these visions can take place at any time, but I have come to realise that I am but a piece in a game that the gods continue to play. It leaves me questioning what my purpose is in this world.

An almighty headache starts to come over me, which I know is the aftereffect of the vision. The light from outside forces my eyes shut as my ears start to ring. It has been a long time since a vision affected me in such away. In fact, the last time it was this bad was when I took the lifeforce of the cook's apprentice all those years ago. That had replenished me instantly. Perhaps that is what I need right now. I rush across my room and draw the curtains, darkening the room. That at least makes my surroundings more bearable, and I look at my freshly made bed with its plump pillows and yakula fur throw. The posts of the bed reach to the ceiling, a veil hanging loosely around them. This will be my solace now. I only hope that in sleep, I am not haunted by my latest vision.

Collapsing onto my bed, I let the softness of the yakula fur wrap around me. It is like falling into a warm bath, offering me comfort in this bleak moment.

As I try to rest, my mind starts to race, not about the vision, not about my aching body, but about Rhagor's face. About the cut he received when he was too busy slamming plates like a petulant child.

I have watched Rhagor closely ever since he first took control of Laith's body. He has always stated that he is immortal, that he cannot be defeated. People have tried to assassinate him but the power he wields is like nothing I have ever seen. I have watched through the years as the body of a young man filled out, became leaner, stronger. His hair grew and his beard lengthened down his face, rendering him an attractive man. But in all this time, I have never once seen him bleed. Up until now, I have believed Rhagor when he told me about his immortality. But when the shards of that plate cut his cheek and drew fresh blood, it raised the question: If he can bleed, can he die?

My door opens and I sit up. Who dares enter my room unannounced? My vision is blurred, but I blink until I can make out Vaya's form. She looks pale, like she is about to faint.

"What is the meaning of this, Vaya?" I demand. She may be my only trusted maid, but that does not give her the right to enter my room so freely, without invitation.

She is out of breath, panting as she tries to gather herself.

"What is it, Vaya?" I say as I sit at the edge of my bed, fighting back yet another hot flash. It is strong enough to make me wonder how my clothes have not ignited into flames.

"I bring news," she says, a quiver in her voice. "Of Osar."

"Of Osar?" I repeat, my heart sinks to the pits of my stomach. "Are they . . .?"

Vaya shakes her head at my question. "There was an incident, a fire. A body was found in the ruins but it was that of a local man. Yaelor and the child, their bodies were not found."

I breathe a sigh of relief, but it does not settle my racing heart. "What happened? How did the fire start?" I ask hastily, forgetting my own rules that I have set.

"They do not know. They are saying that a man has been murdered and that guards have been out searching for her. A bounty has been placed on her head and that of her daughter."

"They don't know where they are?" What exactly have I been paying them for all of these years? Ever since I found them hiding, I have done what I must to keep them safe, to help keep them hidden. It is the least I can do for everything that I have done in my life. When I learned that Yaelor had given birth to a child, it gave me a window of opportunity. Perhaps a chance to recompense for the sins of my past.

"They must have escaped in the night, whilst their home burnt."

"I cannot stress to you the importance of finding them," I say

"Yes, my queen." She bows her head and offers me a polite curtsy.

"And Vaya?"

She raises her head to look at me and I offer her a warning look. "Mention their names out loud within these walls, and it will be the last thing that you do." There is a coldness in my voice. She knows the rules. Rules that exist to protect my sister and my niece. It is why communications are only written, and in code. I read the messages, then burn them. Updates on Gillam's development are one of the only things that I look forward to as time passes by slowly in this castle.

Vaya looks shaken by my words. "I'm sorry, my queen," she says before leaving me to my thoughts.

So much for sleep. How am I meant to rest and recover from my vision now? If these visions don't kill me, it will be the stress of knowing that Yaelor and Gillam are out there alone that does. Anything could happen to them. I need to know they are safe again. I cannot rest until I know that they are.

So much has happened today, and although I am exhausted, I know that I have much to do before I can finally rest. But how? How am I meant to find them, how am I meant to hide them again, without them realising I am involved? I need to keep them away; if he were to find out that the child shares the blood of his host, I know all too well what he would do to her.

The blood, Gillam's blood. That's how I can find them.

I hastily head to the door and make my way across the

castle to the dungeon where I keep my grimoire, my findings on my necromancy magic. A power that many would say I have mastered, but I know there is so much left for me to learn about this ancient blood magic.

When I reach the dungeons, they seem quiet. These days, there are not as many wails as I am used to. I traverse the dark, dank halls until I eventually reach my study. The room smells damp, tinged with blood and the soft scent of heather to ward away any spirits that may take umbrage at the experiments that I conduct here.

I remove a stone in the wall. It scrapes with resistance, but it is light enough for me to move, and I place it on the ground, revealing a large hole in the earth behind it. Within it sits my leatherbound grimoire. I am certain that there is a spell I have cast before, one that will help me locate my niece. I pull out the grimoire with both of my hands and wrap my fingers around it. It has been some time since I have felt the need to use it, and it is cold to the touch as I trace my fingers over the surface, the hairs on my arms standing on end. There is so much knowledge in this book now. Knowledge that I alone discovered of the magic, of all the spells that can be cast through channelling people's blood.

I carry the grimoire to my desk, and with a click of my fingers, I ignite two black candles that sit on either side of it.

I open up the book and scour through the pages until I find what I am looking for. Hundreds of diagrams and entries where I have documented what has worked and what has not, how best to get the results I desire. Transference magic has become one of my main capabilities. I proved that in the battle of Eltera where I nearly died on more than one occasion.

My eyes widen when I reach the page that I have been looking for, a tracking spell. One that requires blood.

I read through my notes to reacquaint myself with the spell, and I know what I must do. I blow out the candles, then make my way to my room where I deposit my grimoire before heading to Rhagor's chambers.

A few minutes later, I find myself outside of Rhagor's closed door. My chest heaves, but I must do this, for Gillam more than anything. I knock on the door and wait for a reply. This is the most brazen I have been with Rhagor. He does not suffer fools; if he figures out what I am up to, he will snap my neck before he asks me any questions.

"Yes?" his voice hisses and it sends a shiver down my spine. I push open the door to reveal myself. I am wearing a plunging yellow gown, the fabric thin and distracting, with a low cut revealing exactly what I want him to see. I have never lain with Rhagor. He seeks his pleasures elsewhere, all the more reason to be careful. He is untrusting enough without me giving him more reason.

I show him the bowl of water in my hands.

"I couldn't help but notice you cut yourself earlier," I start, as much confidence in my voice as I can muster. "I thought I would come and clean it for you."

Rhagor is slouched in a large chair. He looks tired. His hair is long and messy, and his thick beard is uncombed and unkempt. Far from the pristine appearance you would expect from royalty, let alone a god. He is shirtless, sitting in just his pants, his chiselled body on full display and leaving little to the imagination. He has a needle and thread in one hand and a mirror in the other.

"It is a good job I turned up when I did," I say. "You are going to make a mess out of that handsome face of yours."

It is a face that was strange to accept when Rhagor first

possessed him. Laith had been an adversary of mine, but he was courageous, brave, and kind to those whom he was loyal. To see that same face speak with such hostility and venom was difficult to overcome.

"You do not speak a word of this to anyone," Rhagor growls.

"My lips are sealed," I say with a tease before I move to kneel beside him. I meant what I said – it is a good job I arrived when I did, otherwise he would make an even bigger mess of his face. Blood runs from the gash on his cheek, down his neck, and across his chest. Some is fresh but some is darker, crusted and congealed as it sticks to his chest.

Rhagor looks less than impressed with my being here. I can feel the anger emitting from every part of him at the knowledge I have. That he can be wounded would not be something that he would want everyone else to believe. What a tangled web we weave.

I squeeze the cloth and begin cleaning his cheek and the blood that clings to his chest. His breathing is slow and laboured, frustration tinged with hesitation in every breath that he draws. In this close proximity, I think about how it would feel to draw a dagger across that throat of his. With him gone, I would be Queen Regent. I would hold all the power.

"It will leave a scar," he complains. "I can't allow anyone to see this, I will not have it."

"Perhaps next time you will calm that temper of yours. Perhaps if you shared with me, your queen, what it is you desire, I could share the burden that so clearly weighs down on you." I wring out the cloth, allowing the blood to drain into my bowl.

I have what I came for.

Rhagor raises his hand and grips my wrist, squeezing it tightly. His strength is incredible and I grimace from the pain. If he were to squeeze much harder, I fear that he would shatter my bones.

"Why is it I feel as though you are scheming, Morgana?"

"I mean only to serve. It is all I have done since you returned to this world. I have done everything you have asked of me, and I will continue to do so." I do not lie with my words. I have been a good servant to Rhagor, and he has provided me with what I desired my entire life – unquestionable power.

So why is it now that I am a queen, I feel more like a slave than I ever have?

Rhagor doesn't reply, he simply growls under his breath.

When I am done, I drop the cloth in the bowl and make to leave.

"Are you not forgetting something?" Rhagor asks, a menacing tone to his voice.

I smile. "Of course." I put the bowl back down and walk to the front door where a guard stands outside. He is young, fit, and in his prime. A handsome man with thick, black hair and a chiselled jawline. He stares forward at the wall, his hand wrapped around the hilt of his sword, ready to draw on it at any moment.

"In here," I tell him. "I need your assistance."

The guard does as he is told and enters the room. He freezes to the spot when he sees Rhagor sitting in his chair with a gaping cut on his cheek. The young man's eyes widen further when he then notices the bowl of bloody water on the table.

I start channelling my power, my fingers bending unnaturally as I tangle with the dark magic that I wield, magic that comes at a cost. Pointing one hand at Rhagor and one at the guard, it only takes a brief moment to feel the connection, and the gash across Rhagor's cheek slowly reverses and transfers to the guard. The guard grits his teeth and winces as the skin on his cheek tears open and starts bleeding. Within seconds, Rhagor's wound is completely gone.

"Nobody will ever know," I say, giving the god a forced smile.

He stands from his chair, displaying his powerful physique, and walks towards me. "He does," he says as he passes me, a sinister grin on his face. Meanwhile I pick up the bloody bowl and cloth, ready to make my leave.

"I – I won't say a word," the guard protests, a fear in his eyes that only serves to make Rhagor's grin even wilder. There is a menace in the king's eyes as he steps in front of the guard and pulls a dagger from his waist.

"Open your mouth," he demands.

The guard does as he is told. I can smell the fear as he sweats and trembles.

His screams do not affect me as I watch Rhagor cut out the guard's tongue. Such a shame. He was such a handsome young man. I suppose he should count himself lucky that he still lives. Rhagor is cruel and torturous. Perhaps it would have been kinder to kill the guard. But this is how Rhagor works.

17

MORGANA

The murky depths of Lochwater Mere conceal the lair of the Each-uisge, a shape-shifting water horse that lures unsuspecting riders onto its back before plunging into the lake, devouring its prey, leaving nothing but a liver bobbing on the surface.

-Brynn Trevellian, Horrors of Lochwater Mere, 147 KR

The bowl of water containing Rhagor's blood sits on my workbench beside me, deep in the dungeons beneath the city of Askela.

My hands tremble. This spell has to work. My niece's safety depends on it.

Death and despair linger in the air, and a sickening taste of dampness clings to the walls. The depth of depravity I have sunk to in these dungeons has all but committed my soul to the afterlife, for what I have done here is unforgivable. I will spend the rest of my life making up for the atrocities that I have committed.

Safe with the knowledge that I was manipulated by the gods through a false vision, I cannot see what is real and what is not. Was it only Rhagor who reached out to me in my visions, or is there another god at play? What I can say is that I will no longer be a pawn in their sick games. They may have guided me through tainted visions, but it was I who made the decisions that I did, and I will bear the consequences of my actions.

I have long ceased the torturous experiments that I conducted in order to enhance my necromancy skills, but that does not mean I have stopped practising magic.

I pull out a mortar and pestle and I begin adding different ingredients and grinding them together into a soft, delicate powder. Then I plunge my hand into the crimson bowl containing Rhagor's diluted blood and pull out the cloth I used to clean his wound. I wring it out a little before holding it over the mortar and pestle, squeezing the contents into the mixture. I toss the bloodied cloth back into the bowl when I am done with it.

This has to work – failure is not an option.

I have practised this spell before with varying degrees of success in accuracy, so I know that this spell will only allow me to know where Yaelor and Gillam are in the here and now. What's more, it works far better with the blood of both parents, so even if I tried to use my own blood to track down my sister, the accuracy could not be guaranteed.

If they are on the move, all I can do is make a prediction about what direction they travel, and hope that it is the right one. Whatever happens, Rhagor cannot understand or learn of the importance of the child. Despite Vireo's best efforts to keep them both hidden all these years, this has only been achievable because of me. None of them are aware of the things that I have done to ensure that they remain hidden and well out of the sights of Rhagor.

The mixture starts to sizzle and hiss like meat on a hot pan. The smell is acrid and stings the back of my nose, leaving a nauseating, vile taste on my tongue. A thin trail of smoke wisps into the air and I allow the potion to rest until I know the mixture is ready.

I unroll a map of Levanthria on the other side of the workbench. It is old and fraying at the edges, and slightly damp from the cold, wet air. The map isn't in the best condition, but it will suffice for what I need it for.

I place the mortar and pestle on one corner of the map, a book on another, a skull in the top left, and an empty vial on the bottom right to keep the parchment weighted down.

Then I concentrate my energy and allow just enough magic to flow through my body before picking up the mortar. I start chanting a basic incantation, repeating it over and over again until it sounds like nothing more than the mutterings of a crazed woman.

I tilt the mortar and allow the congealed mixture to pour onto the map. This has to work. After all, the child bears the same blood as Laith, and I can only hope that Rhagor's possession of Laith's body has not altered the blood somehow.

It is through this blood tie that I will find her, and it is through this blood tie that I will keep her safe, for she is also bound to me. For as long as I walk this world, I vow to always keep her safe from those that would seek to do her harm.

I want Gillam to live a free life, to be able to make choices of her volition, free from the burden of false visions and prophecies. I can only wonder how I would have turned out had I not been tainted by these gods' visions that have haunted me since such a young age. How many times have the gods pitted man against man, kingdom against kingdom, all for the sake of their own games?

My fingers tingle as my magic flows down my arms and channels onto the map of Levanthria. I watch as the congealed blood begins to shift across the map, splitting into two. One section moves faster than the other, leaving a thin trail with mucus and plasma on the parchment, sliding towards Askela where Rhagor is located.

The rest of the blood moves slower towards the village of Osar where I know my sister and niece have recently fled. Given how long it may have taken for word to reach me, they must have been on the road for at least a week. Vireo played the dangerous game in re-homing them so close to Askela, but I do understand their decision.

I find myself holding my breath as the blood continues to traverse the map as if it were a living creature. It slides north, towards the mountains of the Gondoron Pass. Surely Yaelor couldn't be so naive as to take her young daughter through one of the most dangerous passageways in Levanthria? During the years that she has lived in Osar, someone would have passed on stories about the dangers that lurk within those mountains.

Then my heart sinks when, to my horror, the blood stops moving within the pass itself.

I fear for the dangers that they may be facing at this very moment.

Without hesitation, I jump up from my desk, knocking my chair over. It crashes loudly in the hollows of this chamber, the wood echoing off the stone floor.

I must get to Yaelor and Gillam, before it is too late. The

longer they're in that pass, the less their chances of survival.

As formidable as my sister is, she has long left her life as a warrior. She will be out of practise given the sheltered life she has been living, and even if that were not the case, strength alone cannot guarantee one's safety somewhere as dangerous as the Gondoron Pass. Even fully furnished caravans must travel the pass with a body of armed mercenaries – mercenaries who are well versed in dealing with the savages and monsters that inhabit that land.

My heart races as I rush towards the courtyard, my footsteps echoing down the hallways like a pebble skipping across the surface of water. When I reach outside, it is dark, and a couple of guards look panicked at my presence. They immediately stand to attention, holding their weapons tightly by their sides as they bow their heads at me.

"I need a horse," I say as I rush past them, the trail of my dress billowing behind me in the wind.

"My queen, a storm is looming, it is not safe to travel. Not until the morning, at least," one of the guards protests and holds out his hand to try and stop me in my tracks. I knock his arm away, a surge of anger rising up from the pits of my stomach.

"Ready my horse," I command. The guard would be foolish to not heed my words. I will not hesitate to snuff his life out in an instant should he show me such insolence again. "Now!"

The guards stumble out of their surprised stupor and quickly begin to assemble my horse.

The seconds that pass feel like an eternity. My thoughts race as I think about a million different scenarios that Yaelor and Gillam may be facing in the Gondoron Pass by themselves.

The portly guard approaches me with my steed in tow as the other rushes to make sure that my saddle is attached properly. When the guard passes me the reins, I snatch them from him like an ungrateful child.

"My – my queen," he stammers, his voice gravelled and deep.

The second guard – a tall, muscular man – offers to lift me onto my horse. I don't think he means to be patronising, but in my heightened state of frustration, my anger flares. I am not some damsel in distress. I am Queen of Levanthria. I am the calm before a storm. I am the fury when need be, and I do not need the aid of any man to achieve my goals.

I push him out of my way and climb onto my horse.

"Where is it you go, my queen?" the portly guard asks. "What should I tell the king?"

I can't help but laugh. "Tell your king whatever you want. I bow to no man." There is an air of defiance in my tone as the wind whips up around me. In this moment, I do not know if it is a natural storm brewing, or if it is my own magic. Within moments, the rain starts to lash against my skin. My horse bucks as if sensing my agitation, and I steer it towards the castle courtyard gates. I set off frantically through the streets of Askela, without a care for anyone who may find themselves in my path.

I must get to my sister. I must help them in whatever way I can. Whether they know it or not, I could not bear the thought of something bad happening to either of them. It would be something that I would not be able to forgive myself for.

Gillam's bloodline is too important. But she needs time to mature, to become strong enough.

With Yaelor and Gillam's safety pressing at the forefront of my mind, I know that I will ride through the night if

I have to. And so the most frantic journey of my life starts with the burning thoughts in the back of my mind:

Rhagor cannot learn of their existence.

He cannot learn of their importance in this game of the gods.

18

VIREO

"Keep up, and remember what I said. If you fall behind, I will leave you behind," Gregor calls from over his shoulder as we reach the edge of the loch. The speed at which he presses forward is impressive given his age and appearance, his powerful frame not holding him back. I consider myself fit and healthy and I find myself panting for breath as I struggle to keep up with him.

"I didn't realise it was a race to get to the loch," I say, sweat dripping from my face, my tunic soaked from the exertion.

Gregor laughs. "This curse only lifts every five years, they say. If we miss this window, it will be another long wait. I cannot afford to let that happen this time. She has taken too many lives, has walked these lands for longer than is natural."

His words feel somewhat hypocritical if Gregor is in fact as old as the legends say. He must be at least two hundred years old. Forgive me for saying, but that doesn't feel entirely natural.

"What do you get from all this?" I ask when I reach him. He stands with his hands placed on his hips as he takes in a huge gulp of air through his nose.

"Redemption," he says, peering at me through his piercing blue eyes. There is a sadness within them, but I dare not press him further.

"Sounds like we are seeking the same thing, friend," I say with a solemn smile. "I help others so I may one day repay the cruelty and greed I once showed in this world. Maybe we will both find what we are looking for today."

Gregor laughs again. "I have come to think that no matter how hard I try, no matter how many demons I slay, it is not enough to appease the gods."

"Don't get me started on this," I tell him. If the gods cared about us mere mortals, they would not leave our lands in such a sorry state.

Gregor kneels on the ground and turns his head as a gentle breeze ruffles his thick hair. He stays in this moment as I watch on wondering what he is doing.

"There is a storm coming shortly," he says, "no doubt it will reach us as night falls. I am certain that tonight is the night. The beast will be free of its curse to walk amongst these trees."

"What do we do now?" I ask, feeling a strange blend of nervous and excited. I have never hunted a monster before. I can only imagine how hideous she truly is.

"We wait, by the water's edge," Gregor says, removing his satchel from his side. He opens it up and retrieves a black tunic, and his eyes do all the smiling as he tosses it to me. "Here, you are going to need this," he says.

Catching the worn tunic, I open it up to see the gold insignia of Askela embroidered into the centre and I trace my hand over it. Once I would have worn this with pride.

Now it reminds me of everything that I hate in this world, gods and kings.

"Why is it that I need to wear this?" I ask, confused. Then it dawns on me. "You intend for me to be the bait."

"Why else would I have agreed for you to join me?" he says with a serious tone.

There is a ruthlessness in his tone that I would have admired once. Gregor is doing what he must to capture this beast. He is doing what is needed in order to ensure that no more lives are taken by the creature. Well, maybe it will take one more life if I am to be used as fodder to draw the creature out.

"Are you serious? I am great with a sword and a bow. I assure you, I could be a better help than a decoy."

"You are a mortal man, Vireo," Gregor says coldly, "and as such, you have no powers which would help you defeat something as powerful and strong as the Beast of Bragoa. Put on that tunic, draw it out, and then I will do the rest."

I can tell by his tone that he sees no other use in me, but if I can help in any way, I will, so I remove my torn cloak and tunic before throwing on the Askelan garb. If the legends are true, Gregor is a formidable warrior, and if I can prove to him that us mortals are capable of putting up a fight against these creatures, that we are not as defenceless as he perhaps feels, then maybe, just maybe, there might be a way to get him to help us in our fight against Rhagor.

The first thing I notice is the musk that clings to it, then the itch as the fabric scratches against my skin. The odour is less desirable than I would have liked – it smells as though it has been worn to good use.

"You could have cleaned it," I say.

"Don't be so delicate," he says as he looks out towards

the loch, its darkened waters seeming unnatural in themselves.

It has been a well-known fact that the waters have been tainted for generations past, with no one either brave enough or stupid enough to try and fish in these parts. The water casts a dark sheen as the sun begins to set, and Gregor tosses a small stone into the loch. The surface of the loch looks like tar as the stone skims across, smashing slightly before disappearing into the depths. It is a wonder that anything at all can survive in these waters.

I step to the edge and a darkened reflection stares back at me, one with worn eyes and a dirtied face. I am already weary and yet my quest has only just begun.

"I wouldn't get too close, Vireo, especially when you are wearing those colours."

Heeding Gregor's warning, I step away from the water's edge, not wishing to tempt fate any more.

"We will set up camp over there."

"By camp you mean hide within the trees and rocks," I say.

"When night falls, you will take a leisurely stroll. If I have my timings right, she will attack you on land, and that is where all I need you to do is get yourself to a safe place. I will do the rest." Gregor makes his way to the tree and takes a seat in the dirt, resting his back against the large trunk. He pulls a small block of wood and a knife from his satchel and begins whittling. "I will do what I can to keep you safe, but I cannot guarantee it," he says.

"I will help you, Gregor, but on one condition. If you defeat the creature, you will owe me one favour."

Gregor lets out a sigh and simply nods. "Very well," he says in a gravelled tone. "I don't suppose I would be able to kill the damned thing without your aid." With this, he continues to whittle away at the wood.

I find myself lost in time as he sets about carving the wood with the expertise of a master woodworker, with nothing more than a carving knife.

When dusk falls, there is an eeriness to the woodlands that sit on the periphery of the lake. Silence surrounds me as I take a walk through the trees, nothing but the moonlight above to help light my path. It sits at its fullest, its haunting light and energy that surrounds it giving my surroundings an unsettling glow.

There is nothing around. No animals burrowing in the ground, no birds nesting in the trees, as if they recognise that this place is devoid of life. The only thing I can hear are my own baited breaths and footsteps in the dirt as I walk around aimlessly.

I walk for an hour, slowly and cautiously. After all, I do believe bandits frequent these parts, and as skilled as I am with a blade, I would not last two moments on my own if a group was to set upon me. I clutch my hand tightly around the hilt of my blade which is tucked into my belt.

It is amazing, the tricks that the mind plays on you when you are in a heightened situation. I freeze in my tracks when, without warning, the hairs on my arms stand on end. It is as though my most basic primal instincts have kicked in, and I stop to weigh up my surroundings. My heart thunders against my chest as shadows formed by the trees trick me into thinking that someone is here.

"You are being ridiculous," I mutter under my breath. I have no doubt fought worse over the years, different creatures from the forest as well as the natural forces of Rhagor.

Why is it in this state I feel so vulnerable? Then I remind myself that I am alone, that I do not have men and women fighting beside me.

Heavy footsteps catch my attention, and without hesitation I spin on the spot and fetch my sword around to be greeted by two hatchets being brought down on my head. The steel of the hatchets rings against my blade, the force of which sends a shockwave of power down my forearms. As I bring my blade back upright, I look for my attacker, but I am greeted by nothing more than the shadows and the patter of rain as it begins to fall on me. The timing could not be any worse as the rainfall in an instant drops heavy, as if the clouds are emptying themselves in a hurry.

Dirt splashes from the ground as I continue to circle, staring into the shadows for my attacker.

"Who goes there?" I shout, rain cascading down my face, stinging my skin.

I hear footsteps to my right and turn as a shadow races past me. This time I feel a pain in my thigh when I am not quick enough to react. I drop to one knee, keeping hold of my sword as best I can, my focus on finding my attacker.

An almost childlike cackle rings out from the trees, cracked and broken as though the sound that they form pains them, like water sits in their mouth.

No human could move that fast.

"Show yourself, beast!" I demand, bringing myself to a standing position and adopting a defensive stance.

"Why?" the voice hisses. "Your forces hid in the shadows, they attacked us at night, why should I show you any courtesy?"

"I have done you no harm," I say.

"Yet you wear the colours of your kin," the voice cries in

pain, as if choking on her words. "The colours of forces that I have sworn vengeance against."

"Vengeance," I say, putting the pieces together. "So you were wronged."

Without warning, the shadow runs from the trees at an alarming speed, their hatchets out to the side this time. I bring my sword up again, and this time the blow sends me backwards into the mud. The creature is too strong, too powerful for me.

No sooner do I roll onto my back, I find her diving onto me as though feral. The stench of death clings to her as her form is revealed by the moonlight. Her skin is pale yet coated in the muck from the water, her hair knotted and tangled, frustration forming under her right eye and down her cheek. She bears her sharpened teeth at me as she hisses at me, bringing her hatchets high above her head.

A green glow of light flashes from the side and once again I hear heavy footsteps approach us. With a roar, Gregor barges into the beast with more force that a battering ram and sends her soaring from me. She crashes into a tree and lets out an almighty shriek, her neck bent at an unnatural angle, along with one of her arms and her leg. With an agonising snap and a crack, they fall back into place, and she lets out a gargled grumble of frustration and ire as her focus switches from me to Gregor.

"The hunter," she growls. "It has been some time since we crossed paths." She leans her head to one side then the next, as if inspecting his form.

"Except this time you are in my terrain and not the water." His voice is powerful and commanding as rain continues to lash against us. His face and body is illuminated by his broadsword which he reaches for and removes from his back. To my amazement, the blade is engulfed in an unnatural green flame, the sight of which keeps me frozen to the spot in awe. Gregor was right. There is nothing I can do in combat to aid him.

I spent a lifetime not believing in mystical weapons, only for this to be the third one that I have come across.

"One of us will not make it through this night," Gregor warns.

"If only it was that easy," the beast hisses, and then she flies through the air at Gregor and their weapons meet. The green flames kiss and sizzle against her skin, but she seems undeterred. The two of them fall face to face as they snarl at each other, and I cannot help but feel that there is more history between the two than I am aware of.

Gregor pushes her back forcefully before taking a wild swing with his sword, but the beast ducks underneath, then slams one of her hatchets into Gregor's stomach. As he turns, so does she, and she smashes the other hatchet into his back with a snarl. Gregor grunts in pain but continues to stand tall, despite two hatchets being buried in him.

"Foolish hunter. I am cursed by the gods. Bound to walk these lands to enact vengeance on those that slaughtered my clan." She rushes forward and slices down Gregor's chest with razor-sharp claws that protrude from her fingers, shredding his thick coat.

"You are not the only one bound to this world by a curse," he says as he slams a thick fist into her. "Leandra!" he yells.

"Silence," the creature hisses. "How is it you have come to learn my name?"

"What do you think I have been doing with my time since our last encounter? I am a demon slayer, a monster hunter. I would be foolish if I did not try and learn as much as I can about the creatures that I stalk." Gregor brings his flaming broadsword around the front of him, ready to strike, his eyes unmoving from the creature he has named Leandra.

"They slaughtered us like cattle," she says. "What was I to do? I was dying and desperate to see those responsible for my clan's demise to see my fury. As I begged the gods to allow me this, one of them answered. The pain and agony that I endure every day is worth it just so I can spill the blood of my enemies."

"But for how long must you do this? When will you be satisfied?" Gregor asks.

"There is no end. As long as I can walk this land, the ground will turn crimson with the blood of Askelans." With this, Leandra's gaze turns to me with a hunger in her eyes, and the corners of her mouth curl into a cruel smile.

She looks at me as though she is a ravenous animal seeking to devour its next meal. I don't intend to sit around idly and wait to become a feast, so I pull out my bow and ready and arrow as fast as I can, then pull the string back tightly before releasing my fingers. The arrow flies towards her, but she drops her shoulder with unnatural speed and dodges it.

Grinning, she sets off towards me, both hands outstretched, and I swear that the claws in her hands grow longer as she roars whilst running towards me. I pull out another arrow and fire it at her. This time it lands square in her shoulder and knocks her slightly, but she continues her run, teeth bared and snarling in anger. I am amazed at the hatred she displays towards me when I have done nothing to wrong her. I draw on another arrow and fire it at her, piercing her stomach. She doesn't even flinch before she dives through the air at me.

I find myself pinned, using my bow to bridge as much

distance between me and her. She is feral, her jaw snapping as she desperately tries to shred my skin with her hands. Growing frustrated, she pulls my bow from me and snaps it like a twig, grinning at me. I brace myself to meet my maker. I have never fought anything as fierce or as terrifying as this creature.

My last thoughts are of Gillam. At least we will be reunited and she can tease me once again in the afterlife.

Maybe I can even see Allana again, though it has been so very long.

Before she has time to take another step, Gregor slams into her and pins her to a nearby tree. He has his sword on its side, pressing it against her, and her skin cracks and burns as she squeals in agony.

"This need not be the way, Leandra. I can free you from this curse. But I need you to will it, I need you to wish it." The sword's flames burn even brighter than before, and Gregor's face strains as he struggles to keep the flailing Leandra in a pinned position.

"Why should I repent? I vowed an oath. I swore to shed the blood of Askelans," she rasps, struggling against him.

"You want revenge?" I shout as I step towards her. "I assure you that I share a common enemy in the god who sits on the throne of Askela. Rhagor."

Leandra's eyes draw to me and I know I have her attention.

"Rhagor?" she says the name as if she recognises it. "He is the bringer of war?"

"And he rules Askela," I say, taking another step towards her. "Listen to my friend Gregor here. Be free of this curse, and help me bring Rhagor's tyranny to an end. You will have your fill of honour and bloodshed on the battlefield, away from those who are innocent in all of this."

"Tricks," she hisses and flails against Gregor. "You speak only to distract me."

"Listen to him, Leandra!" Gregor roars. "I do not offer to break curses so easily. My job is to vanquish the darkness, and there is plenty of that in your heart. But there is also light. Why else would you seek to honour your clan by slaying their enemies?"

"Lies!" she hisses again, all the while trying in vain to push herself free. The skin across her chest is blistering from the flames and she continues to writhe.

"Tell me, Leandra, did you agree to this when you asked the gods to help you?" I ask her. "Did you ask for your body to be transformed in this way, to be bound to these lands for an eternity? If there are good gods out there, they did not listen on the day you needed them most. You asked for vengeance, and whichever god did this to you has manipulated you. Tell me that you want to live like this. Gregor can help you. I can help you." Desperation clings to my voice, and I cannot believe that I am trying to now recruit the Beast of Bragoa to lend aid to my fight.

Leandra stops fighting against Gregor and lets out a pained cry. "You are right," she says as if a weight has been lifted. "Do what you must, monster hunter."

Gregor steps back from her and for a moment, his position tells me he is tempted to cleave her head off whilst she is in this submissive state. Suddenly I wonder if he really meant what he said, or if he was merely trying to disarm her with his promise.

"This will hurt," he warns.

"You do not know the meaning of pain," she says as she lowers her hands to her side and closes her eyes to embrace her fate.

Gregor opens up his hand and it becomes wrapped in

the same flames that coat his sword. He growls as though the magic he draws on pains him, and then he steps forward and slams his hand onto Leandra's face and neck, gripping her tightly.

She starts to convulse violently, crying out in agonised pain, but Gregor uses his free hand to press her back into the tree, dropping his sword to the muddied ground in the process.

Darkened veins track throughout Leandra's body. As whatever darkness is within her begins to draw towards Gregor's hand, he pulls his hand away, coaxing the darkness from her body as though weaving fine silk strings. It begins to coil and shake violently in the air. When it is pooled together, he spins on the spot, tossing it between himself and me. Whatever it is, whatever magic or curse this is, the mass starts to crawl along the ground towards me, moving of its own volition.

Gregor lets go of Leandra who drops to the ground, silent in unconsciousness, and he scoops up his sword, then slams it down on the blackened mass. With a shriek and squeal, the flames engulf it aggressively, burning so brightly that I need to shield my eyes. Then the squealing dies down to nothing and so do the flames. Gregor is panting, his hands braced against his thighs.

"All in a day's work," he says.

19

RHAGOR

In the mist-shrouded lands of Hyborea, the legendary Golden Fleece is said to possess the power to heal any wound, no matter how grievous. Woven from the shimmering wool of a divine ram, the fleece is coveted by kings, heroes, and desperate souls alike. Many have set forth on perilous quests to claim the fleece. But few return.

-Lyra Frostwind, Myths of the Frozen North, 209 KR

I wake from my slumber surprisingly refreshed after a night of vivid dreams. I stretch out in bed and appreciate the comfort that the finer luxuries in life afford me. I still find this whole notion of sleeping a strange phenomenon. After all, being bound by a human body has its draws. I question whether it is something that I will ever get used to; this body still feels like some form of prison, although not as confining as the stone tomb I was confined to for nearly two millennia.

That does not mean that I am happy with my current

situation. I'm mainly making the best out of the tools and resources at my hands. The sword that I wield is key to my power, but as long as I am restricted by the human body of the one they called Laith, my former strength remains out of reach. Only the gods know the power that I could wield if I were able to channel that magic through my own body.

Yesterday was too close for comfort. They cannot see that this body can be wounded. If that became common knowledge – if people were to discover that a god can bleed – I have no doubts in my mind that they would soon turn against me.

Right now, the only person who knows is Morgana. When she first entered my room to help me with my wound, I thought it might be a sign of her growing loyalty to me.

And yet, I have always known Morgana to serve her own agendas. As much as she has proved her worth over these years, her knowledge that I bleed like any other man in this world gives her far more power than I would care to allow.

Although we are married in name only, never having consummated the marriage, I do feel that I know my wife better than she realises.

What exactly is Morgana going to do with the information she now holds? If she knows I can bleed, she will assume that I can die. After all, this body is only a vessel and I its captain.

She must be dealt with. Today.

I stare at my sword that sits on the stand on the opposite side of my chamber, its gold handle moulded perfectly to look like a serpent wrapping around it. A singular red gem is embedded on either side where its eyes should be. It is a thing of beauty, and something that I am tremendously proud of crafting, of honing my magic and coercing my power to be retained in such a confined space. After all, it did prove to be a masterstroke, for I didn't trust my mother – but I did not expect her to turn my body to stone in her desperation to see me fail.

I can only hope she can see me now, see the monster that she created. She is to blame for all of this, she is to blame for all the suffering that is to come.

I feel the corner of my mouth tug into a wry smile as I get out of bed and move across the room to stand in front of a large, ornate mirror. I look at my own reflection, admiring my rugged physique and slender frame. The muscles on this body look as if they are carved from stone.

There certainly could have been worse bodies for me to possess.

I rub my hand over my cheek and trace my fingers where there should be a scar, yet nothing is there. I laugh to myself, my gaze fixed onto my own eyes, and I wondered why it feels like it is still a stranger that looks back at me. Thick, matted hair fills my head with curls that billow down my face, accentuating the sizeable beard that I have grown. The man who looks back at me is clearly one reaching mature adulthood, but the wisdom in the eyes staring back at me is mine.

I smirk, and I hope in this moment that Laith, the true owner of this body, is able to witness and see everything that I see. He should be grateful. How many humans get to walk alongside a god?

I sigh as my thoughts return to Morgana. Business needs attending to.

I quickly get myself dressed into my tunic, put on my boots, and fasten my sword to my belt before setting off to

Morgana's chambers. The quicker I silence her, the quicker I can have breakfast. I am ravenous.

The guards stay out of my way as I march down the hallway. They know better than to cross my path when I'm in this frame of mind. They know better than to get in the way of a god.

When I reach Morgana's chamber, the two guards give me a subtle nod before stepping to the side to allow me access. I push the door open without bothering to knock.

She is not there, though her bed is perfectly made. Something doesn't feel right. I scan the room, wondering where she could be at such an early hour.

A maid enters the room carrying a pile of towels folded neatly in her arms. She looks surprised to see me standing over Morgana's bed.

"Where is she?" I ask.

"I don't know, my lord," she says with a panicked expression in her eyes. "I just came to wake her."

"Tell me, do you have any clue where she may be at this hour?" My voice is menacing and I can feel my jaw tensing.

"No." Her voice is trembling with fear. There is something, though – a quick glimpse to her left, towards Morgana's dressing table.

"Is there something I should know?" I ask, and the maid cowers out of fear.

"No, my lord."

If I wasn't a god, maybe I would believe her. Unfortunately for her, I am, and I don't.

I step towards her, grabbing hold of her throat with my left hand. "Where is she?" I repeat, anger seething from my tongue. I apply just enough pressure to make her tremendously uncomfortable whilst still allowing her to speak, but she says nothing.

She's loyal, I'll give her that. Loyalty is something that this world lacks. What I would give to have someone to confide in, but unfortunately that is not the world we live in.

I give the maid a polite and courteous smile as if this is all just one big misunderstanding, loosening my grip on her throat.

Then I lean in close. "You only draw breath in this moment because I allow it." I walk across the room to the vanity table where a brush, comb, and various other utensils are lined up neatly to one side.

I pull open a drawer and scan the insides but see nothing of importance. I watch the maid's face as I open up a second drawer, savouring her look of terror.

This time when I look down, something catches my eye: a frayed piece of parchment, charred around the outer edge.

"Now that is interesting," I muse, looking back at the cowering maid. "What do we have here?"

The colour drains from her face as I lift up the charred paper. Other than a couple of letters on the outer edge of the parchment, there is nothing legible.

"What is she hiding?" I ask, anger pouring from my mouth. If there is one thing I detest, it is being played like a fool.

"Noth –"

The maid does not have a chance to finish her reply because I have already lunged across the room. I grip her by the throat once more and turn her head to the side, leaning in to whisper through gritted teeth, "This is your last chance. Life or death. You decide."

"I choose life," she gasps.

"Go on then. What is it that Morgana is hiding from me?"

"A child, she's hiding a child, that's all I know."

I let go of the maid and she turns to flee, but before she has the chance, I draw my sword and bring it straight down the centre of her back. Her blood spills all over Morgana's pristine rug, rendering the cream colour crimson.

If only Morgana knew how easily her maid turned on her.

The question is, who is this child, and why would Morgana hide it from me?

Whatever is going on, it is clear that Morgana has been playing a game with me.

A game that I do not intend to lose.

I storm down to the courtyard, screaming and shouting her name. "Morgana, Morgana!"

The guards are startled by my rage, and I can feel the hatred and anger coursing through my body, my hands curled into fists. What exactly is she up to? I will not allow whatever plan she has to disrupt my own, for I have come too far, I am too close to achieving my goal.

In the courtyard, the guards tremble with fear; they know that one wrong word could be their last breath.

"She left, my lord," one of them says. He's so nervous, his eyes cannot meet my own. "In the dead of night. She – she was in a rush. Said something about bowing to no man."

My blood boils. "Which direction did she leave?"

The guard points a shaky finger towards the gates to the dungeon. "She came from the dungeons, my lord. Then left through the main gates."

With this news, I march towards the dungeons, knowing exactly where to go. My steps are quick and hurried as I traverse the corridors of this wretched place. Morgana's very own hellscape. She cannot judge any of the things I have done, given the atrocities that she has committed in the name of furthering her magic in these very walls.

In the dark chamber of her laboratory, I find her table overturned, but the rest of the room looks in place. A slab of wood to the right has bloodied leather straps hanging loosely from it, and the table is stained with the blood of previous residents.

It has been some time since I have known Morgana to frequent the dungeons, something that makes me more curious about what she was doing down here. I am drawn to her desk where what looks like an old map is rolled out. I immediately move to examine it.

Rather interestingly, there are two congealed trails of blood that look like they've travelled from one side of the map to the other, like a slug leaving a trail. When I inspect the map closer, I see that one of the splotches of blood falls upon Askela. A smaller lump of congealed blood has stopped over the Gondoron Pass.

Then I notice the bowl of water that has been knocked over, leaving diluted, bloody water all over the cobbled floor. I recognise the bowl. It is the one Morgana had with her when she came to clean my wound last night.

"Just what are you up to?" I muse aloud as I try to piece this puzzle together. Clearly, she wanted my blood for something, but why?

I place my hands on the edge of the desk and lean in to sniff the parchment. I can smell traces of whatever magic she was conducting here. When I examine my congealed blood on the parchment, once again my eyes jump from Askela to the Gondoron Pass, then back again.

Then I understand. The scent of the spell still lingers in the air like a cooking pot. Had I not been involved in the very creation of magic in these lands, I would not be able to sense it.

This is a tracking spell.

Who is she tracking, and more importantly, why is she using my blood to do it?

Do I follow her to the Gondoron Pass, or do I forge ahead with my plan? I cannot allow myself to be distracted, but my curiosity is piqued.

Morgana, what is the game you are playing?

Is she after the amulet? Does she know what I need it for? Either way, when I get my hands on her, I am going to squeeze the very last breath from her with my cold, callous hands.

20

ZERINA

"Zerina!" Darmour calls after me as I make my way back towards the ship. I cannot stand by the side of that scoundrel any longer. My body shakes with an anger in the pits of my stomach like nothing I have felt since I sent one of the ships of the King's Fleet to the depths of the ocean.

I will not allow my sisters' names to be spoken with such disregard. Ulrik knows exactly how to hurt me.

"Zerina!" Darmour calls again, and then I feel his firm grip around my arm. "It is too dangerous to go storming off on your own!" he scolds as he pulls me back towards him.

"Let go of me!" I shrug out of his grasp. "I think it is quite clear that I can handle myself, Darmour."

"Aye," he agrees, "you are just about the most powerful spellcaster that I have ever had the pleasure of meeting, but that does not mean that you are immune to danger. We have no idea what kind of creatures inhabit this island. As powerful as you are, what would you do if you happened upon a trap or something worse? Don't let your anger blind you that your powers are enough to prevent your death. I care too much for you to see that happen."

"Or are you just doing as your master commands?" My words are born from my anger towards Ulrik, and I curse myself for lashing Darmour with my spiked tongue.

His eyes dampen at my words, but there is a steeliness to them that reminds me that it would take far more to dampen his spirit.

"I am sorry," I say, "I did not mean to."

"Yes, you did. You would not have said those words if you did not mean them on some level. I am first mate on *Esara's Revenge*. Something that I take pride in. By my honour, I will follow the captain to the ends of the world. Without honour amongst thieves, what do we have?"

How can Darmour be so misguided? I understand his viewpoint and he certainly lives each day fulfilling his role as first mate. Surely he must know that there is a line that should not be crossed, even in the name of honour?

"Zerina, we sail the seas as free men and women of the world. Unbound by the social constructs of society, not restricted by the borders of territories and kingdoms. If I allowed anger to guide me, how long do you think I would have lasted in this world? It is through a clear mind that I am able to make decisions, able to lend my advice to the captain, to you."

"And what would happen if what Ulrik says were to come true?" I ask.

Darmour cuts a puzzled expression, mulling over my words. Finally, he responds, "I don't understand what you mean."

"If you were put in a position where you had to choose, between your captain and me, who would it be?"

When Darmour's shoulders drop and he turns from me,

his disappointment visible in his usually vibrant blue eye, I know I have pushed him too far.

"The fact you would genuinely even ask that . . . Maybe it is best to end this conversation here, Zerina, before things are said that cannot be undone."

I could kick myself. At times I know I speak like a petulant, spoiled child. I know I do not mean what I say, so why do I push him away? Darmour is the kindest man I have met other than Ulrik – the real Ulrik. Darmour and I have been through so much together, found so many treasures, tasted the finest food, travelled to distant places. But the hardest thing for me to accept is that of all the treasures and luxuries of the world we have discovered together, there is still one thing more precious to him above all else. Something that you cannot quantify with silver or gold, for my heart belongs to him and no one else.

"If you choose to carry on this path alone, I will not stop you. But I will not stand by and watch you put yourself in harm's way," Darmour scolds. "And for once, I will not follow you. Not if this is how you are going to be. The captain is hurting. They are not thinking with clarity. That is what I bring. The clarity I can offer is the only way I can think of to ensure the crew's safety. And yours." Darmour continues to speak with his back to me, walking away. "I would have thought you of all people would have known that. After all, there is only you and I who carry the burden of knowing Ulrik's true identity."

"Darmour, wait."

Darmour continues across the open sands, towards our trodden path. Despite my temptation to leave, I know when I am wrong and when I need to listen. Reluctantly, I follow.

Guilt already creeps over me for how I have spoken to Darmour. He has shown nothing but loyalty to me and to

Ulrik, and it is something that should be admired and championed, not chastised and used as a whip to lash him with.

Darmour picks up his pace without a glance behind him.

Ahead of him, I see Ulrik disappear into the dense trees, using their cutlass to carve through the thick vines that block their path. Have they found something? Following Darmour and the rest of the crew, I watch as one by one they disappear into the trees. Darmour and I fall into step behind them.

Then our surroundings grow darker, as if we have stepped into another world.

The sounds of the forest become nothing more than muffled noises in the background, dampened by our surroundings. The sound of water gushing ahead of me becomes the focal point of my attention as I arrive behind the crowd formed by the crew. At the front of them stands a beaming Ulrik, who stares into the brightest infinity pool that I have ever seen.

It is enough to make me want to dive straight in. Maybe it will help me wash away the plethora of negative feelings I have been carrying for some time now.

I meet Ulrik's eyes, and their smug smile tells me that this is exactly what they have been searching for.

"Thank you, Zerina," they say, and I almost stumble backwards from their words. They have not thanked me for anything in a long time. "For burning my treasure map. It was only once the map was gone that I heard the flowing waters of this fall and witnessed the blue lagoon beneath."

"What exactly is it?" I ask, pushing my way to the ledge where Ulrik stands.

"An entranceway." They point out to the centre of the falls, casting me a cocky look. "Will you join me?"

"You know I will," I sigh. Now my own curiosity is piqued. "But how will we get inside?"

"We climb." Ulrik looks up at the steep, uneven rock face. "At least if we fall, we will be able to have a nice swim in the lagoon." They give the water that flows past us an untrusting stare. "Any men or women brave enough to test these waters? I do not trust that the gods who created this entranceway would make it so easy to access."

Unsurprisingly, no one steps forward.

Then: "I'm happy to go first, Captain." Prious, a slight man who looks as though he has seen better days, steps forward, offering to lead the way.

"Very well," Ulrik says, motioning for him to take the lead. "Tell me, what is your name?"

"P-Prious," he stammers.

I swallow down my annoyance that Ulrik does not even know the names of their own crew.

"Prious here has shown bravery before the rest of you. Let it be known that when we have found our treasure, he will receive an extra cut of our spoils. The gods reward the brave." Ulrik raises their fist into the air and the crew cheers as though we are readying ourselves for battle. I have been into far too many caves of wonder to know that battle could be precisely what we are heading towards.

Prious nervously places a foot onto the rock to the side of the ledge, then grips the rocks above him, the whites of his knuckles making me wonder if he has a great fear of heights.

Refusing to look down, Prious shimmies across the rock and moves towards the cascading waterfall, the force of which would send him sprawling if it were to connect with him.

With a grin, Ulrik follows behind, planting their foot on a stone that protrudes from the fall and pressing down on it before taking a leap of faith.

Then my eyes are drawn to Darmour's hook, a constant reminder of the hand he lost in Zarubia. "Will you be able to scale this wall?" I ask. "You can wait here with a couple of the crew members if need be."

"And miss all the action?" he says, but he doesn't give me his usual smile. "I will be just fine." He raises his hooked hand and gives it a slight wave. "If anything, this thing will give me an advantage."

"Very well." I follow Ulrik's path and cling onto the rocks with my fingertips, shimmying across the ledges. I am followed by Darmour and the rest of the crew as we slowly make our way behind the lip of the waterfall. The noise is unforgiving as the water pours over the cliff above us by around a metre. My focus remains on Ulrik, who displays far more agility than I do as they traverse the rocks with relative ease, as if they find rock climbing as simple as walking.

I take a step to my side but my foot slips, and small rocks spill from the wall into the waters below. I gasp as my heart sinks, but luckily I am able to regain composure.

"You okay there?" Darmour asks.

I do not answer. I am no damsel in distress. With a steely determination, I continue, this time being certain I am not stepping onto a loose stone.

"What are you doing?" I hear Darmour ask.

I turn around ready to chastise him, to tell him that I am perfectly capable, but then I realise he is not speaking to me.

Nate, a middle-aged crew member with sagging skin around his waist, is leaning out from the rock face, reaching for the water.

"If these waters are blessed by the gods, I want to taste them," he says. "Maybe they will grant me some divine powers." He speaks oddly, as if encumbered by the weight of childlike dreams, as if he is not himself.

I of all people know that such magical waters do exist, but it is not worth the price that needs to be paid. Orjan was proof of that.

Nate beams as he scoops up a handful of the waterfall and brings his hand quickly to his mouth to drink. Some of the others look as though they are ready to follow suit, until Nate's face contorts faster than the water that flows past us.

He splutters, then breaks out into a hoarse, rasping scream.

"What is going on?" Ulrik demands.

Nate's skin begins to peel back and dissolve, revealing a bloodied mess. The sound of his sizzling skin is as traumatising to hear as it is to witness. He continues to howl in pain, grabbing his throat until he emits nothing but silence. His eyes roll back and he stoops towards the waterfall.

"It's acid!" I warn. "The waters are formed from acid." I am grateful now for avoiding the temptation to launch myself into the pool below.

Darmour desperately uses his hook to catch Nate's flimsy jacket to stop him from falling, but it only seems to prolong Nate's agony as his head buries into the water. The rest of the crew watch on in horror as the waterfall turns crimson, melting away Nate's head at alarming speed until only his skull is visible.

"Let him go, Darmour!" I cry, worrying that the weight of Nate's body is going to take Darmour with him.

"I am sorry, Nate," he says, pulling back his hook. Nate's body falls through the waterfall, splashing water onto Darmour's arm. Speckles of acid burn through his shirt and he snaps his hooked hand back to the rock face, grimacing with pain.

Below, at the foot of the waterfall, the turquoise lagoon turns red, and my attention returns to Ulrik. The rational choice would have been to formulate a new plan, but Ulrik continues to press forward, unbothered.

The acid water is all the motivation I need to follow him as quickly and safely as I can. Unsurprisingly, one or two of the crew who had not started their climb decide to stay where they are.

"Down here," Ulrik calls. To my surprise, they have descended at least ten feet. "The opening is here," they say before disappearing inside.

Not wasting any time, I continue across, then descend as carefully as I can. The waterfall behind me is close enough to kiss my neck, sending a chill down my spine. The hairs on my arm stand on end, and my chest feels as though it may explode at any moment as I concentrate on my descent. When I see the cave opening, I draw myself level and shimmy across, hugging the wall until I am able to plant my foot onto a solid surface. As I do, Ulrik grabs hold of me and pulls me inside.

"Are you hurt?" they ask.

"I am fine," I answer. "Which is more than I can say for Nate."

"He knew the risks when he joined the crew."

I can't help but tut at how callously Ulrik disregards Nate's death. They probably didn't even know Nate's name.

Ulrik reaches for an unlit torch that is attached to the walls of the cave and turns to face me, extending the tip of it to me. "If you may," they say.

With a crack of my wrist, I channel my magic and ignite the torch, illuminating our immediate surroundings.

I fear for what lies in this cave, but Ulrik has a wide-eyed look of excitement. I can't help but wonder once more what it is that seems to be bringing a joy about them that I have not seen in years.

21

YAELOR

Elestrar, a mortal scholar, delved too deep into forbidden arts, uncovering secrets never meant to be known. The gods, fearing her knowledge, offered her a choice: accept godhood and lock away her dangerous secrets, or face oblivion. Choosing godhood, she became the keeper of forbidden lore. Her ancient tome coveted by those who delve into the darkest and deplorable magic.

-Thalia Duskweaver, Scribe of the Great Temple, 48 KR

Our home is a pile of rubble. The walls remain, but everything else is gone. Everything I have worked for all these years, gone. All down to some arse who took umbrage with me standing up to him.

"What now, Mama?" Gillam asks. She hugs me, and my arm is wrapped around her.

I don't have any answers for her.

"Are you okay?" Trivor reaches us, his face panicked as he takes in the embers that dance in the night sky.

"That fucking pig came back," I say sharply. "He attacked me, he did this." I wish he still lived so that I could draw his final breath once more.

"Where is he?" Trivor asks as others rush to our burning home.

"He is inside. I was defending myself, Trivor."

Trivor looks down at my bloodied hand, then back at me. "Others might not see things that way."

"Why would I set my own home on fire, my livelihood?"

"Others will call for you to be put on trial, especially if there is a body that will be found in the rubble."

"That can't happen," I say, holding Gilliam even closer to me. I can't allow her to be on her own, and we are meant to be keeping a low profile. A trial would achieve the exact opposite of that.

Trivor looks at me, then our burning home. There is a kindness in his heart that I wish only more people shared in this world.

"They will not believe you," he says, "especially when your daughter attacked his son yesterday. They will only be looking for an excuse, they will hang you."

"You can help them see reason. You have authority here."

"I won't be able to protect you, Yaelor. If I try to intervene in any way, they'll assume I'm protecting you due to . . . ulterior motives." He looks away, embarrassed.

"Someone fetch the guards," a voice calls that I don't recognise, and more shouts follow.

"Come with me." Trivor takes me by the arm and pulls me away. I take one last look at the burning home, at the flames that continue to burn anything that remains. Perhaps Dronsar's bulk will fuel it for a bit longer.

I follow closely behind Trivor as he leads us towards his house. He opens his front door and ushers us inside before closing the door behind him.

His living room is dark, with only the dull light from a lamp in the corner, its flame almost extinguished. I have never been inside his house, and I find that it is not as tidy as I thought it would be. There are papers scattered all over the table that sits in the centre of the room, some with written words on them, others with drawings. His humble quarters are a reminder that Trivor is not a noble by birth.

"He said that this day might come," Trivor says.

"What do you mean?" I ask.

"Vireo," Trevor sighs as if he has released a great burden. "Ever since you arrived here, I have been watching you, helping influence those in the town so that you and your daughter would be accepted."

I am shocked at what Trivor says. I know that Vireo helped source somewhere for us to start a new life, somewhere for us to blend in, but I thought that was where his influence ended. He has visited a few times over the years, hiding in the shadows, but never once has he told me of his connection with Trivor.

"I don't need watching over," I snap, angered by this breach in trust. "Tell me, have any of our conversations over the last seven years been real?"

Trivor rushes to a cabinet and pulls out a bag and some fresh clothes. "Here, you are going to want to get dressed. I have food and water you can take with you, it should last you a few days if you ration it well. There is coin, too. Vireo left it here for you, in case anything happened and you needed to leave."

It is all too much. Just a day ago, we were talking in the

smithy, we were laughing together, and now my home lies in ruins, a man is dead, and we must go on the run.

"Yaelor, I have grown fond of you over these years. I have always respected you. Vireo may have recruited me to watch over you at first, but I continued to do so of my own accord. You are strong, stronger than any woman I have ever met. Perhaps in another life this could have led to something. I always thought . . ." But he stops himself and looks away. I can see the pain in his eyes. "Go. Take your daughter to safety."

"Mama, I'm scared," Gillam says. "Where are we going?"

"Home," I say. We have no other option. We have to make our escape and return to the Forest of Opiya.

"I will do what I can," Trivor assures me. "Maybe I can convince them that this is an accident, but as you will have left, they will likely assume your guilt."

"So we are damned if we leave and damned if we stay?" I fume as I take the bag and undress, changing my clothes.

Trivor does not look away.

"Have you any whisky?" I ask.

Nodding, Trivor goes to another cabinet and pulls out a bottle and two glasses. He pours us both a drink, but instead I reach for the bottle and pour its contents over my injured hand. The sting is harsh, but it is the best I can do to clean it for now. Trivor hands me a clean cloth, and I wrap it around my throbbing hand.

"You must go while it is still dark," he says, passing me the glass. We share a drink, and then I head for the door, clutching Gillam's hand.

"Thank you," I say, looking over my shoulder. It saddens me to know that this is the last time I will see him. It saddens me that after all this time, we are to flee to the forest once again. This was our chance at a new life, a chance for freedom. Maybe I was foolish to leave the forest in the first place. Perhaps Gillam would have been better with a life in the Forest of Opiya with Vireo, a life away from me.

I open the door and give one last look from the darkness. The coast seems to be clear, and in the distance, I can see the orange glow of our former home, of a life now lost. I tried so hard to blend in here. We built a good life.

"I don't think anyone has seen us leave. That will give us until at least the morning before they realise that your bodies are not in the ruins. There is a horse, around the back. Take it."

I give Trivor a nod, and his eyes dampen as if a spark within them has died on this night. He has shown us a kindness in our hour of need. I will not forget it.

I pull Gillam outside with me and we walk around the house until we reach the back where a horse stands by a hitching post. She is a large, black horse and has a nervous energy around her. I have not ridden in so long, but I stretch out my hand and place it against her head. My touch seems to calm her.

Grabbing hold of Gillam, I hoist her into the air and onto the horse's back before untying the lead from the hitching post. Then I heave myself up with difficulty, using my good hand. Ahead of us, there is nothing but darkness.

I heel the horse and we set off at speed into the shadows.

Many hours later, my back is pressed against the bark of a thick tree, its dense network of leaves giving us the cover we need from the rain as we try to get some rest. Gillam is snuggled into my side with my arm wrapped around her. She was so distressed when we rode away from our life, but now that she is asleep, she looks peaceful, like all the worries in the world have been lifted from her.

On the horizon, the sun begins to wake, drawing first light. As much as I would like to let Gillam rest for longer – and for myself to get some sleep – we are still closer to Osar than I would like. Would they have already searched the smithy? Would they have already found that we are not there and dispatched a search party?

My heart beats faster with every thought that I give it, and I know I have given my daughter as much time as I can for this moment.

I give her a gentle shake. "Come on, Gillam, we must leave."

"I'm so tired, Mama," she says as she squeezes me a little tighter.

"You can sleep all you want when I know that you are safe. For now, we need to ride." She rouses, and we ready ourselves to leave, eating some of the bread that Trivor stored in our satchel. I allow Gillam to have more than me. Once we are done, we set off once again, but not at a gallop this time. I do not wish to exhaust our horse too quickly. The journey ahead is far too long on foot.

"You said we were going to a forest?" Gillam asks me as she sits in front of me. Her hands are pressed against the horse's mane.

Up until this day, I have shielded her from everything. She is just a child, and too young to know the burden that is placed on her. My life is insignificant, but hers . . . Hers is more precious that she will ever realise. I don't think this solely as a mother; I say this with the knowledge that Laith is her father. The man who now reigns over all of Levanthria as its ruler and as its god. How am I meant to tell her this? She knows nothing of her past, the ties we have, the Forest of Opiya, the Barbaraqs – none of it. She is blissfully unaware, and in that innocence comes serenity.

I dread the day she finds out that our life was a lie.

22

ORJAN

In the far-off continent of Xian'sur, the Obsidian Citadel is said to house the Mirror of Souls — an ancient artefact that allows the viewer to speak with the spirits of the deceased. Many have sought its power, hoping to glean wisdom from the dead, but the mirror exacts a heavy toll, draining the life force of those who gaze into it.

-Zhan Qiu, Relics of Xian'sur, 197 KR

Daylight fades away, bringing with it the shadows that we will need to sneak back into the ruins of Hora. The night sky is as kind as it can be, given our situation: thick clouds hang heavy above, obscuring the moon from view, casting little light. We stopped at a ravine east of Hora, far away to let Codrin think we have left. He will not be expecting us to be so foolish. Now we find ourselves walking on foot, approaching the boundaries of Hora, the all-too-familiar scent of ash and cinder lingering in the air like a warm plague.

We are crouched as we approach, keeping our steps as light as possible. I glance over at Rior. "If we are caught, we'll be traitors to the king," I tell him. "We won't be able to return to the way life was. You do not need to do this, Rior. You may return to Eltera, find a girl, settle down."

Rior smiles. "And miss out on all the fun?"

"Where has that caution gone that you were showing earlier?"

"I can't exactly leave you to do this all on your own, can I?" he says. "After all these years, you have grown on me, Orjan. I can see that hard exterior of yours softening to me, too."

His sarcasm draws a laugh from me, and I appreciate his humour in this moment. What we seek to do is madness. We are defying Rhagor himself, and I dread to think what he will do with us if we are caught. The best thing I can hope for is that he never finds out I was involved – if we even succeed.

We have already surveyed Hora as best we can from afar. As expected, work has grounded to a halt for the night, but as we draw closer to the opening of the tunnel, we can make out two guards standing on either side of the entrance. The tall woman on the left is alert and staring out towards us. Luckily the shadows hide us well. The smaller man on the right is propped up against his polearm as if it is what is keeping him from keeling over. I don't blame him. No one likes a night watch.

"I'll take the one on the right," Rior says with a grin, switching sides with me. Of course he will. "Remember, Orjan, these guards need not die."

He has a better moral compass than I do.

We separate, and I follow the shadows until I can see the soldier from the side. Her focus in the dead of night is to be admired. Still, it has done her no favours, as she has not noticed me creeping up on her. I nod to the far side and Rior walks silently towards the other guard. We need to time this perfectly.

I reach the woman from behind, wrap my arm around her neck, and squeeze with my forearm. She is strong. Rior would no doubt have struggled with her, but I pull her back towards me and hold firm until she falls unconscious before dragging her through the mud and into the shadows.

Rior is panting when I return to the entrance. I pull the torch that is fastened to the wall and raise it ahead of me, lighting up the tunnel.

"Have your wits about you, boy," I growl with a throaty rumble. "We still do not know what awaits us on the inside."

When we step inside, all the outside noise vanishes and we find ourselves in true silence save for the steps of our own boots in the mud. There is a wet, earthy smell that clings to the air as we navigate steps downwards which take us deep beneath the village and the temple ruins above us. The ground is soft and slippery, forcing me to concentrate on each step that I take to stop myself from falling on my arse. The tunnel is narrower than I would have liked, bringing with it an uncomfortable claustrophobic feeling.

If the tunnel entrance was to collapse now, that would surely spell the end for me and Rior, but the desire to learn what it is that Rhagor is looking for is too much. It draws me in like a moth to a flame. And like a moth that bothers those in the light, I intend to cause whatever hindrance I can to the false god king. Whatever the consequences this will bring for myself.

Ahead there is light, and as we approach, I can hear the sound of pickaxe against stone. They are still digging, still working into the dead of night. When we reach the bottom of the tunnel, I stay out of sight as I observe what it is that is going on down here.

"We are nearly through," a croaky voice calls.

"Hurry, then," another voice replies, shrill in comparison. "Imagine the rewards we will get if we are the ones to find it."

"Gold a plenty and freedom from this role."

"We can only wish."

Both of them are foolish for even beginning to think that Rhagor would offer them any form of kindness. He is incapable of such a thing.

"Have you not thought what he would do to those with the knowledge of a sacred artefact that he is so desperate to seek?" I say as I step out from the shadows, startling the two workers. "With Rhagor, death is the only kindness that he deals with."

There are four at work in total and each of them stop what they are doing to turn towards me. Each has a pickaxe in their hands.

"So much for the element of surprise," Rior sighs. "I wish you would warn me when you do these things, Orjan."

"Now you are faced with two options and I hope you are wise enough to make the right decision," I continue. "Option one, you lower your pickaxes and leave without saying anything to anyone. You will not report that we were here. We will have a look around and leave. Option two –"

I am cut off from my words when a stumpy, well-built worker strides at me and takes a swing with his pickaxe. I step to the side, managing to dodge the blow as compressed air passes between us. The man loses his footing and stumbles, and I grab the back of his dirt-filled shirt, then pull him back towards me, tossing him at another man who approaches me with anger in his eyes.

"It's the dragon!" another worker says, this time a woman who has to adapt quickly as Rior is already upon her with both his swords drawn. The third worker chooses to focus on me, forcing me into a three-against-one situation.

"Codrin will string you up like a ragdoll for all to see," he snarls as he stands opposite me, fingers gripped tightly around his pickaxe. The other two men lie in a groaning heap on the ground.

I reach for my morning star and take no time adopting a defensive stance. "They already tried that once with me," I growl, emitting a threatening grumble from my throat. "Have you not heard the stories?" I swing forward and the man tries to block my attack. My morning star splinters the pole of his pickaxe, leaving him with nothing but a piece of wood in one of his hands. This doesn't deter him, and he reaches for a dagger strapped to his leg and tries to bed it into my chest. I grab hold of his arm with my free hand, wrapping my fingers around his forearm. Squeezing tightly, I let my clawed nails embed into his skin to his pain-filled howls before slamming my morning star against his head.

My momentum causes me to turn and I face the other two who are already advancing on me. One has replaced their pickaxe with a sword. I ready myself, but the more slender one is quicker than I give him credit for, and he dives into me, slamming me into the wall. Earth falls from above us as the solid wall behind me vanishes and we smash through into a darkened open space.

Losing my footing in the rubble, I fall backwards and drop my morning star in the process. A flash of light fills my vision as my head bounces off a rock, and my vision becomes blurred in an instant. A strange, metallic noise rings in my ears from the blow.

"Fuck!" I growl as I roll onto my side. I am greeted with a boot to the chest. The force isn't great but it's enough to wind me and knock me onto my back as I gasp for air. The guard jumps on top of me with something in his hands. I realise it's a rock and he intends to stove my head in with it.

I reach outwards but don't feel my morning star, so I press my hands against his throat, my reach clearly catching him off guard. He slams the rock against my head and I see a flash of light again, but I tighten the squeeze around his neck until he drops the rock from above his head.

The squeeze is unforgiving and he desperately claws at my hands, trying to force himself free, but he has no chance of survival now. With a crunch, I feel his throat collapse as I crush his airways, and his eyes widen before I throw his body to the side.

When I sit up, the last of the three men is standing before me. His eyes widen before his mouth opens and fills with blood. When he looks down, a sword is protruding through his chest. A second blade pierces the back of his head, forcing its way out of his mouth, and the man hangs in the air suspended in time for the briefest of moments. He slides off the swords and crumples to the ground with an earthy thud, revealing a blood splattered Rior behind him, calm and collected in his demeanour.

Rior grins. "You're getting slower with age," he says as he sheathes his swords to his back and reaches for the torch in the first chamber. "Where are we?" He steps through the hole in the wall and offers me a hand, which I accept.

We are standing in a big, open chamber, large enough

for me to question how the temple that once stood above had not collapsed the ceiling.

The room itself feels strange. Smooth ridges line the walls and ceiling as if something has created this space. It does not give the air of a natural cavern. Ahead of us, a larger opening sits at the top of crumbling stone steps, a form of light cascading out from within.

I beckon Rior to follow, and we climb the steps slowly and cautiously. It would not surprise me if the next chamber was laden with traps. The last few steps have crumbled away, leaving nothing but a plate of broken, uneven stone. Beneath us, a formation of jagged rocks protrudes where I can see the skeletal form of some four-legged creature that has already met its end here. I throw myself across, just about reaching the ledge on the far side, then heave myself upwards.

Rior walks to the edge and looks at the drop before looking back at me. "Crazy bastard, you didn't give that any thought."

"If I did, I would have hesitated. Come." I wave him over.

Rior takes a few steps back and shakes his head as if disagreeing with himself. Then he runs and vaults over the gap.

I reach down and grab him by the wrist just in time as he slams against the crumbled rock face.

"That was close," he says, wincing as I pull him up. "Thanks."

I give him a nod, then turn and head for the chamber. The air feels thicker here, and there is an unnatural tinge to our surroundings.

My eyes light up when I enter through the opening, and a strange gust of air pushes back against us.

"That's it," I say, fixing my eyes on the artefact.

Across the room, a necklace sits displayed on a stone slab. When I approach, I stand in awe of the craftsmanship that has gone into it and wonder what it is made from. It is in pristine condition, as if time itself has not touched it, as if not one speck of dust has lain to rest on its surface even though it has remained buried underneath Hora all this time.

"Is that bone?" Rior asks as we stand over the ancient amulet.

The centre is carved into the shape of some form of creature, its mouth snarling in a roar, ridges of bone forming a solid necklace that seems more like an ornament than a piece of jewellery. The carving of the beast looks as though it would sit below the neckline towards the top of the chest, with offshoots of sharp-looking bony tendrils.

"What now?" Rior asks.

I find myself drawn to it, as if some magic-infused charge pulls me towards it.

"Orjan, be careful, we still don't know what that thing is capable of."

"Either way, we need to take it and keep it away from Rhagor." I find my speech slowing as I speak, drawn as I am to the ethereal glow that surrounds the bone necklace. A whispering noise chews away inside my mind as if a thousand souls try to entice me into donning the amulet.

"Orjan?" Rior says, but I am unresponsive to his words as I reach out and take hold of the necklace.

A charge of energy pulsates up my arms, shocking me to my core. My arms seem to move of their own accord as I instinctively place the necklace over the top of my head.

"Orjan! What are you doing?" Rior protests but his words are muffled.

I am entranced, unable to focus on anything else other than the artefact, responsive only to the whispered words I hear in my ear. As the necklace sits on the nape of my neck, it is as if it comes alive. The bone tendrils sink deep into my skin and a searing pain greets me. I grab hold of it and try to pry it free, suddenly seeing sense as the artefacts binds with my skin.

My skin sears as if it is on fire, and the heat travels underneath my skin, pulsating in wave upon wave. It is all I can do to cry out in pain. It is unbearable, and my body jolts, twists, and cracks as I fall to the floor, slamming my fist into the ground over and over again. The pain feels as though it lasts an eternity. Each second my desire for the suffering to end, for my life to end, intensifies.

And then it stops as quickly as it started.

I pant heavily as I stare into the stone ground, my blood and sweat mingling with the dust and debris. I gasp for air as if it is the first time in my life that I breathe.

Something feels different. I reach for the necklace to find it still there, and I trace my fingers along the edge to feel that the bone has buried itself into my skin. What is this fresh curse that I must now endure?

"Orjan?" Rior repeats, and as I turn my head, his face falls ashen as if he has seen a ghost. "Your – your face," he stammers as he points a trembling finger towards me. "You're human."

23

ULRIK

Zerina casts a look of intrigue and apprehension as she walks beside me down the darkened tunnels carved under the waterfall. The air inside is cool and damp, with a faint smell of earth and musty decay, one that reminds me of the Elven skeletons we faced in Voraz.

The walls of the tunnel are jagged and uneven, forcing us to stoop low as we all move forward. The darkness is thick and oppressive, seeming to press in on me from all sides. Moving slowly, I rub my fingers over rough rock walls, my senses on high alert.

My eyes strain as I continue to peer through the darkness, the warmth from the flickering torch in my hand kissing my cheek, bringing a gentle glow to my skin.

"A waterfall of acid," Zerina says to my left. The sound of our footsteps echoes loudly through the cave, reverberating off the rough rock walls and ceiling. The sound seems to linger in the stillness of the cave, as if each step leaves a mark on the very air around it.

"Not come across that one before, how the gods

continue to surprise us," I reply, my concentration remaining on the darkness outside of our periphery.

"Nate was a good man, a good pirate," Zerina says, her voice solemn.

I don't know why she bothers getting to know them. I have no doubt that the majority of the crew would gladly stab me in the back given half the chance. Still, even I was tempted to touch the waterfall, the alluring pull of the lush waters drawing me in like a Venus flytrap. Luckily I had my wits about me. I do not trust the gods, not when I am so close to a treasure that threatens to tip the natural balance of the world.

"We won't even be able to bury his body," Zerina sighs. Something that she is keen on doing when members of our crew fall. Whether that be on land or at sea, she insists on it. A service that I have never bothered to attend.

The rest of the crew move slower than us, apprehensive with our surroundings.

"Zerina, we are likely to lose more on this treasure hunt," I muse, my voice skipping down the tunnel like a pebble across calm waters.

"That does not mean that we shouldn't pay our respects to our fallen brothers and sisters."

"They are not my brother or sisters," I growl. "They are criminals who would likely be met by the noose or living in poverty if not for the protection that sailing under my flag brings."

And the less you know about someone, the less it hurts to lose them.

"I forgot that your heart is blacker than the shadows in front of us," Zerina snipes, her voice crackling with frustration.

I ignore her, and we continue to move down the tunnel

in silence. The ground begins to slope slightly so I lean back to balance my weight out. The stone is dry so I do not need to worry about slipping, but that doesn't mean one of the blundering fools behind me won't come sliding into me.

When the ground finally levels out, I pause for a moment, the hairs on my arms standing on end.

"What is it?" Zerina asks.

I stop and try to listen but the heavy footsteps of the crew behind me echoes off the walls.

"Shhh!" I tell everyone, raising my finger to my lips. Turning my head, I listen intently to our surroundings. A light breeze grazes over my face and I close my eyes to embrace it.

"We are in an open space," I warn. "Have your wits about you." I know that the people who hide their treasures in lost caves do not make them easy to access, let alone find. The fact that I am searching for one said to be hidden by the goddess Nareva herself draws concern from me. Still, it will be worth the risk. I would fight to the ends of the earth for this treasure. I already have. What is one last labyrinth?

"What now, Captain?" Darmour asks, his eye fixed on the darkness.

"These torches don't provide enough light. Zerina, is there anything you can do?" I ask.

"It is stone floor. Unless there is something to ignite, my flames will not remain for long. Not without eating into my own reserves. Besides, the last time I checked, none of the crew were able to walk through fire."

Zerina is right. As much as I do not trust this space, we have no option but to press forward.

"I have an oil lamp," Darmour says, retrieving the item from his satchel. He holds it out for Zerina to light.

With a snap of her fingers, Zerina creates a flame that ignites the lamp, giving a greater glow of light around us.

"Come, I will lead," I say as I step into the room. I can tell by the way our voices bounce off the walls that the room is large. Gripping my torch tightly, my eyes dart between the ground and ahead of me. The darkness beyond my torch is like nothing I have ever seen, as if the darkness is more than a lack of light; it is a void between this world and the afterlife.

We have a few torches between us as the crew forms a line behind me and we make our way through the dark, dank cavern.

"What is that smell?" Zerina says, scrunching her nose.

"Death," Darmour answers. "Captain, I do not have a good feeling about this."

I smell it too, but I ignore his warnings and focus on progressing forward.

I stop in my tracks as the sound of footsteps scurrying over stone catches my attention to my left, then to my right. The noise becomes louder and louder.

Something is surrounding us in the shadows.

"What is it?" Zerina asks as we stare into the void. Chattering noises like grinding teeth and nails against stone continue to grow around us.

"Keep your wits about you! We are not alone!" I reach for my cutlass and the rest of the crew do the same as their worried murmurs grow amongst their ranks. I do not blame them; there is nothing worse than being faced by a threat that you cannot see. It still does not compare to the demons that ravage my mind. It is why I do not fear death. I embrace it, I will it. If you are not bound by fear, you are free from the shackles of consciousness, and that is truly what makes me dangerous.

The scurrying footsteps grow closer. Members of the crew tremble as they point their blades towards the darkness.

With a scream, a woman is dragged into the shadows, her cries growing further and further away from our group until she eventually falls silent.

A fat man at the rear attempts to break away, falling back towards the direction we came from. I watch as a long, silvery arm materialises and wraps around his neck, then hooks him away. He doesn't have time to scream as I hear his skin tear and the sound of his body dragging against the stone floor.

"Move!" I demand, rushing forward, keeping my torch stretched out in front of me. On the periphery of the darkness, I can see more and more silvery, scaled limbs as they crowd around us.

Shit, there must be hundreds of them.

They do not, however, push into the light as I wave my torch around, forcing them to dart to either side of me.

"They do not like the flames!" I call back as I continue to press forward. High-pitched wailing echoes around us, joined with the screams of our crew members as they fall behind or allow themselves to be consumed by the darkness. A raw and primal cry, filled with fear and pain, that seems to reverberate endlessly through the cavernous space.

"Keep going!" I take a wild swing with my cutlass and find it meeting with the body of one of the creatures. It drops in front of me and I vault over it. I only manage to catch a fleeting glance, but its head is larger than a human's, bald with strange lumps on the surface of the skin. Its eyes are large and white with no pupils. They are blind, I realise as I continue to wave my sword, hacking and slashing at anything that falls in my path.

Footsteps echo behind me. I have no idea in which direction we run, I just know we need to get out of this cavern.

With a flash of red light, the cave momentary illuminates, and I see a mass wave of white eyes surrounding us, bodies pressed compactly against each other as the creatures fight to try and get to us.

They shriek in some form of pain or discomfort as they all attempt to shield their faces from Zerina's magic.

One of the creatures falls into my path, writhing around in agony as its skin blisters under my torchlight. I am not quick enough to react and my leading foot clips its body, sending me crashing to the ground. My arms and legs throb as I tumble forward across the surface of the cold rock, desperately trying to hold onto my torch. A gap has formed between myself and Zerina, and as I scramble to my feet, a blast of fire magic explodes from her fingertips, illuminating the dark cave with a searing blaze of light. The flames shoot out in all directions, casting flickering shadows across the rough stone walls and ceiling. It is enough to light up the cavern, and the creatures scramble away to the edges of the wall as they try in vain to create some distance between them and the light.

"They do not like your magic, Zerina!" My voice is hoarse as I try and force a shout through the shrieks and wails. Darmour and Zerina reach me with the rest of the crew behind them, and Zerina helps me to my feet.

"Over there!" Darmour points to a tunnel out of the cavern about fifty feet away. The only problem is, there is a wave of these hideous creatures between it and us.

"I hope you have plenty of your flame magic left!" I say.

Zerina smiles. "It is like Zarubia all over again."

What I would have given to be able to see the destruction she rained down on the battlefield against the oncoming Zarubian army. I was only privy to a flash of light, being that I was inside the keep when she unleashed her untethered fury.

"Let's go!" Darmour cries as he moves forward, holding his oil lamp in front of him.

I follow behind and the creatures move to the sides once more, Zerina saving her magic only for those that try to brave the light to slash at us with their elongated claws.

Another scream comes from behind as they continue to chew through our men like a giant at a buffet. We can't afford to lose many more. We have already lost too many at this stage as it is.

As we reach the entrance to the tunnel, damp air emanates from within, as if the tunnel is breathing. Strangely, it feels warm and sticky, not the cool, refreshing breeze I am accustomed to in these places. I spin and stand at the entranceway, holding my flaming torch high above my head. Chattering teeth and swinging claws draw closer than I would like. I jam my sword into the chest of one of the creatures and it lets out an ear-splitting shriek that causes me to wince and nearly drop my torch.

"Hurry!" I shout as I shepherd the crew past me. I count only seven of them and I am shocked at the number we have lost.

"Is this everyone?" I ask.

Zerina gives me a nod.

The creatures push towards the cavern entrance. They are unforgiving in their pursuit of us and my mind races as I think of a way for us to progress down the tunnel without them snapping at our heels.

"Step aside, Captain!" Darmour says as he pushes past the rest of the terrified crew. I do as he says, and he swings his arm, his lantern hanging from his hooked hand. He smashes the lantern into the ground.

The clever bastard!

Oil from the lamp courses along the stone at the entrance, igniting into a shield of flames in front of us. The creatures continue to reach for us frantically, but each one that comes forward recoils with blistering skin, only to be replaced by another creature trying their damnedest to shred us.

"It won't give us long, but hopefully we will be able to get some distance between us and them," Darmour says, sweat shining on his brow.

Zerina runs past me, her left arm illuminating with a familiar molten glow. As she reaches the entrance to the tunnel, she claps her hands together and a flash of white-hot burning light erupts in front of her, filling the cavern.

I turn my head and shield my eyes, but even from behind her the heat is immense. My skin stings from the power of her flame magic.

As the fire magic spreads, the air is filled with the sound of crackling flames, the roar of heat, and the cries of the monsters as they are incinerated. The intense heat fills the cavern with a wave of warmth that is almost suffocating.

The flames of the fire magic dance with a life of their own, licking and leaping across the surfaces of the cavern, consuming everything in their path. The sound of destruction is deafening, a cacophony of shrieks that echoes off the walls and fills the air as everything within the cavern is incinerated.

As Zerina's magic begins to die down, the cavern is reduced to a charred and smoking ruin, with little remaining of the creatures that stalked us. The air is thick with the smell of burning and charred flesh, and the ground is covered in the ash of the fallen.

Zerina drops to one knee, using the wall of the tunnel to brace herself, but Darmour is quick to her side to help her.

"That was incredible," he says, beaming. "Will you be okay?"

I am not surprised by the toll the magic has taken on her. I have never seen her cast such intense flames. My jacket feels warm enough to the touch that I fear it might ignite itself as I reach for Zerina's flask at her side and pass it to her.

"Thank you," she says before taking a drink of the ancient Elven waters that it holds within. Her strained face lifts and her pained expression subsides as she allows herself to stand freely from Darmour's arm.

"I think we need to be thanking you," I say. "Come, we have treasure to find."

24

JORDELL

Necromancy, the darkest of all magical arts, has been forever banished from our lands. This vile practice involves the manipulation of the dead, forcing their souls to endure unspeakable torment as they are torn from the afterlife and bound to the necromancer's will. Such power is an abomination against the natural order

-Grand Master Alaric Greyward, Journal Entry 62 KR

When I come to, the first thing I do is laugh and heave as water spills from my mouth. How can it be that I survived that fall?

I find myself washed up on a river's embankment, but I have no clue where I am. I try to stand, but my body aches as though it has been battered by a storm. The weather feels calm and the sound of the river pushing past behind me makes me question once again how I have survived, especially given my weakened state.

My staff. Where is it?

The whole reason why I tossed myself off the edge of

the keep was to keep that blasted staff safe. My eyes dart about me as I desperately search for it. The gods only know what I will do if it has washed even further downstream. My mind ruminates on all of my lost notes, my research that I have had to leave behind from the last eight years. Research that is now confined to my fragmented mind.

I look to the skies and close my eyes, savouring the breath of the wind that kisses my face. So long ago I worshipped the very gods that now choose to taunt me. I denounce them. What have they ever done for me other than bring me pain and misery?

I step forwards, but my foot catches on something and I lose my footing. When I slam against the ground, my head hits a rock. In this moment a flash of bright white erupts in my eyes and a strange sensation falls over me. It is as though I am bathing in the warmest of waters, the aches and pains in my body vanquished and leaving me in a state of comfort. In this moment, my mind rests, and all the anger, the pain, the anxiety – it all stops and I find myself being drawn into a calming state.

When I open my eyes, I am not on the embankment. I am somewhere else entirely. Nothing but whiteness surrounds me, but my feet feel planted to the ground, earthing me, centring me. The ground where I stand and my surroundings are blended into one, and I take a tentative step forward, half expecting to fall into oblivion.

"Am I dead?" my voice stutters as I speak aloud.

"No," a calming, soothing voice of a woman replies. "You have lost your way, lost your faith, Jordell Torvin. I am simply here to help you get it back." Her voice is like honey, soft and sweet as her words wrap around me like a warm hug.

"Lost my faith?" I argue, my temper still flared from my

thoughts before I fell. "I have lost everything, I have achieved nothing. I followed, I obeyed, I did everything I was told to do since I was a child. Worship, believe, and bring a greater good into this world. Look where it got me." Spittle leaves my mouth and I have no choice but to question my sanity. After all, I am arguing with nothing but a voice in void filled with nothing but the brightest of white light.

"The knowledge we share, the things that we show you, it is all to help guide you down your path. We cannot walk the path for you. How those who we touch react to our ways is something even the gods cannot control." The voice remains calm and collected, still comforting.

"Was it you?" I shout out. "Was it you who shared the vision that I saw? The one that led me on a blind quest, the one that created the whole sorry mess that we find ourselves in?"

"That was not me," the voice says. "The vision you shared belonged to the sorceress Morgana. It is a different being entirely that influences her choices. One of darkness."

"So it was all a lie, all a trick, everything that I saw in that vision. The battle, the sword, everything."

"I cannot say, as it was not me who foretold that war," the voice explains. "That war is coming. It is going to happen, so not everything that you have seen is false. But what you have seen was a manipulation in parts."

"Manipulated by who?" I ask, spinning on the spot as if doing so will allow me to catch the form of whoever it is that speaks to me.

"You already know the answer to that question. You have already met him."

"Rhagor," I say. To speak his name out loud brings a

wave of anger about me that I could never have imagined myself capable of when I was younger.

"Yes," the voice says, and I sense a tinge of indifference in her voice. "Rhagor manipulated that vision to meet his own ends. You, however, were not meant to be part of it. After all, it is Morgana who he controls, who he bends to his will."

"What do you want with me?" I say with a trembling voice. "I have already given everything that I have, and in return, I have lost everything. I now stand before you a broken man."

"And I applaud your resilience. You have done what you thought necessary with what has happened in your world. However, this has been impacted by a god who chooses to walk amongst humans. Something which is forbidden and cannot be allowed to happen. This is where I need you to find your faith, to help stop Rhagor and see to it that he is banished from your lands once again."

"So I am to be nothing but a pawn again, in this sick game that you all play." My frustration continues to simmer like water splashed on a hot stone. "You expect me to be blind and to not see? You expect me to be a plaything of the gods?" My voice echoes as my tone rises to a shout. I have had it with the manipulation, I have had it with dedicating my life to lost causes. I want to be free of it all, be free of this life. I could be sent to the afterlife for all I care.

As my words fade, there is no reply, only me and the void that I stand in. "Is that it? Is that all you have to say?" I call out. I know that this god is no different from the one that abandoned me when I needed them the most. How many lives have been lost because of their inaction? How many lives have been lost because of their manipulation?

"I understand you are hurt, that your belief has gone,

but I am here to ask of you to help. To find your faith, reclaim it as your own. In doing so, I know there is a light within you that can bring about a peace to this world that has not been seen for over a millennia."

The voice's words continue to remain calm, despite the venom that spews from my mouth. "Jordell Torvin, I believe that you are key in all of this and always have been. You have the power to end Rhagor, and so bring balance back to your world and ours."

That leads me to my next question. If the gods have infinite power that cannot be rivalled, why is it that Rhagor remains here in our world? Why is it he chooses to parade around as king, inflicting pain and suffering? "What does he want? What is it he is hoping to achieve?" I ask.

"That I cannot answer, for I do not know. Just know that in order to stop him, I need you to find your faith. Reclaim it and make it your own. I am simply here to help guide you, as it is clear to see that you are truly lost."

Just how does she intend to guide me? And why now, if she could have shown herself at any point in the last ten years?

"Because you seek death now, and it is not your time," she answers me as if reading my thoughts. "I am here to stop that, to spark the light within you, and although this may take time, I know it will grow. You simply need to be started on the path."

"And what is this path that you speak of? What is it you expect me to do?" I demand. How can she expect my faith to reignite at her whim?

"Find the child." Her voice is different this time. Rather than echoing around me, it feels more present, and then I realise that the voice comes from behind me.

When I turn, I am greeted with the face of a beautiful

woman, the most beautiful that I have ever laid eyes on. There is a familiarity about her as well as a magical glow around her. She offers me a kind smile and takes hold of my hand.

"You need to find the child, the child is key in all of this. The journey to her will help you find your faith again." She pulls my hand forwards and I find myself sitting bolt upright.

My breathing is heavy and I pant as if I have been holding my breath. The sound of the nearby river cascading past me grounds me back to this world. Was all that but a dream, did it really happen? I wince as I bring my hand up to my head and inspect the lump I have there from my fall. When I look at my fingers, they are bloodied, and then the dull ache throbs in my head, deeply and unforgivingly. I simply knocked myself out and had a strange dream. That is all.

I allow my blurred vision to steady itself, then let out a sigh. I may be alive, but I am well and truly lost. When I stare down at my boots, I see the root that I must have tripped over protruding from the ground, and in frustration, I kick down at it.

To my surprise, it moves.

Crawling towards it, I let my hands sink into the sand of the embankment and grab hold of the root, pulling it free. It is not a root at all.

It is my staff.

"What are the odds of that?" I say aloud as I inspect the staff. There is barely a blemish on it. I had fallen some way into the river and have no clue how far it then took me. I cannot see any sign of Zakron's Keep, yet here is my staff, with me when I am at my most lost.

My mind goes back to the conversation that I held in

my dream and the words that I was left with before waking up.

Find the girl.

Rising tall, I grip my staff tightly and plant it into the ground. It helps brace the strain on my injured knee as I take my first step forward.

Was my dream my subconscious? After all, it was Vireo who told me of the child. Maybe in my unconscious state, my mind recalled the recent conversation.

There was no doubt a reason for Vireo bestowing this information on me, and I draw back to his closing statement before he left.

The town of Osar, he had said.

Taking my staff being with me as a sign, I look up into the sky and say, "Very well, I will look for the child." And with this, I take another step, and another, my new path forming ahead of me.

Find the child.

What happens next, I do not know, but maybe in finding her I can find some form of redemption for my failings with Laith. I would say only the gods know, but I have still not forgiven them or forgotten everything that I have been through.

I have no clue where this new path leads, where it will take me, but at least it offers me some form of direction.

I follow the track away from the embankment and towards the trees and hills ahead of me. My first step will be to find passage across the water and back to Levanthria's mainland. And then from there, across the coast to Osar.

And suddenly I remember that Codrin and his forces are probably combing this area for me.

I have no time to waste.

25

MORGANA

Te Boneless, a formless mass of animate flesh, is said to ooze through the narrow sewers of Greywick, seeking prey to engulf and digest. Many a drunkard stumbling home from the taverns has vanished, only to be found as picked-clean bones come the morning. This is my next stop, I must find it, I must destroy it before more fall victim.

-Gregor Yerald, Hidden Journal Entry, 92 KR

I only have the moon to help guide me on my path. Its glow clears the darkness ahead of me as I race towards the Gondoron Pass. Ominous, dark purple clouds line the horizon. That is never a good sign.

Despite everything that I have done to get to where I am today, I would cast it all aside in an instant. I would give it all away just to make sure that Yaelor and Gillam are safe.

It seems crazy even to me, given the lengths to which I have gone to attain the power I now hold. The feeling is strange to me. I have always been a selfish woman. Everything I have ever done in this life has been for my own benefit. But a part of me changed the day that I learned that my sister was still alive, that she didn't perish in the fires that ravaged through my village when the Barbaraqs destroyed everything I hold dear. A part of me awakened that had long been hidden, locked away in the darkest chambers of my now blackened heart.

For the first time, I began to wonder how my life could truly be, or what it could have been had we not been separated in childhood. Upon learning that my sister had borne a child – that our bloodline would continue, our family name no longer vanishing without a trace – I discovered an almost maternal instinct within myself that I did not know existed.

I was quite quick to figure out who the father was, and despite Laith's body no longer being in his own possession, Gillam is arguably the heir to the king that now sits on the throne. I knew right away that this was something I needed to keep hidden.

At first, I protected Yaelor's secret for my own agenda, knowing that one day, I would be able to leverage my knowledge of Gillam's existence for my own advantage. But as time passed, I found myself yearning to be a part of their lives – not because I wanted to use them for my own purposes, but to find out whether I am capable of the one thing that I've always kept locked away: love.

I look at the stars twinkling in the night sky and find my eyes stinging with tears that well like lakes in a hidden forest. Tears that for so long, I've never let anyone see. More than anything, I just hope that they're okay. It took me a few years to find them, and although they don't know it, I've done everything in my power to keep them hidden from ever being discovered by Rhagor. If I do not protect them – if Rhagor discovers them – all my planning will be for nothing.

I let out a cry of frustration, my throat rasping as I release a scream into the dark void that surrounds me. I find it helps me, it grounds me, it centres me and allows me to regain control of my fleeting thoughts.

Up ahead, I see a singular large tree. With the moon behind it, the solitary tree looks haunting in its appearance, with mist sitting eerily on the ground around it. The tree is leafless and seems to be dead, its aged branches reaching out as if beckoning.

Something else catches my attention as I continue to ride at speed.

The shadowy figure of a man, standing at the base of the tree. It is impossible to make out further details in the darkness.

The man doesn't move. The harder I stare, the more it seems like he's looking in my direction. Is my mind playing tricks on me? Perhaps this is a sign that I am in dire need of rest, having been awake for the best part of two days.

Slowing my horse, I shake my head and close my eyes. When I open them again, the tree remains but I no longer see the man, and I breathe a sigh of relief, not sure why the sight rattled me so much to begin with.

When I finally pass the tree, it is quite clear that no one was there and that my mind was simply playing tricks on me.

So why is it when I look ahead once more in the far distance, I see the same shadowy shape simply standing on its own within the darkness? Still and unmoving. I focus on the shadow, questioning my mind once more. It must just be the shadow of a nearby shrub or rock.

Even though I am certain it is nothing more than a

figment of my tired mind, I find myself pulling my horse to the left to veer away from the path so that I do not pass the shape that lies ahead. I keep my eyes on the shadowy outline as I continue onwards, still unable to make out any details. The hairs on my arm begin to rise, and an icy chill shivers down my spine from the base of my neck.

Then, whilst staring at the shadowy figure, my heart speeds up slightly as I swear I see its head turn slowly to face me.

I heel my horse as hard as I can and we set off at a sprint across the plains. I change course so that I do not pass anywhere near the shadow. For all I know, it could be a bandit trap, and despite being as powerful as I am, I do not have time for any distractions. I need to get to my destination without delay and ensure that Yaelor and Gillam are safe.

The cold air rushes into my face and my heart beats so fast, I fear it's going to rip from my chest. I cannot explain the icy fear that grips me at the sight of the man in the shadows.

I avoid looking across to see if the shadowy figure is still there, instead choosing to focus on the distant mountains that leads to the Gondoron Pass. My horse pumps heavily as I continue to push it harder than ever before.

Once I've created enough distance that I see nothing but my own solitude, I slow my horse down to a trot and sit back down in the seat, panting as if I myself was the one running instead of my horse.

I let out a sigh of icy relief, my cold breath lingering in the air as I lean forward and rub my horse's neck, trying to calm her.

"There, there," I say. She's breathing heavily and although I know we can't fully stop, I understand that if I do not slow down our pace, I will end up having to do the rest of the journey on foot. "What on earth was that?" I mutter under my breath.

Out of nowhere, my horse rears up in the air and neighs so loud, it is as though she screams out in pain. I grab hold of the reins tightly to keep my balance and try to bring her back under control.

"Calm down," I plead, but she rises up again, and I barely manage to keep hold this time. She has never behaved like this, and I tell myself she is merely feeding off my own agitation.

I feel like I'm hanging on by a thread, and seconds feel like minutes as I continue to wrestle to keep my horse under control. She continues to buck as if she herself is trying to dismount me.

Finally she drops back onto all fours and pads the ground. She lowers her head, and although her breathing is still erratic, she seems to be calming down. I look around frantically, searching for whatever it was that had her so spooked. The night sky is haunting, a light green aura being cast along the skyline. It sits heavy in the sky like a warning. If only I could read the stars. There is nothing around us as far as I can see, but I keep my wits about me nonetheless.

Something definitely doesn't feel right though, and I think for a moment before my attention is once again grabbed by the dried leaves that spin on the ground, blown around by the breeze that is growing. How exactly are there leaves when there are no trees around?

I can see the Gondoron Pass ahead of us. The top of the path looks as though it is being kissed by the moonlight, casting a reflective light that bounces across the plains between us, giving it the impression that it is a lake and not land. Under different circumstances, I might have stopped to take in the beautiful view, but once again, my chest sinks into the pits of my stomach.

In the distance, I see what looks like the same shadowy figure looking straight at me, except this time, white eyes as bright as the stars in the sky burn into me.

Then my eyes dart to the left and right of the shadowy being. Two more figures stand on either side of the first. No sooner do I notice them, their eyes light up with the same brightness of the stars, and it sends a cold shiver running through my body. I have not felt a chill like this in my body since I first started wielding magic, before the days where I learned to channel my power through other people's bodies, before I mastered my necromancy.

When I blink, they are suddenly much closer to me.

"If you value your lives, I suggest you do not come any closer!" I call out loudly into the silence of the night.

I've no idea what kind of magic they're using, but it must be some kind of cloaking spell for them to remain hidden as if they themselves are shadows. I've heard of rogues mastering this kind of magic to help them steal. Perhaps this is all they intend.

"If you plan to rob me, I hate to let you know that I have nothing of value on me. And if I did, you would be foolish to try." I attempt to sound as confident as possible, but despite my best efforts, there is a small quiver in my voice.

Silence passes between us.

I stand firm, staring back at them. The worst thing I can do in this situation is show them any semblance of fear.

Then the main shadowy figure in the centre of the three seems to open their mouth, or at least I think it's their mouth. Bright light that matches the eyes is released as a terrifying croaking noise fills the void between us. Once again, the hairs on my arms stand tall as the croaking becomes louder and louder until the shadowy figures take one step towards me in tandem, perfectly uniformed. The other two creatures then open their mouths too, emitting the same light but different tones of the same croaking noise.

It sounds like a death rattle.

I should know. I have tortured enough people in my life and heard it enough times.

My horse is exhausted, but she needs little encouragement to set off at a sprint towards the Gondoron Pass. I am not waiting around to find out what game these people are playing or what magic they are wielding.

The croaking continues but grows more and more distant before finally stopping. When I look over my shoulder, my heart thundering against my chest, it seems that the figures once again have vanished.

This time I am not taking any chances, and I do not intend to stop until we reach the Gondoron Pass.

I can only pray to the gods that daylight will greet me soon.

26
ZERINA

The art of binding a soul to an item is a closely guarded secret, known only to a select few. This ancient practice involves the use of powerful enchantments and rituals to anchor a willing soul to a physical object, allowing the soul to persist naturally beyond the death of its mortal body.

-Excerpts from the private journal of Enchanter Lyriel Mistweaver, 83 KR

The waters of Treventine help renew my magic stores, but even with the aid of those enchanted waters, my body aches. Although the waters prevent my body from succumbing to the full aftereffects caused by magic use, my arms and legs ache as if I have been running for days on end. As we continue to traverse the darkened caverns, I walk of my own accord, despite Darmour's best attempts to support me.

Ahead of us, Ulrik leads the way, their torch flickering

beside them, lighting one side of their face. Their eyes are wide as they search for whatever it is we are here to find.

My hand is clasped tightly around my own blade. Nothing in the large cavern would have survived my blast of fire, but that does not mean there are not more of those hideous creatures waiting to strike us from the darkness.

Ulrik continues to press forward with vigour as they navigate the narrowing tunnels. Above us, glass-like crystals draw from above like shards of ice. Normally they would be enough for Ulrik to stop in their tracks and collect; after all, we need anything we can sell to maintain our voyages and keep the crew happy. The fact that Ulrik does not stop tells me that the value of the treasure we are looking for far exceeds that of anything we have ever found.

"Are you okay?" Darmour asks. "I notice you are limping a little."

"I will be fine. That spell just took it out of me is all. My legs tire, but it is no different than what the rest of the crew will be feeling, having hiked all this way." For some reason now that Darmour has drawn attention to my limp, it feels more prominent as we continue our journey through the shrouds of suffocating darkness.

"How many did we lose, Darmour?" I ask, my thoughts returning to our fallen brothers and sisters. "I counted at least eight." We have not had the opportunity to regroup as we have been pushing forward. It is simply not safe enough here to stop.

"Including Nate, eleven," he says quietly.

Pain erupts in my heart as I anguish over those who have greeted the afterlife. We have never lost so many members of our crew in one go. Even when we have battled other ships, or the ocean for that matter, we have never suffered such heavy losses. The burden of responsibility suffocates me as though I breathe through thick fabric, and it is all I can do to stop myself from bursting into sobs. My eyes fill with tears that roll silently down my dirt-ridden cheeks. Using my thumb, I wipe them away and take a deep breath. Those poor men and women were our responsibility. They followed us here, knowing our reputation as pirates, as masters of the ocean.

Tales of our exploits and the treasures we have found have reached across Levanthria. A fearsome pirate with a heart as black as obsidian and a witch more powerful than any seen this side of the Dyran Treaty, which saw magic outlawed.

I understand the risks that comes with living as a pirate. We are not free to make a home anywhere. To do so would likely bring us an early death. After all, Ulrik is the Kingslayer. The bounties on our heads are so high, bounty hunters would be onto us as soon as we stepped foot on Levanthrian soil. We have not even been able to return to Voraz because of the dangers of being captured by the pirates that frequent her shores.

In a strange way, since leaving the Pendaren Hills, Voraz became my home away from home, and it saddens me that we are outcasts, unable to rest for longer than a few days anywhere, let alone form any roots for somewhere to come home to. How I long for the days where it was just me and my sisters, my sweet Briasse and Lyrissa.

What I would give to be able to hold their hands, to have idle conversation and go about my day carrying out boring, monotonous chores. How my life has changed since those days.

Darmour's rough hand greets my own as we walk and I give it a light squeeze before interlocking my fingers. It grounds me and comforts me. It is as though he can read my troubled thoughts, and I cast him a thankful smile. His rugged jawline is speckled with black and grey stubble and his eyed shine in the torchlight.

"I think I am done, Darmour," I say quietly and under my breath so as not to draw the prying eyes and ears of the crew.

"We are pirates. We are never done."

"I don't want to carry on like this."

Darmour seems somewhat flustered by my words, his grip on my hand loosening. "We have already spoken about this. Please don't put me in a position where I have to choose, Zerina."

"I will not put you in that position," I say, our echoed footsteps growing louder, which tells me that we are potentially reaching another cavern. I turn to see our bedraggled crew shuffling behind us. "I just . . . I do not want to lead any more of our crewmates to their early graves." Graves is putting it kindly. The eleven souls we lost today do not and will not have any form of grave, their bodies lost to the traps of this godforsaken cave.

Nate, Figuera, Freya, Colt, Bravo, Joriah, Moran, Verul, Nash, Drean, and Guella. Each of their names will live with me for the rest of my life, each of their faces burnt into my memories like a searing iron. Every night that I close my eyes after this day and the next, I know that I will be greeted by their own looking back at me. In my nightmares, they will blame me for their deaths, for not being able to return to their families, or at the very least, send coin back to them.

Some of them had what I long for more than anything: a family. I would be lying to myself if I said it wasn't something that I had been thinking about, having a family. And in a fleeting moment my mind takes me far away from these death-filled caves and brings me a moment of mental reprieve that I embrace wholeheartedly. It is a place I see as my home, an escape from the life that I live now, somewhere that I know will bring me peace and solitude.

Nestled amidst a lush, verdant landscape in the heart of the countryside stands an enchanting farm cottage that seems as if it is frozen in time. The walls are constructed from a harmonious blend of aged fieldstone and weathered bricks, covered with patches of emerald moss and tendrils of ivy. A vibrant thatched roof with an aged patina gracefully arches over the cottage, providing a canopy for the whimsical, leaded glass windows that peer out at the surrounding lands.

A white picket fence, adorned with fragrant climbing roses, circles the quaint home, as if protecting a hidden treasure. Beyond this fence a thriving small holding of animals, each adding their own unique charm and character to this dream. Majestic horses graze peacefully in the meadows, their coats shimmering in the warm sunlight that dapples through the canopy of the surrounding trees.

In the nearby paddock, a small flock of plump, woolly gnarwools lazily graze, their bleating voices harmonising with the soft rustling of leaves in the gentle breeze. A gaggle of geese splashing around in the pond and the soil surrounding it, leaving trails of webbed footprints in the soft, damp earth, whilst a few inquisitive ducks dip their heads beneath the water's surface, searching for a tasty morsel.

It is as though I am there, and I take in a deep intake of air, my muscles relaxing at the sound of clucking chickens scratching at the ground for seeds and fluttering about in their coop, a rustic wooden structure adorned with hand-painted signs displaying their names. A sturdy, aged barn stands proudly nearby, its weathered wood and peeling red paint bearing witness to the countless seasons it has endured. It is a home, it is my home, one that I have longed for so long, one that more than anything I wish to become real.

Peering inside the window in my vision, I see the fuzzy outline of Darmour. I am unable to make out his features through the glass. What I do see is the forms of two children running towards him inside the cottage and him scooping them up in each of his arms. My heart swells to an ache that I cannot describe, the longing for what I can see almost unbearable.

"Zerina, Zerina?" Darmour's gravelled voice snaps me from my daydream. It felt so real, perhaps my mind is playing tricks on me given the strain of my magic. "You were miles away then."

"You have no idea." I smile as the craving for the life I have seen in this moment pushes harder than ever before to the forefront of my mind. In this moment I know that the conviction is true and that when we are done with this treasure hunt, I will start about the process of finding somewhere I can call home, where I can raise a family.

"Over here!" Ulrik calls. They are some distance ahead of us as their voice echoes down the tunnel towards us. Even from this distance, I can see that they are excited by something.

Quickening my pace, I reach them and breathe a sigh of relief at the natural light that is forcing its way through the far side of the cavern.

The air is cool and damp, the scent of damp earth and ancient stone lingering, as if the very walls of the cave held secrets of times long past. The only sound to break the profound stillness is the slow, steady drip of water echoing through the cavernous space, each drop weaving an intricate symphony of solitude.

From the depths of this abyss, a glimmer of light emerges, casting a faint glow upon the rocky walls of the cave. The wall's hard surface is an unyielding, cold canvas of rough-hewn rock, its jagged contours and intricate mineral patterns telling the story of countless aeons etched into the very bones of the earth. As the tunnel leading to the outside world meandered through the cave, the delicate tendrils of sunlight grow stronger and more insistent. The light dances and flickers, casting an ethereal net of illumination as it filters through the narrow passage, traversing a labyrinth of stalactites and stalagmites that loom like ancient guardians of the subterranean realm.

The view takes my breath away and as I focus on the ground, I see vibrant green vines and foliage have coated the surface like a fine quilt. There is natural life here. The air is fresh and crisp, and a slight salted taste in the air tells me that we are not far from the ocean.

"We're getting closer," Ulrik says, a look of joy on their face making them almost unrecognisable. The expression is short-lived, contorting into a scowl. "If only I still had my map. Careful as we enter," they say with a guarded tone, their eyes scanning the open area for signs of traps. "I do not trust the gods that created this place."

"Yet you insist on stealing treasure from them."

"It is not stealing," they say sternly, dark shadows casting across their face. "I can assure you that if we find this treasure, it is the gods themselves who have willed it."

"Let's go then," I say in haste, stepping onto the blanket of green leaves as I enter the cavern.

"Zerina, don't be so brazen. You need to have your wits about you," Ulrik calls after me, but I continue forward. The sooner we find this blasted treasure, the sooner we can escape and I can go about living my life, free of this burden.

"Careful, Ulrik," I tease. "The crew will think you care for my wellbeing." I cast them a mock salute. "Wouldn't want to ruin your fearsome image."

Ulrik glowers, an unforgiving grimace possessing their face.

Darmour taps Ulrik on the shoulder and walks past them into the cavern behind me, a sly smirk hidden under his pursed lips.

I give Darmour a playful wink as my confidence soars like a griffin dancing around the mountaintops.

The ground is soft underfoot, a sponginess which I presume is due to the canvas of leaves that decorate the surface. The leaves themselves are surprisingly tacky, however, and my boots stick to the surface, to the point where I notice string-like silk separating between the heels of my boot and the ground.

There is a perfumed smell in the air that I find alluring, a welcome reprieve from the stench of death that has assaulted us since we got here. I continue my way across the surface of the cavern towards the light at the other side.

"Zerina," Ulrik calls after me, but I care not for conversation with them, and I walk playfully away.

"Zerina!" Darmour repeats, an air of worry and concern in his voice that stops me dead in my tracks.

"What is it?" As I turn, a sudden pressure consumes my ankle and I howl in pain as I fear that my leg is about to snap. A thick, green vine with thorns protruding from its viscous green skin has wrapped around my lower leg.

With a scream, one of the crew members is hoisted into the air so fast that I cannot see who it is. Their screams billow around us, sending the rest of the crew into a fearsome frenzy. At once they rush forward, seeking to cross the cavern as quickly as possible as the green canvas of the floor slowly begins to move.

In an instant, the leaves and vines come to life. Spiked tendrils start whipping at Ulrik, Darmour, and the crew. They hack and slash wildly at anything that comes near them, severed vines crumpling in heaps around them like coiled rope.

These vines are the trap, lying in wait, the verdant tendrils springing to action as a sinister snare, eager to consume any unsuspecting souls who dare to tread upon its seemingly innocent surface.

We dared, and now we are paying the price. But I will not allow our crew to suffer.

With a flick of my wrist, I seek to channel my magic down my right arm. If there is one thing I know will help us in this moment, it is my fire magic.

Nothing happens.

I stare at my hand in confusion. I snap it around again, but yet again nothing happens, and a sinking feeling erupts in the pit of my stomach.

With a snap, the sinewy vine wrapped around my ankle slams me to the ground, then pulls me helplessly through the cavern. I struggle in vain against the unyielding pressure of its grip. The eerie echo of the vines manoeuvring around through the thick, condensed leaves makes the thick mass appear alive, as though the ground is breathing. My futile struggles do nothing as I am dragged across the leaf-strewn floor, the gnarled, living tendrils reaching out like malevolent arms, brushing against my body and entangling my limbs even further as I struggle.

I focus my mind, the varying vines now wrapping around my arms, suppressing me from reaching for my sword, and I panic as they begin to coil slowly around my waist like a python. Panic consumes me as I wriggle around in vain, completely helpless as I fight against the vines that threaten to consume me.

In desperation, I try to channel my magic again, but nothing happens.

Something is not right.

"Zerina!" Darmour races towards me with his arm outstretched, his pace slowing as thinner vines grapple with his ankles. He brings his cutlass down, and I swear I hear a high-pitched shrieking noise as if these very vines feel pain.

"My – my magic!" I stammer. "It's not working!" I can always feel it pulsating through my body, coursing through my veins. But right now, right when I needed it most, I cannot feel it. I feel empty.

The vines continue to bind me, growing tighter and tighter around me, moving up to my chest, tightening with a relentless grip that seems to possess a vicious intent. Desperation shrouds me as I struggle to breathe, my head feeling as though it is going to explode. In this moment, I swear I hear ethereal chatter amongst the leaves as though the vines are communicating.

The sharpened steel of Ulrik's cutlass rains down from above, hacking into the thick tendril that coils around me. With a nightmarish squeal, the vine's grip loosens, and Ulrik brings down their cutlass again and again until they are able to hack through the thick vine. As the pressure subsides, I roll onto my side and gasp for air, shrugging my arms until I am able to force the vines away from me.

Ulrik offers me a hand, but my eyes widen at the sight of the large, gaping mouth behind them, spiked teeth protruding as more vines reach out for them.

"Look out!"

27

JORDELL

I walk for three days and nights, with no sign of Codrin or his men. I can only assume that they think I am dead. After all, how can anyone survive that fall? I *should* be dead. Part of me wanted that fall to kill me, for perhaps in the afterlife, I will finally have the peace that I so long for.

As I walk, I replay the conversation with the mysterious woman, wondering if I am a fool to heed her words. Am I that shrouded in darkness that madness has taken a stranglehold of me? Did that conversation truly happen or did I imagined it? Not for the first time, it occurs to me that I might be following the path based on nothing other than a figment of my own imagination.

The cut to my head throbs deeply and I can smell the iron of my own blood that clings to my face from the open wound as I make my way towards Levanthria.

I used to be a man that believed and had faith in the gods that watched over us, but that blind faith has been eroded like the cliffs near Zakron's Keep, constantly assaulted by the unforgiving ocean until nothing but a crumbling mass remains.

This is how I feel, this is how I have been left by everything that has happened. All the pain, all the destruction, the death. No matter what I have done, it has always followed me. My own actions were the catalyst for the very thing I had fought for so long to stop from happening. I have lost everything. Everyone I held dearest. My mind, my will, my faith. And I have only myself to blame.

Find the child. It is my mantra now as I find myself moving with a steady stride towards an obscure fate.

Previously I had a corrupted, tainted vision that sent me on a fool's errand, but this time it feels different. This time, a deity has spoken to me directly.

That, or I really have succumbed to madness.

The girl is key, Laith's daughter is key. Maybe in finding her, I can somehow find a way to bring my son back and free him from his prison.

I stop for a moment and look around me. Above me is a canopy of foliage and I am surrounded by dense trees making it impossible to map and track where I am heading. I haven't explore this land but I know that if I keep walking, I will at some point reach the ocean, though I am beginning to worry, for it is taking longer than I would have expected.

The sound of the water is calming as the flowing water navigates the terrain, carving its path through the stone in the ground to forge a new path through persistence and time.

Ahead of me, I notice that the stream appears to widen. I continue to follow it, reaching into my satchel and retrieving a wild mushroom I foraged, which I pop into my mouth. It has a thick, meaty texture to it with an earthy taste. It is not the most pleasant of flavours, but a few of these are enough to keep me well sustained for the time being.

When I reach the river's mouth, I breathe a sigh of relief as a gust of air brushes over my face. It is a sensation that I savour for a moment as I feel my long beard move from the force. I crouch down and splash my face with water. It is crisp and refreshing, and it helps to revitalise me.

I can taste salt on the air now, and soon enough, I can see an opening from the trees ahead revealing the clear, bright blue sky, and below it, open water.

When I finally emerge from the forest, there is a rock formation to my right, a red rock that looks to be crumbling as though it is made of sand. I rub my hand over its surface to find the texture is rough, with hundreds if not thousands of tiny porous holes. My legs ache tremendously, my body still battered and bruised from my escape at the keep, so I take the opportunity to sit on the smaller rock and rest. I spend the rest of the morning eating some more mushrooms and drinking plenty, wondering how I am supposed to get back to the mainland of Levanthria.

"Am I going to have to fashion a boat myself?"

"How long would that take me?"

"It would be too long."

I voice my own racing thought as a feeling of defeat quickly replaces my relief. I could fashion a small boat from fallen trees in the woodlands. It may take me a while, but the main question would be, would it be strong enough to get me across the expanse of ocean that separates me from Levanthria's mainland?

As I sit thinking about my next steps, movement catches my eye. Small grubs are popping up from the holes in the large red stone beside me, and I find myself transfixed as multiple grubs stretch out of the holes before popping back inside. They are thick, grey, and worm-like in shape. They reach out as if trying to touch the sun itself, and I can't help but start to hypothesise why they would do this.

A commotion in the trees startles me, and I instinctively reach for my staff, waiting to see what woodland creature seeks to use my saggy bones as dinner. Not that they would be able to eat that much meat off my malnourished body.

"Show yourself, beast!" I yell, grasping onto my staff so tightly that my knuckles whiten as the wood groans under the strain. Nothing comes as I approach, other than a strange grunting noise, along with further movement as the shrubs by the trees shake.

It could be dangerous, yet I find myself drawn to it, my curiosity getting the better of me. When I reach the shrubs, I use my right hand to pull the foliage to the side, all the while keeping my staff firmly pointed in front of me.

"Oh," I say in surprise as an owl-like bird flails around in the dirt, tangled in the shrubs. It is not feathers that grace its body, however, but hardened, deep-purple scales.

The animal, I realise, is a growlite, and one of its wings is injured. It is as much akin to a dragon as it is a bird. A creature so incredibly rare that if I were on the shores of Levanthria, I could sell it for a heavy amount of coin.

When the growlite spots me, it opens its pointed jaw to give me a warning growl, but instead it releases the least intimidating noise possible. It is more like a chirp, and I cannot help but smile. It is only a youngling, no bigger than a chicken.

"Here, let me help you," I say, reaching to pull away one of the branches that is trapping its wing. "How in the world did you end up here?" As far as I know, growlites are not native to Levanthria. In fact, it should not be anywhere near here.

As I try to pull on the branch, I can see that the creature's wing is at an unnatural angle. The creature snaps at my finger, and I just barely snatch my hand away in time. The growlite may be small, but its teeth are still sharp enough to shred skin from bone.

"This is going to hurt," I warn as I quickly lunge forward and pull the horned branch back, allowing the youngling to move more freely. With a grumble, it rolls sideways, freeing itself from the shrub before stretching out one of its wings to try and intimidate me.

"Well, aren't you a hostile little thing," I chuckle as I notice its other wing remains tucked up into its side. A patch of blood soaks through the scales and drips onto the ground.

All the while the growlite remains defiant, its good wing outstretched, its teeth bared as it emits a quiet, threatening hiss.

Holding my staff forward, I focus my magic and a soothing feeling rushes through my arm as the tip of my staff glows gently. I lower my staff to focus my power on the creature and help it with its suffering, channelling my healing magic into its injured wing.

The creature's hisses and shrieking slowly stop as a bright, focused light temporarily limits my vision. When the glow at the tip of the staff subsides, I am faced with a much calmer growlite. It cocks its head from one side to the other as if weighing me up, both its wings now tucked to its sides tightly, blending perfectly with its body. It may be aggressive, but it is such a beautiful animal.

With a squawk, the growlite stretches out both of its wings in perfect symmetry and gives them a good flap, sending forward a slight gust of air that sprays dust in my face.

"Well look at that," I chuckle to myself as the growlite continues to flap its wings as if testing them.

For one, fleeting moment, I consider how easy it would be to subdue the creature and take it with me. After all, I have not a coin to my name, and I will need gold to secure passage to Osar. Despite its small size, I could sell it for a hefty sum.

But as I peer into the creature's eyes, I know I cannot do such a thing.

"Your wing is healed, so you can be on your way," I say as I turn to walk away from it, safe in the knowledge that I am not at risk of being eaten by a wild beast.

When I reach the rock where my satchel sits, I turn to find that the growlite has followed me, its tiny footprints scattered in the dirt behind it. When I make eye contact with it, it makes a soft clicking noise that seems to come from its throat.

"You can go now, it is safe to fly," I say, "Your wing is healed."

The growlite tilts its head to one side as it studies me, then it hops closer, skipping from one foot to the other whilst keeping balance using its outstretched wings. The sight makes me laugh; I always imagined that growlites would move with more grace.

I stare back at the creature with nothing but fascination, wondering what it could want from me.

"Are you hungry?" I ask, and I reach into my satchel and pull out one of the mushrooms. "Here, try this."

The growlite looks reluctant for a moment, but then it skips even closer to me, takes in a few hurried sniffs, and lets out a squawk of disapproval whilst skipping backwards once more.

"You don't like mushrooms, that makes sense." Leaning back onto the large red rock behind me, I remember the worm-like grubs I was watching just a few moments before.

"I wonder," I say as I use my staff to generate some heat from above the rock. To my surprise, my idea works, and at least twenty of the things stretch out of the rock, reaching for the warmth that my staff is now producing.

Fast, excited clicks come from the growlite's throat. It skips quickly towards the rock, grabs hold of one of the grubs, and pulls it from the hole, tilting its head back and swallowing the thing in one. It gives another sequence of fast clicks and rumbles which I ascertain to indicate happiness, and then it dives straight in for another.

I watch as it eats grub after grub, counting at least twelve that it eats in quick succession.

"Wow, you were hungry," I say as it eats another before finally skipping away, tilting its head at me once more.

With another squawk, it flaps its wings and hops on the spot from one foot to the other before bowing its head almost as if it is thanking me.

"You are quite all right," I say. I lower my staff and allow my magic to fade, and the grubs return to their home. Slowly, I lean forward and give a polite nod of my head to the creature. Now that it has a full belly, it will surely be ready to take flight. I reach down to my satchel and place it over my shoulder, ready to move on.

"I wish you well, friend," I say. As I set off, the creature emits a strange, sad whistling noise.

As I turn to face it, the growlite flaps its wings again and clicks come from its throat. To my surprise, it shuffles towards me, and when it reaches my feet, it bows its head at me once more.

Tentatively, I reach down slowly to pat it on its head, and this time, it does not snap at my hand. Its scales are softer than expected, and I rub my hand down the back of its head. It raises its neck and pushes itself into my hand, moving its head from side to side, like a bear scratching its back on a tree. Again, it makes the chittering noise, and I think the growlite is happy.

"Be on your way," I tell it once more. "No doubt your mother will be looking for you." I look to the sky above and wonder if its mother is already searching for it. Given that the people of Paldera are renowned for riding these things, it leaves little to the imagination about how big they can become, and I do not fancy an encounter with an angry, protective mother.

I start walking, but the creature continues to follow me, its scurrying feet scratching against the dirt.

"You are not going to leave me alone, are you?"

The growlite shakes its head in delight.

I heave a heavy sigh. "Come on then."

28

ORJAN

Kaelis Vore, once a fabled bard, sought to create the greatest epic ever told. Her mortal life ended by disease before she could complete her song. In death Kaelis was to become the patron of bards, storytellers, and all those who strive to create something greater not just for themselves but for others who seek to change the ways of the world.

-Dante Wordforger, Scribe of the Great Temple, 55 KR

Can it be true? After all these years of suffering, is my curse finally broken?

There is a deep, burning pain across my collarbone where the necklace has embedded itself into my skin. But it is a price that I am willing to pay, to be free from my curse.

My skin tingles with a strange sensation. The cold, crisp air stings against its surface, like I'm experiencing the sensation of air for the first time.

Like I'm a snake that has shed its skin.

"I can't believe it," Rior says. His eyes are wide and childlike, seeing magic for the first time. "How can this be? How is it that the curse is lifted?"

We find ourselves in an abandoned shepherd's hut around halfway between Hora and Eltera. The roof is barely hanging on, but it will provide us with all the shelter we need for the remainder of the night. Not that I will get much sleep given the rate at which my mind is now racing.

"All I know is that it has something to do with this artefact," I say. If I can lift this curse as well as disrupt Rhagor's plans, then this night has been a success indeed.

We managed to get out from the ruins beneath the city of horror with ease, the shadows giving us the perfect cover in the night.

The only question now is where to go next.

Rior sits by a makeshift campfire, the gentle glow from the flames kissing the underside of his chin. I, however, find myself clinging to the walls on the far side of the shepherd's hut; my skin is too sensitive to the heat now that my scales are gone.

Rior stirs a pot of stew, and for the first time in as long as I can remember, I find my stomach growling with anticipation of enjoying a meal without my tastes being dampened by the wretched curse that has plagued me for so long.

It's a vegetable soup with potato and leek, and it has never smelled so good. I feel myself practically salivating at the prospect of eating it. For so long I have eaten out of necessity, without enjoying it. Now I am eager to see if everything is back to what it used to be. If I can enjoy flavours once more.

"Do you think it's permanent?" Rior asks as he continues to stir the stew.

"I cannot say." It feels strange to hear my own voice without the reptilian rasp that I have become accustomed to. Even my breath no longer hurts my lungs, and I feel truly free, as though the world has been lifted from my shoulders. "We still don't know what this magic is, or what Rhagor wants with this artefact." I look over my hands, still in disbelief that it is not scaled skin that I see. I rotate them back and forth, fearing it is only an illusion that threatens to disappear at any moment.

This has to be one of the most powerful artefacts in the known world if it holds the ability to dispel a curse. I can't begin to imagine what Rhagor plans to do with it.

Zerina tried for years to lift my curse. Even though she was the most powerful witch on this side of the world, she was unable to find any form of magic that could free me from my burden. So the fact that an artefact like this exists, and that Rhagor knows of it, leads me to question what exactly he intends to do with it.

"Here, take this." Rior ladles some of the stew into a bowl and passes it across to me.

With trembling hands, I take the bowl from him, but my hands are shaking so much that I risk spilling the contents all over the floor. Bringing the bowl up underneath my nose, I take a deep inhale of breath and savour the exquisite smell that erupts in my nostrils. Leek and potato has never smelt so good, and it warms my insides before I even taste it.

I raise the bowl to my lips and tip the contents into my mouth, but my mouth rasps with a painful burn and I cough and splutter.

"Careful," Rior scolds me like a parent with a child. How the tables have turned.

My mouth feels as though it is on fire, and the roof of

my mouth throbs from my over-eagerness. Even then, the taste of the leek and potato stew explodes in my mouth like I am tasting food for the first time in my life. "I can't help it, it tastes so good," I gasp as if my tongue is swollen. I raise the bowl to my mouth again, this time taking a more delicate slurp of the stew. If this is how food tastes, I can't wait to sample all the other delicacies that life can offer me. It is as though my tastebuds have been cleansed, like I am experiencing flavours for the first time in my life and it feels amazing, exhilarating.

In this moment, it is as though there is only me present in the room as I continue to slurp up the stew, not caring how much of it ends up on my chin and my tunic.

"Easy, Orjan, there's plenty more left. You're eating as though it is your last meal," Rior says with concern.

"It feels like it is the first," I say, lifting my eyes to greet Rior with a smile.

"Well, that confirms to me that the curse is broken," Rior laughs. "You seem to have regained some semblance of a sense of humour. Do I even know you?"

I can't help but laugh myself as a warm sensation overcomes me. My cheekbones ache as I do, and I'm left with this smile wide enough to open the gates of the afterlife. The noise feels foreign to me, the feeling feels foreign to me.

Before I was cursed with the appearance of a lizard man, my real curse was the affliction of excess drink. But this curse, too, has seemingly escaped me. For the first time that I can recall in years, I do not have the temptation to drink at the first opportunity.

I pass Rior my bowl and he scoops some more stew into it before passing it back to me. This time, having learned my lesson, I blow onto each spoonful before sipping it lightly and more delicately than before, savouring the explosive flavours. I could quite happily eat this all through the night.

My senses have gone into overdrive and as much as I enjoy the sensation, it is overwhelming. Rain lashes against the roof of the shepherd's hut, and cold air prickles my skin. And yet, I am grateful for the icy sting, for it means that I am human once again.

The wind also picks up outside and I fear for our horses that are tied up to a nearby tree without the same form of shelter that we find ourselves in.

"In all seriousness, Orjan, what is the plan? What are our next steps?"

I do not answer right away. In truth, I hadn't thought this far ahead. Never in a million years had I imagined being freed from my curse. I had accepted my fate, accepted that I would walk the world as a cursed lizard man for the rest of my life.

My main mission now is to keep this artefact out of Rhagor's hands.

"It won't take long for Codrin to put together that it was us who took the amulet," I say. "We need to get back to Eltera quickly and formulate a plan. We should assume that Codrin will send word to Rhagor. Starting today, we'll be enemies to the crown. They'll try to track us down, of that we can be sure."

Rior grins. "But you're forgetting one thing."

I look up at him, confused. "What?"

"They'll be searching for a lizard man, not you. That will buy us some time." Then his expression changes to concern as his eyes are drawn to the artefact that is embedded in my collarbone. "Does it hurt?"

I trace my fingers across the bone necklace. The finger-like tendrils that have buried deep within my skin feel as though they have wrapped around my bones, becoming one with my anatomy. Just touching the surface of the necklace feels as though I am rubbing my fingertips over my own bones, and the feeling sends a wave of nausea from the pits of my stomach. I give the necklace a light pull, wincing from whatever magic this is. I can't see how it can be separated from me now. Lost for words, I simply give Rior a subtle nod in answer to his question.

"I am surprised that Rhagor seeks such an artefact, given that he's an all-powerful god."

Rior's sarcasm forces another laugh from me.

"Just know that whatever you decide to do, I will remain by your side, Orjan. You will always have my swords."

I give Rior another smile. "And for that reason, I know that I will sleep well tonight." I place my bowl by the fire and shuffle back against the wall of the shepherd's hut before stretching and placing my hands behind my head. I lean back and close my eyes, embracing sleep.

Time passes as though I have only blinked. When I open my eyes, there is a natural light coming in through the open doorway. I have slept through the entirety of the night as though I'm being housed in the most luxurious of environments. I find myself fully refreshed, and for the first time in as long as I can remember, I am excited to see what the day brings, despite the danger that will follow me from stealing this ancient magical artefact.

Sitting upwards, I arch my back and stretch. Loud, audible cracks rise up every notch of my spine and it is so satisfying. I stretch my neck to the right, then the left, each time getting another audible, satisfying crunch as I loosen my aching bones.

Rior is slouched against the opposite wall from me, his head resting against the stone. Drool pools on the left-hand side of his mouth and he breathes so delicately, I question if he is alive.

"Good morning," I say, but my own words startle me. The voice I project still feels foreign to me, and is one that I simply do not recognise. This is going to take some getting used to.

Rior stirs and looks around the room with his hand already clasped around one of his blades.

"At ease," I laugh, "I didn't mean to startle you. Did you sleep well?"

"I managed a couple of hours," he replies, raising his tunic to wipe the spittle that has lined his chin.

He's the best squire I could have asked for, and I know that he would have remained awake long after I slept to ensure that I was okay before finally resting himself. He has become a truly selfless man, one that I am proud to have by my side.

"Thank you, Rior," I say without elaborating. "It is something I don't tell you enough."

Rior smiles. "What have you done with Orjan?" Then his gaze shifts to the amulet. "You have been blessed by the gods, Orjan."

"It's about fucking time," I laugh. "Come, let's ready the horses. The sooner we get to Eltera, the sooner we can eat."

"And drink?" Rior asks. One thing he has picked up from me is his willingness to indulge. Although he can handle his ale far better than I could at his age.

Normally I'd have pitcher of ale or even a glass of spirits

alongside my breakfast, but the urge no longer consumes me. I feel truly free. "I think I'd rather keep a clear head, especially with the danger that no doubt awaits us in the future."

"Well," Rior says, "you will insist on pissing off the gods."

"Rior, we cannot allow whatever this artefact is to fall into Rhagor's hands. If that means I have to go into hiding for the rest of my life, it is what I will do, if that is what is needed to keep our people safe. Levanthria deserves so much better than him, and one day I believe a true king will sit on that throne."

It still pains me to see my former squire Laith possessed by that false god, to watch him parade around and carry out atrocities. If Laith was aware of the dreadful acts being committed by his own hand, he would be truly devastated.

Then the thought dawns on me. What if the power harboured within this artefact could free Laith from Rhagor's cruel grip? What if this artefact could bring him back and put him in control of his own body once more?

I only know of two spellcasters that may be versed enough in magic to help me with this artefact. One of them is Zerina, but she could be anywhere in the world at this point. The other is Morgana – and I have no clue where her allegiances truly lie.

"You have the look of a man who has just thought of a terrible idea," Rior says as we exit the shepherd's hut. We walk over to our horses and untie them from the nearby tree where they stand grazing on the wet grass. Rior reaches into his saddlebag and pulls out two apples which he promptly gives to each of the horses.

"You're right," I say, "this might just be the worst idea that I have ever had."

To carry through on what I am thinking, to act on the very thoughts, would be the definition of stupidity.

To ask for Morgana's help and opinion on whether this artefact could bring back Laith would run the risk of allowing this necklace to fall into Rhagor's hands.

But I have to try.

29

YAELOR

Large mountains form on either side of us as we navigate through a winding road that seems to have no end. The mountains are tall and formidable, and some are kissed with snow at the very tops, whilst some reach far higher, stretching into the clouds as if they are stairways to the gods themselves. The road is rocky and uneven, and our horse struggles with the terrain. On a few occasions, I have heard it cry out in pain, and I know that if I push it much harder, it runs the risk of injury. The days since we left Osar have blended into one another, making it difficult for me to know how long it has been since we left in the dead of night.

Gillam sits in front of me on the horse. Both her legs are draped over the same side of the horse to the left, and her head rests against my chest. I can only hope her dreams grant her solace.

I glance down at the top of her head, listening to her muted breaths. The lengths I would go to protect this child do not bear thinking about. Her safety is all that matters.

It is warm here, with the sun kissing my skin. My arms

redden from exposure to its glaring stare. The ground is still wet from the storm that passed overnight, making it even harder for our horse to navigate. Above us, ravenous-looking birds circle around in the sky, searching for a carcass from which to pick whatever meat they can. I wonder if they are circling us, waiting for us to collapse and give up so that they can feast on our bodies. Other than that, I see no other signs of wildlife. Occasional trees are scattered around, along with shrubs and bushes that seem like they are in desperate need of a drink, as if they get no nourishment from the barren land that we pass through.

My stomach growls and I know that I must eat soon. My head thunders from dehydration. What rations we have left, I'm saving for Gillam. Of course she does not know of this, and I would not burden her with it. After all, she is but a child, and too young to deal with the situation that we are faced with. The pains are getting worse, however, and before long, I will be forced to stop just so that I can hunt for food. I have no clue how far away we are from the Forest of Opiya.

There is no sign of the woodlands in the distance. All I can see are rows upon rows of mountains. I have no map and I have no familiarity with this land. Nothing but the northwestern stars to guide me.

"Mama?" Gillam groans as she stirs from her sleep.

"I'm here," I say.

"How far away are we?" she asks, her voice broken and dry.

"Not far now, child." I retrieve a flask of water from the satchel and pass it to her. Gillam takes a drink, then passes the bottle back to me. I only take a small sip, not wishing to waste the water and unsure when I will be able to refill it.

"I had a dream," Gillam murmurs. "One where we lived in a castle. I had the biggest bed and it was so comfy."

"One day." I smile as she looks up at me through her big, vibrant green eyes. She is such a beautiful child, and as much as she reminds me of her namesake in character, in this moment, I see how truly vulnerable she is. After all, she is but a child.

My eyes drift the road ahead and tiredness creeps up on me. I don't have time to sleep. To do so runs the risk of the guards of Osar catching us up. Even though I'm certain of my innocence in this whole situation, it is not something that I can prove, not something that others will believe.

I am an outsider. That's how it will always be.

"What's that, Mama?" Gillam points into the distance, drawing my attention to the mountains.

"What's what?"

"Up there on the cliff." She sits upright, more alert.

I notice a flock of birds suddenly fly out from the treetop where they were sitting. The tree sits high up on the cliff's edge. A perfect vantage point, from a hunter's point of view, anyway.

"Well done, child. We must have our wits about us at all times."

"Do you think it's an animal?" Gillam asks. She's too young to understand the dangers that we face, the harm that strangers would seek to do to us. It is something I've always strived to keep her safe from, but unfortunately, given our current situation, I feel that she's going to need to grow beyond her years.

"It's probably just something hunting the birds," I lie. I slow the horse down, wanting to preserve its energy in case we suddenly need to bolt. Forward is the only way. We can't turn back; that would lead us straight towards the guards that are on our trail.

We continue on the track and I keep a fixed eye on the tree ahead of us, looking for any signs of danger, but I don't see anything.

"There's so many birds." Gillam points to the scavenging birds that continue to circle us, blissfully unaware of the reason why they do this. It is not a conversation I'm ready to have with her, as I do not want her to feel that everywhere we look there is danger. Even if that is actually the case, I need to try and protect her from that truth.

I notice the shadow first. It cuts down from the cliff edge onto the ground in front of us.

Someone is up there, someone is watching.

"How many birds can you count?" I ask, wishing to keep her distracted. Gillam starts counting aloud, and by the time she reaches the eleventh bird, my grip on the horse's reins has tightened.

"Gillam, I want you to hold on real tight to the horse's mane. Keep yourself tucked into me, but press your body down on the horse's neck. I'm just going to pick up the pace a little."

Multiple shadows catch my attention, covering the ground in front of us from the clifftops above.

This is an ambush.

"Yah!" I whip the horse and kick my heels into its side as we set off at a gallop. The horse is tired, but she has served us well so far. I can only hope she has enough energy to get us out of this pass.

"Mama?"

"Keep your head tucked down!" I tell her as an arrow flies past us, barely missing the horse's back. "Shit!" I curse as I heel the horse once again, trying to make it run as fast as it possibly can.

More arrows start to rain down on us.

"Mama!" Gillam shouts. The panic and fear in her voice break my heart.

"Close your eyes!" I tell her as we continue to navigate the terrain, weaving from side to side, trying to keep our movement sporadic so they cannot predict our trajectory.

Arrows continue to hail down on us, and then I start to hear the words of our attackers.

"Don't let them get away, they will fetch a pretty price," a man's voice booms through the pass.

The last thing we want is to fall into the hands of slave traders. The gods only know the kind of things they would do to us.

Our horse is fast, and we're soon past the cliff's edge where they are firing at us from, but that does not deter them. Their shouting and jeering grows louder, and when I look over my shoulder, I see that there are three on horseback trailing behind us. One of them has an arrow pointed straight at us.

He fires his shot, and it barely misses us as I press forward to shield Gillam as best I can.

As fast as my horse is, it is also tired. Two of the horsemen quickly gain on us, manoeuvring so that one is positioned on either side.

"Let's not make this more difficult than it needs to be!" one man calls. He has an air of arrogance about him, and by the way he is taking charge of the situation, I assume that he is the leader.

"Well I much prefer the chase, so run as much as you want! It'll make it all the more worthwhile when we catch you." The horseman to my left's voice is shrill and sinister.

If only they knew what they were letting themselves in for. Why is it that I have managed to evade a fight for the last eight years, yet now I find myself in them in quick succession?

"Keep your eyes closed and keep a tight hold of the horse's mane," I tell Gillam.

Then I reach for one of my hatchets. I pull it free from my side just in time as the horseman to my left tries to pull me off the back of the horse. That is his first mistake, thinking it would be so easy to stop us. I turn and take a wild lunge with my hatchet and feel it connect with his forearm as he yelps like a pup.

"Fucking bitch!" he snarls as he falls back.

I'm not taking any chances though, and before he has a chance to regroup, I hurl my hatchet at him and it buries deep into his chest. He is flung backwards off the back of his horse and he slams into the ground with a sickening thud.

I quickly glance over my right shoulder and see that the leader along with the archer fall back slightly, clearly understanding the risk that I pose with my hatchets. The only problem now is I only have one.

Another arrow flies past us, this time a lot closer than I would like. The pass is unforgiving and relentless as we continue to hurdle down the path, jumping over rocks, shrubs, anything else that gets in our way as we desperately try to escape.

A searing pain erupts in my shoulder and I am knocked forward. I cry out in pain as my body slams against Gillam's back. I know in an instant that the arrow has pierced my shoulder, and it is only my adrenaline that fuels me now. My right arm falls limp, no longer able to hold on to the reins.

I feel myself start to slide off the horse, and my heart sinks.

"Don't stop running!" I yell.

And then I fall.

"Mama!" Gillam cries. Her panicked expression is the last thing I see before I slam into the ground. The world tumbles around me, and I feel every stone that I bounce off as my body ricochets off the ground.

When the spinning stops, I try to pick myself up, but the pain in my shoulder is intense and the rest of my body has exploded with pain as though I have been trampled by a herd of wild horses. When I look up, two men are standing over me on horseback.

"Shall I chase after the other?" the man with the bow says. He is bare-chested except for a chest strap and shoulder pauldron, and his eyes are ravenous as though he has not fed and I'm his dinner.

"Let her go," the leader says. He's a lot older, with long, greying hair and a face covered in scarred pockmarks. He hops down from his horse and stands over me. "People like you, you've always got to run and make things difficult. People like you always have to learn the hard way." His face contorts into a sinister smile, and then he leans down and crashes a fist into the side of my head. A flash of light is immediately greeted by darkness as I begin to fall into unconsciousness.

At least they do not have Gillam. They can do what they want to me, just as long as she is safe.

30

RHAGOR

The Thieves Guild thrives in the shadows of our city, a brotherhood bound by secrets and treachery. They slip in and out of the most heavily guarded places, bending shadows to their will and vanishing from sight. No guarded treasure is safe from them, and those who doubt their power do so at their own peril. The Thieves Guild is real, and I have seen them with my own two eyes.

-Confession of Samir Quickfingers, 97 KR

"What do you mean, it's gone?"

The wall behind Codrin crumbles as I slam him against the cold stone. Just when I thought things could not get any worse. Not only have I uncovered Morgana's scheming, but it would appear that someone feels it appropriate to take something that belongs to me. My hand is gripped tightly around Codrin's throat, my leather gloves groaning under the strain as I contemplate ending him where he stands.

Codrin is a strong Elven brute, but he is still no match for the strength that I wield. To my surprise, however, he does not fight back. Oh, I can see the hunger in his eyes. How he longs to punch me for having the audacity to grip him in such a way. I can see the frustration that burns deep within him about how he has to freely accept someone manhandling him. But he knows he is powerless. He only draws breath because I will it, and oh, does he know it.

His Adam's apple rubs against the palm of my hand as he tries in vain to draw breath. Heated anger spills from my mouth like a dragon spewing flames.

"Who is responsible for this?" I demand. "Who would dare defy me, who would dare steal from me?" My words are slow and aggressive, my fury getting the better of me. It is a struggle to not destroy everything in this room.

Codrin merely chokes as he tries to form words, spittle falling from his mouth as his eyes start to become blood-shot and bulbous. Realising that he doesn't have the capacity to respond to my questions, I loosen my grip, but only barely, just enough to allow him to speak and gather minimal amount of air.

"My lord, when the workers arrived in the morning, they were greeted with nothing but death. All those digging through the night had been murdered. They notified me straight away and by the time I arrived, it was clear that the amulet had been taken." Codrin splutters in between words, his breaths rasping.

I look away from him and clench my jaw tightly, taking in a deep inhale of breath to steady my frustration. "Well, were there any signs of who did this?" I ask. "After all, there was only you and your men that knew what you were doing there. In fact, as far as I'm aware, there was only you who was aware specifically what it was that I desired."

Codrin breathes heavily, trying his hardest to draw as much breath as he can through the little opportunity that I have afforded him. His eyes bulge so much that I wonder for a moment whether they will pop from his skull. This is no less than the stupid Elf deserves. His insolence and failure is simply not acceptable.

"My lord," he croaks.

I ease off that little bit more before letting go of his neck entirely, allowing him to stand freely and draw breath. For now, anyway.

"You must have some kind of inkling. It was quite clear you were from the King's Guard, and everyone knows that you are the steward of Askela. I find it hard to believe that anyone would have knowingly raided that tunnel. No one would be foolish enough to take the very thing that I desire most." If I could burn Codrin simply with my eyes, I would as I give him a deep stare. I am surprised to find that aside from struggling for breath, he is somewhat undeterred by my violence. He does not appear shaken or scared, and for some reason I find that an admirable trait. It is why he makes such a good foot soldier. "Tell me, was anything untoward found in the day prior to this theft? To this treason?"

Codrin pauses, then his eyes ignite with light. "There was the lizard man," he growls, his frustration almost as severe as my own. "He appeared with his squire, apparently angered by the destruction of Hora. He was most aggrieved. I was waiting for him to start a fight. But he knew better."

"Orjan?" I ask. I'm usually terrible with names. I have no need to memorise them because most people are insignificant to me, but the lizard man has always stood out because of his repulsive appearance. They tell me his curse comes from the sacred waters that he stupidly drank in Treventine. I do not recall who his squire is, nor do I care. All I wish to know is where the fuck he is, and where the fuck my amulet is. "Did you not think it wise to lead with this information?" I scold, spit leaving my mouth as I dress the Elf down.

"How can we be sure that it was him?" Codrin asks. "He knows full well what the price would be for his treason. After all, he has had the same warning as all the other stewards of the lands of Levanthria."

"It is too much of a coincidence that this lizard man turns up at the dig site ready for a fight, and then the next day the amulet that you were searching for has mysteriously vanished. You should have sent the fucking dogs straight to Eltera."

And another thought dawns on me: What if that witch is working with him? She must be, it is too much of a coincidence.

"I can send men straight away. I assure you, I will tear that city to the ground until we find it."

In this moment in time, I have little faith in Codrin. Luckily for him, I find myself stretched thin. Not only do I have Morgana to deal with, but there is still my plan to enact. And while it is an inconvenience that the amulet is now missing once again, this is something I need Codrin to resolve so that I can do what I must.

"You have a few days," I growl. "Further failure will see you meet your end, and it will not be the pleasant way. Consider me displeased. You will take your man and ride to Eltera without delay. When you are there, you will do whatever it takes to get the lizard to hand over what is mine."

"And if he doesn't?"

"Then you will kill as many people as you see fit until he hands it over. When he does, you can force him to watch you destroy the entire kingdom before bringing him to me. I want him to watch everything he holds dear be burnt to the ground before I end his miserable life. When I am through with him, he will beg me for mercy. Death will be a kindness for the inconvenience that he has caused me." There is a deep growl within my voice as I feel my nostrils, my anger, surging like a volcano, ready to spray molten ash across the land. Gods, how I despise these lands, how I hate having to walk this plane in a mortal body. But everything is coming together, and that amulet is key to me enacting my revenge.

"Yes, my lord." I can see the fury in Codrin's eyes. What else did he think I was going to say? He should be grateful that I let him live despite his failure. I have ended the lives of so many for so little in comparison. This is his biggest failure yet. If it wasn't for the fact that he keeps these lands in order, I would have ended him a long time ago. Without Morgana here, I have no one that I would trust as a suitable replacement, and besides, I kind of admire how he likes to shed skin from the bones of those who wrong him. It's just something I would never tell him.

"Is there a reason why you are still in my presence?" I growl.

Codrin gives me a slow nod before exhaling deeply, clearly keeping his temper under control. "No, my lord," he says before turning to leave.

"And Codrin?"

The Elf stops in his tracks and I almost see him shudder with anger before he turns to face me.

"Do not fail me again," I warn. "I assure you it will be the last thing you do."

Codrin does not speak another word before he exits, but I can tell by his tense muscles that if he had the opportunity, he might well try to end me.

But I am a god, and he is a mere mortal.

I have had it with this world. It tires me. It bores me. For eight years I have bided my time. For eight years, I have waited for my revenge. Even after two thousand years being imprisoned in stone, eight years in this wretched body has felt like an eternity. Being bound by the laws of man when I am a god. By the time I am through, the world will remember me. Well, what's left of it anyway.

With that, I ready myself for what I must do next. I do not have time to chase down Morgana and find out what it is she plans or why she sent her pet lizard to steal the amulet from me. I will deal with her later. For now, I have more pressing matters.

My chest flutters with excitement at the mere thought of what comes next. It will be something that my dear sister will never see coming. After all, she is almost as responsible as my mother for the torture that I have endured, and I cannot wait to see her face when I land on her doorstep. I will make her pay for what she did to me.

I had hoped to wait until I had the amulet in my possession before proceeding with my plan. But thanks to Morgana's scheming, I cannot risk waiting any longer.

It is time for me to inflict a little bit of chaos.

31

ULRIK

I dive out of the way just in time as this creature attempts to make me its dinner. Although I manage to avoid its snapping jaws, the side of its head catches me in the back and sends me hurtling into the pile of sticky leaves. As I pull my hands away, sticky, saliva-like goo stretches from my palms to the leaves.

Rolling onto my back, I look up at the latest test that the gods have laid down before us.

It is as though the cave itself has sprung to life within the confines of the cavern as stones, leaves, and vines merge together, wrapping and binding until it forms a giant humanoid shape.

"It's a golem!" I roar in warning at my crew. Having dropped my cutlass, I reach for my belt and withdraw a dagger, the one that my brother gave me on Voraz all those years ago. I know it will keep me safe.

I rush to Zerina who is removing the last of the vines from her torso as she clambers to her feet. She retrieves her own blade just as the golem finishes revealing its form. The brutal stone golem, a sentinel of the underground world, stands tall and menacing, its body an amalgamation of jagged rocks and boulders, bound together by the sinewy strength of vines and leaves. Its hulking form, reaching over ten feet in height, is a patchwork of stone, each piece unique in colour and texture, collected from the various geological layers within the cave. Moss and lichen, vibrant greens and muted greys, cling to its surface, giving the golem a sense of life and connection to the subterranean world it inhabits. A life that the gods have given it.

The golem's limbs, thick and powerful, resemble craggy tree trunks, but they are made of stone, their surfaces marred by scratches and gouges from the countless battles it has fought. The vines and leaves that bind its stony frame weave in and out and their roots dig deep into the cave floor, anchoring the creature as if it is drawing nutrients from the earth itself, from the skeletal remains of those that have tread this path before, now revealed through the peeling back of the leaves.

Its head is a rough, irregular boulder, with deep, hollow sockets for eyes that glow with an eerie, otherworldly green light. The cavernous mouth, a jagged crack in the stone, is set in a snarl, and above its head, the tangle of vines and leaves forms a crude helmet. This thing is not just a golem, it is a stone guardian.

As the brutal stone golem moves, the sound of grinding stone echoes through the caverns, a slow and deliberate rhythm that is both unnerving and awe-inspiring. The vines and leaves flex and twist, allowing the golem a surprising degree of mobility and agility for a creature composed of rock.

"What the fuck!" Darmour curses as he reaches my side. "How in the blazes are we meant to fight this thing!"

Darmour verbalises my own thoughts and I eye the

golem frantically, trying to think of a way to best this thing. "It is times like this that I am grateful for Zerina's magic," I reply, a cocksure arrogance to my words.

"I wouldn't count on that," Zerina says with a trembling voice as she looks into the palms of her hands. "Something is wrong, with my magic, with me."

Panicked groans filled with anxiety escape from the crew. They know all too well that flesh against stone never ends well.

"What's wrong?" I ask. "What do you mean?" I know she should still be able to channel her powers. I watched her drink the water from the Treventine fountain, and that is usually more than enough to replenish her reserves. I have never seen her magic fail her.

Zerina takes another determined step forward and squeezes her knuckles tightly, but nothing happens and she lets out a gasp of surprised exasperation.

Before we have a chance to do anything else, the golem heaves one of its large arms, the vines wrapped around it like muscle and sinew.

"Get down!" I roar and drop to the ground as the golem's arm swings over the top of us. The force of pressurised air that presses over me is a testament to the golem's strength, and I breathe a sigh of relief that it missed me.

Darmour, Zerina, and the others have dropped to the ground to avoid the blow, heeding my command. Save for one.

The older man is simply not fast enough to dodge the blow. With a sickening thud, the golem's arm connects with his body, sending him sprawling through the air to his shrill, pain-filled scream. With a snap, his head bounces off the roof of the cavern and his body slams against the jagged rocks that line the walls. He sticks to the surface as his skin explodes and his blood sprays across the blackened stone, cementing him in the history of this place.

The golem gives us no time to think as it steps towards us. The entire cavern shakes as it moves, the loose stone above us falling and dusting us with layers of dirt.

"Keep your distance!" I tell the others as I hop to my feet, my mind racing with no clue how the fuck we are going to defeat this thing.

With another heave, the golem swings its other arm, this time lower to the ground as if it seeks to scoop us up.

"Fall back!" I cry.

I drop down again, the force of my movement blowing my tricorn hat from my head and onto the pile of bones that decorates the centre of the cavern. Zerina may have lost her magic, but I still have mine.

I plant my hands into the ground and draw on levels of power that I have never before. I have the power to glamour but I need to create something that will buy us some time.

Pulsating energy seeps down my arms, though my palms, and into the ground amongst the bones where I crouch. The energy from my magic swirls around me as I continue to focus and channel like never before. I have taken sips regularly of the same waters that power Zerina, which has allowed me to sustain the form I take. My brother's form. After all, what kind of crew would take commands from an eighteen-year-old woman?

My hands sting as I concentrate on the bones in front of me. I glance up at the stone golem, using it as my inspiration for the glamour that I aim to cast.

The bones quiver, rattling and shifting as they begin to move and form a new shape around me, one that I stand in the midst of. The bones clank around me like a whirling torrent of a hurricane as they start to assemble themselves into an equally terrifying, skeletal golem. I grimace from the levels of magic I am drawing on. I am not used to this, and I only wish that I had the power to summon such a creature, but for now, a glamour will have to suffice.

As the bones continue to wrap around me, I turn to the rest of the crew.

"Fall back!" I say once more, hoping they can hear me through the storm that has formed inside the cavern.

Standing as tall as the stone golem, my skeletal creation is a macabre assemblage of the various species' remains around us: animal, human, and others, pieced together to create the appearance of a formidable warrior. Its body is composed of large, robust bones, their surfaces stained and cracked with the passage of time. Smaller, more delicate bones from long-dead creatures interlock and reinforce the structure, giving it the look of stability and flexibility. My body aches and throbs as I maintain the spell. I just have to hold it long enough to distract the stone golem.

The skeletal golem's limbs are a melding of powerful femurs and tibias, their ends sharpened into lethal points, giving the appearance it is ready to strike and impale any foe. Its hands and feet are an eerie fusion of talons and claws, each finger and toe tipped with razor-sharp keratin. In the dim light, the bones seem to emit a ghostly luminescence, an ethereal glow that only adds to the golem's sinister visage. It is a nightmarish creature.

Atop the golem's bony shoulders, a massive skull with elongated, curved horns serves as its head, its hollow eye sockets filled with a cold, blue flame – the only sign of my glamour. The flames flicker and dance, casting eerie shadows on the cave walls and illuminating the jagged rows of teeth within its maw.

As the skeletal golem takes its first steps, the sound of bones clicking and grinding together echoes through the cavern. Its movements are swift and fluid – after all, this glamour is not tethered by the same physics that bind the stone golem to this world.

To my relief, the stone golem's focus switches to me and my skeletal golem like a primal, almost magnetic force, but then it releases a blood-curdling battle cry that shakes the very cavern that we stand in. I almost lose my footing and my chest thunders with a spike of adrenaline. I feel energised. If anything, this impending battle has pushed me and my magic to a point that I did not think was possible. I feel immortal, like nothing can stop me.

Nothing can or will stop me from getting the treasure that I know lies behind my stone enemy.

With an equally ear-shattering roar, my skeletal golem emits its own battle cry. Focusing on my magic, I glance down at my hands and see that the glamour I take of my brother is starting to fail; I am pushing all my magic into the skeleton golem. For the first time in a long time, I do not see the rough hand I am used to. I see the hand of a delicate, soft-skinned woman.

"NO!" I channel my power again and my hand flickers back to the usual form that I take just as the stone golem takes a step towards me. It rears its boulder-like hand backwards as it seeks to bring it down on the skeleton golem's head. This is my moment, this is my opportunity, and I must not waver, I cannot fail. It is the only way.

As the fist comes bearing down, I raise my hands above me, and the skeleton golem mimics my movements. As the stone golem makes contact, I jump backwards, and the glamoured bones collapse into a heap in front of me, crushed into a plume of dust and shards as they spray around me. The ground shakes as the stone golem's fist smashes into the ground. Through the dust cloud there is only me standing before it, and I can't help but muster a maniacal laugh as I leap onto the back of the golem's arm and race over the surface towards its head, using its arm as a bridge. The uneven surface proves a difficult terrain, and by the time I reach the creature's head, it has become aware of my presence. Wrapping my legs around its shoulders, I lean forward and ram my dagger into its nearest eye with as much force as I can muster. A sulphuric plume of smoke burst outs, tingeing my skin. I have no idea what magic powers this thing, but I know my plan is working. The golem flails around and staggers backwards, raising its arms in an attempt to dismount me, but I manage to keep my balance.

With a heave, I lunge across the golem's face, hooking my left hand into its eye socket and swinging across. Roaring, I ram my dagger into the other eye and another plume of smoke billows out from inside. Then a thick plume of dark purple smoke pops out of its mouth. It has an acrid smell that turns my stomach, one that stinks of death and decay. The golem's form begins to rumble and vibrate as it emits another loud roar, a pained cry.

The stone golem loses its form and the vines binding it together snap and loosen as its limbs start to break away. I find myself hurtling to the ground at speed, so I push myself off from its face, using the top of its chest to give me a platform to turn and dive from.

I slam into the ground in a painful, crumpled heap. A thick plume of dust and smoke that shields the light emanates around me and the room disappears into darkness.

32
VIREO

The soul can then be transferred to another vessel, be it another item or even a living being, should the need arise. However, the process is not without its risks, as a soul bound for too long can begin to fragment and lose its sense of self. Only the most skilled and experienced enchanters dare to attempt such a feat, as to do so is madness.

-Excerpts from the private journal of Enchanter Lyriel Mistweaver, 83 KR

I stare at the woman that sits curled up in a ball by the open fire in the centre of our camp. She is wrapped in Gregor's red cloak as she shivers by the fire.

Her hair is an auburn colour, although it looks like it is coated in tar or whatever sludge it is that contaminated the water she has called home for so many years. Her skin is as pale as ice, as if there is no blood that courses through her body. Light freckles adorn her face and cheeks, and if I was to hazard a guess, I would only place this woman in her late teens.

The once ravenous and snarling teeth have gone. Her hands are bloodied too, but the talon-like claws have also gone. Whatever curse it was that plagued her, she is now free of it, thanks to Gregor. She has been sat by the fire for over an hour and still she has not spoken a word to Gregor or myself. Her eyes have remained vacant and transfixed on the flames that warm us. Is her mind lost now that the curse is broken?

The smoke from the fire billows upwards into the mist that is setting on us. The fire cracks loudly and the smoke is thick. Unfortunately we have needed to use damp wood, but still, fire is fire, and I hold my hands towards the heat, rubbing them together to combat the dropping temperature.

The thicket of trees around us still remains hauntingly silent. There is no sign of owls or any other creatures of the night, and I still remain uncertain whether or not this is a good thing. Gregor is rummaging through his large bag that sits on his sleigh. His yakulas lie huddled on the ground in deep slumber, their breathing laboured and deep. They seem exhausted, and I can't help but wonder how far Gregor has travelled to be here, to free this woman from her curse.

My body aches from the fight, a fight that when I was a child I would not have believed possible. I grew up being told tales of the fabled monster hunter Gregor. We even had a trinket in our house that was said to be crafted by him. A horse, carved from wood, although with age the details of the horse had faded, buffed away with time. It was a trinket that sat in my room with me all through my childhood. I was told that it warded off any monsters that would do me harm. As I reached adolescence, I came to see this as nothing more than a ruse by my parents to help me with the monsters I imagined in my head as a child, turning shadows into creatures that were not there. The stories of Gregor Yerald being just that: tales.

And now I sit with him in the flesh, having just fought against the Beast of Bragoa. A beast that was not a beast at all, but a young woman, cursed for hundreds of years. How many more people like this are there in Levanthria, tainted and tricked by the gods?

I can still feel the warmth and stench of her decaying breath on my skin, and my shoulders and chest sting from the scratches I sustained in the fight. The strength and power of her beastly form was unreal. There was no way that I could have matched her, it was inhuman. Prior to Gregor saving me from her snapping teeth, there was a moment where I had never felt so vulnerable, so powerless. Despite all my training, despite my skill with a bow and a sword, without Gregor here, I would have been torn limb from limb.

Now I realise the gravity of the task I have at hand.

I am readying people to go to war with a god, one with a sword more powerful than I could begin to comprehend, and here I sit, a mere mortal man with no special powers or abilities. I don't possess a shred of magic, and yet the fire within me to stand up and fight for what is right still burns deep within me, thawing away the doubts. I am either brave or foolish, but if what I have seen tonight tells me one thing, it is this: perhaps with the help of these people, those who are gifted with powers and abilities, we do stand a chance. There is perhaps a way to free Levanthria, to not only banish a cruel god but to vanquish him entirely.

Gregor finishes searching through his bag and fetches

some clothes which he places beside the woman called Leandra. He himself wears a dirtied, white-cream shirt, the sleeves of which are pulled up, revealing dark and swirling tattoos etched into his thick forearms. He does not so much as shiver from the cold, as if it does not affect him.

Gregor approaches slowly and crouches down by the woman. "Leandra," he says, his gravelled voice booming in the silence that surrounds us. "Put these on. If the curse is broken and you have truly returned to your human state, then the cold, it will affect you. You do not want to have gone through that painful transition merely to let the cold defeat you. You can keep my cloak through the night. It is lined with yakula fur and will help keep you warm." Gregor wears a solemn look on his wrinkled face, which is weathered and experienced. He looks like a man far older than I, but he has agility, strength, and a large frame that would rival any man in his prime.

Leandra doesn't respond, and her eyes remain transfixed on the floor as Gregor's thick red cloak hangs over her.

"Leandra?" Gregor says as he places a hand delicately on her shoulder.

She flinches, causing Gregor to snap his hand away.

"Sorry," he says, "I did not mean to startle you. You need to dress, before the cold gets to you."

A light enters Leandra's eyes as the vacancy in them subsides. She glances at Gregor before inspecting the clothes beside her.

"I had to guess your size. They may not fit perfectly, but they will keep you warm."

"Thank you," Leandra says. Her accent is different, it is broad and thick. One that I have not heard before, which is strange considering I have travelled much of Levanthria.

She drops Gregor's cloak to stand naked in front of us. Her body is battered, bruised, and scarred.

Without hesitation, Gregor and I turn to avert our eyes in surprise. She is clearly comfortable in her own skin. Either that, or she simply does not care anymore.

I let out an awkward cough as I stare into the dark trees behind me and my mind takes me back to the very stories I was told as a child of the monsters and demons that thrive in the darkness. I find myself getting lost as I wonder if they are all true. Hellhounds, werewolves, vampires. Dragons. I have so many questions for Gregor.

"You can look now," Leandra says, and I turn back around. She has a pair of leather pants that seem to fit her well, and a leather bodice complete with a fur-lined neck. Her arms remain uncovered, revealing three banded tattoos wrapped around her forearm. "This fits surprisingly well," she says. "It is even made in the style of my people." Then a saddened expression washes over her face, and she sits back down and begins putting on the boots that Gregor has also fetched. When she is done, she arches her back and it cracks like a snapping branch, shivering. Gregor reaches for his cloak and moves to place it over her shoulders, but Leandra pushes it away.

"Let me feel the cold for a moment," she says, "it has been so long." She lets out a sigh of relief as she closes her eyes and embraces the moment, breathing deeply and quietly as if meditating. After a moment, she looks at Gregor and says, "You always planned to free me from the curse, didn't you?"

Gregor simply smiles, dimples forming in his cheekbones, and a dry chuckle escapes from the mass of beard that shrouds his face. "I have faced many monsters and demons in my time, Leandra," he says, reaching for a log and tossing it into the fire. Delicate embers dance above the flames like wisps before vanishing. "When I was brought back from the dead, I was given but one task: protect the world from the darkness. Although there was darkness in your heart, through time I have come to realise that this had been warped by a curse. In vanquishing the curse, I removed that darkness," he continues. "We crossed paths over one hundred years ago, do you remember?"

Leandra smiles. "How could I forget? I was driven by hate, by anger. I wanted revenge, and she gave me a way to have it."

I find myself transfixed by the conversation, watching as the two talk like long-lost friends, despite the circumstances, despite what both of them have been through. I fold my arms as the cold continues to bite into me, and my eyes fall on Gregor's cloak. For a moment I am tempted to ask if I can have it if no one else is going to use it.

"You nearly killed me," Gregor says. He raises his shirt to reveal shredded scars on his torso. "It is not often that I retreat from a battle. There was something about our confrontation, something that sat with me for all these years. Something that made me want to come back." He pauses for a moment and smiles at Leandra as he lowers his shirt, tucking it back into his pants. "It was your eyes," he says. "It was those deep-green eyes. Even when cursed, I knew you were still in there. So once I recovered from our fight, I continued on my way, finding more demons and monsters and ridding them from this world. All the while, I researched the Beast of Bragoa, the fables, the folktales, the myths that surrounded your existence. It has taken me a long time, but I figured out how to use my magic to destroy the curse."

"So you always intended this?" I say hastily, interrupting their moment. The two of them turn to me as though they have suddenly remembered that I am present. "You were always going to destroy the curse and free Leandra?" I cannot help but think this would have been useful information for him to share with me before I risked my life.

Gregor simply smiles again, revealing the two dimples on his cheeks. "It is not always a given that when a curse is lifted, that the person held by it survives."

"But the curse helped me avenge my fallen clan," Leandra says. "Who is to say it was a curse and not a gift?"

Gregor sighs deeply. "There are those who walk this world as vestiges of the gods. You could consider myself one of them. I have been bestowed a power, a magic that runs deep in my veins. Some would consider this a gift as my form, my appearance, is not changed. You, however, were manipulated. Your anger and your hatred were used against you in a moment of desperation. It was in this moment that the deity that did this to you took advantage of you," Gregor says. "I believe I know which one it was, too. Did she by any chance have snake-like tattoos that moved around her skin?"

"She was an old hag. I don't recall seeing any tattoos."

"Interesting," Gregor says.

The fact that these two sit and talk about multiple gods is frightening. "I thought gods were not allowed to walk in this world," I say. It is bad enough that Rhagor has unleashed his chaos on this world. To think that there are even more gods that could do the same . . . It does not bear thinking about.

"They shouldn't, it is forbidden. But that does not mean they do not find ways around this, ways of influencing this world and the people that inhabit it. Take Rhagor, for example. He has found a way to link his very essence to his sword, meaning he is able to possess the person that wields it."

My heart sinks at the mere mention of Laith and what has happened to him. I will do whatever I need to in order to free him from Rhagor, to reunite him with Yaelor and the daughter he does not know about.

"You are not the first person I have released from their curses," Gregor says, turning back to Leandra. "I have no doubt you will not be the last."

And I realise this is my moment. It is time to ask the question that has been burning inside of me from the moment Gregor's path crossed mine.

"Your magic," I say to him. "Do you think it could help with Rhagor, could it break his curse?"

"Curse?" Gregor muses. "It is not a curse that he uses. His magic works more like possession. He has taken control of another man's body, through his sword. That is where his power lies."

"The man he has possessed. He was . . ." I pause for a moment, then correct myself. "He is my friend."

Gregor studies me for a moment, stroking his beard. "Tell me, Vireo, do you believe in fate?"

"I would air on the side of caution when it comes to believing in fate, seeing what has happened to my friends and allies who did," I say, holding my hands out in front of the fire once more to let the heat of the flames kiss my skin.

"And I would advise that very caution. But do you not think it strange that our paths would cross on this day?" he says.

He has a point. I am in need of a warrior to take up arms against a god, and it just so happens that I have crossed paths with a fabled monster hunter and a cursed beast – well, a formally cursed beast.

"The gods move in mysterious ways," Gregor says, "and do not take me for a fool that throws my trust naively in support of them. I don't. Not after all I have been through. But I am travelled enough in these lands to recognise what is coincidence and what is coordinated," he says.

"And you think our meeting was coordinated?" I ask. His words resonate with me, and I feel a sense of excitement blossoming in my chest.

Gregor rubs his hand through his beard as he thinks. "There is more at play here," he says. "When we met, you offered to help me, but in turn you asked for me to help you with something. What favour do you ask of me, Vireo Reinhold?"

I feel like Gregor has already aligned all the clues like a constellation of stars that map the sky above us, yet I know he needs to hear me say it. "Eight years ago, we fought in in the Forest of Opiya against the advancing Askelan soldiers. They came for my friend Laith and that blasted sword. A sword my friend Jordell had seen false visions of, one where that very sword would end a Great War before it even started."

My throat grows hoarse as I speak and it feels like I have a knot forming as I explain what happened. "When Laith unearthed that sword, he also released Rhagor into this world. Rhagor took control of Laith's body and we lost our dear friend." I stare into the flames of the fire and I swear I see the battle unfolding in my mind's eyes. I can see Lek, enraged and corrupted by the tainted elixirs that granted him natural magic. "Because of us, Rhagor has been able to commit his atrocities. How many lives have been taken by his rule in the last eight years?"

"I can't begin to imagine what you have been through," Gregor says sincerely.

"I can," Leandra says, a fire igniting in her eyes. "It is what has fuelled me for so long. The curse may have lifted, but my thirst to avenge my fallen clan still remains."

"It is why I am here," I say. "It is why I have travelled across Levanthria. Rhagor needs to be stopped, his reign needs to end. In defeating him, we can bring peace back to these lands."

"And in doing so, you hope to get your friend back," Gregor says.

"I have a plan," I say, my excitement mounting. "I know how to bring back prosperity to Levanthria. How to see an end to the suffering that our people have endured for far too long." I look into Gregor's eyes, then Leandra's. "The question was first asked by a friend of mine, a powerful wizard. One of the most powerful spellcasters in these lands, Jordell. He asked, 'How do you kill a god?' The answer is with people like yourself."

"You can't kill a god," Gregor sighs. "Trust me, I have tried."

"I want to bring us all together," I say. "I believe Jordell was right with his vision, well at least in part. I believe ... I *know* that a Great War is coming."

"And how do you know that, if Jordell's vision was false as you say?"

I stare into the flames. "Because," I tell him, "It is I who intends to bring it to Rhagor's doorstep."

33

ZERINA

A plume of smoke and dust erupts from the epicentre of the battle, a gritty, choking cloud that billows outwards, consuming the cave in darkness. The air is thick with the remnants of the stone golem, the fine particles of rock and earth suspended in the still atmosphere. Silence falls over the cavern, the sounds of battle now nothing more than echoes in the memory.

Moments feel like an eternity as the dust and smoke gradually begin to settle, drifting down like a sombre snow-fall. The cave, once shrouded in darkness, is now bathed in a hazy, dim light.

"Esara!" I cry. I have not said her name out loud for so long that the name feels foreign to me, as if the word spikes my dried tongue. It sticks to the roof of my mouth. My chest heaves and I feel stressed enough to vomit as I race towards her. I care not if the others are confused by the name I cry out.

Slowly, the dust begins to settle, revealing a sight that makes my mind race and a hardened lump form in my throat – a motionless Esara lies amidst the wreckage, still in the glamoured form of Ulrik.

They are partially covered in a shroud of stone debris and wilted foliage, an unnerving sight. One that shows them for what they are: frail and vulnerable. Ulrik's body is clad in tattered, dirt-stained clothing, a thick layer of dirt and debris coating their torn jacket.

I slide on my knees as I reach them and scoop my hands underneath, brushing the thick black hair that clings to their face before lowering my ear to their mouth.

"No, no, no!" I cry as tears flow down my cheeks. "This is not your time!" I am still undecided about whether their move against the stone golem was bravery or stupidity, but I do not care, as long as they survive.

In this moment, Ulrik's glamour threatens to fade, almost flickering into their true form.

"Come on, Esara," I whisper as I continue to stroke the side of their face. The promise I made to their brother comes to the forefront of my mind, crippling me with a lead weight of guilt that presses heavily down on my shoulders. "This is my fault, this is all my fault," I say as tears drop from my face onto theirs, revealing speckled clear skin under the thick layer of dirt and grime.

The rest of the crew and Darmour follow me and circle around us, the cavern drawing silent as I continue to hold Ulrik.

"Don't you dare, Ulrik!" I shout. "Don't you fucking dare leave me! Come on, you bastard!" I hammer my fist on their chest in frustration. "How could you be so stupid?" I say as I thump their chest once again.

With a cough and a heave, Ulrik opens their startled eyes and they sit bolt upright before checking themselves over. I know straight away that they are checking that they still remain in their glamoured form.

"It's okay, Ulrik," I say as they frantically pat themself down and bring their hands to their face.

"Gave us quite the scare then, Captain," Darmour says with a smile, offering Ulrik a hand. Ulrik accepts this and climbs to their feet, dusting themself down. Soot and debris floats in the air like powdered snowflakes as they continue to cough and heave.

"That was some power that you drew on there," I say, managing to muster a smile. I am frustrated by their recklessness but I would be lying if I did not revel in the relief of knowing that they are alive. "I thought we had lost you."

Ulrik does something they have never done before: they bring their hand and rest it on my cheek before thumbing away my tears.

"I didn't realise you still cared." They smile cockily and I know in an instant they are back to their normal self.

I place my hand delicately on the back of theirs for a brief, tender moment before grabbing hold of Ulrik's finger and tearing their hand from my face. With a yelp and a snarl, they pull their hand back and shake it.

"That is for being so reckless and stupid!" I say. Then I reach for my flask and pass it to them. "Drink."

They give me a stern, disapproving look before accepting the flask and taking a gulp of the water. At least I know this will replenish their magic stores so they can maintain their glamour without any side effects.

"Thank you," they say with gasping breath as they pull the flask away from their mouth. "Thought I was a goner then."

"We all did, Captain, but the gods clearly favour you!" Darmour says. "Stories will be told of this day, the day that

Ulrik Thatch took down an ancient stone golem single-handedly, right men?" He raises his hand in celebration and the members of the crew that remain cheer in celebration with him.

"How many did we lose?" I ask, our crew now becoming desperately thin on numbers.

Darmour drops his hand to his chest and bows his head. "We lost two more souls," he says. The remaining crew members do the same, and a silence befalls us for a moment.

"We have no time to waste," Ulrik says, and they head to the centre of the bone pile on the cavern floor where they pick up their tricorn hat. They shake off the dust that coats its surface, then put it on their head and straighten it.

"Come, I have no doubt that we are close now. The gods have tested us and we have made it through this far. I am certain that what I search for lies beyond this cavern, in the next chamber." With a determined smile on their face, they walk past me with only a slight hobble in their step, and I am amazed that they have not succumbed to a more serious injury.

There is such a fine line between confidence and arrogance, but whatever side of the line that Ulrik walks, one thing is clear to me – they clearly have the favour of the gods on their side.

After navigating through the dark and barren caverns, I cautiously follow as we approach the exit of the cave system. My senses are heightened, expecting to encounter more darkness and desolation. Instead, as we step through the threshold, we are met with a sight that leaves me – and the others, judging by their gasps – in awe: an open chamber filled with natural light, waters, trees, and the harmonious cacophony of animal life. Its own ecosystem.

Sunlight streams in through cracks and openings in the cavern's ceiling, casting warm, golden beams on the life below. The chamber, a hidden oasis in a place where life should not flourish, teems with vibrant flowers and trees, defying all expectations. The air is alive with the sweet scents of blooming flowers and the soothing sounds of rustling leaves, a welcome reprieve from the oppressive darkness that has surrounded us until now.

Ahead of us, a crystal-clear stream flows elegantly through the heart of the chamber, its gentle waters joining the symphony of birdsong and animal calls that fill the air. Lush trees, with trunks as wide as houses and leaves that shimmer in the sun, tower above the forest floor, their branches creating a canopy of green that filters the sunlight, dappling the ground with patterns of light and shadow.

Myself and the crew stand at the entrance to this miraculous haven, unable to comprehend how such a place could exist in a realm where life is not meant to thrive. This is truly a place that can survive only with the blessings of the gods, for such a place to exist defies the very balance of nature itself.

Ahead of me, Ulrik's face beams with delight and wonderment as they take in our surroundings. They were right all along. Even if I still do not know what it is that we search for.

Birds of all colours and sizes, of which I have never seen before, fly overhead, their songs calming along with the sound of the waters that run through this place. A creature as large as a bull but with large, curled horns drinks from the river, telling me that these waters are not made of acid.

"It's beautiful," I gasp, my breath taken away by the

oasis that sits in front of us. Only the beaches on the Isle of Voraz have taken my breath in this way.

My eyes are drawn to a stone table that stands in the centre of the cavern, and the light catches something sitting on top of it.

"Is that the treasure you are looking for?" I ask Ulrik, pointing towards the centre of the oasis.

Ulrik smiles a wide smile and straightens their tricorn hat once more. "It is," they say, their eyes sparkling.

Just what is it that has got Ulrik so motivated?

Without hesitation, Ulrik darts through the dense leaves, into the oasis.

"Ulrik, we don't know if there are any more traps!" I call after them, but it is to no avail. If a stone golem isn't enough to stop them at this stage, I don't think anything will.

With my heart pounding excitedly and my breath catching in my throat, I sprint through the exotic oasis on Ulrik's tail, my eyes fixed on the distant stone table where a red jewel gleams enticingly.

I'm half expecting another golem to emerge, but the oasis remains a vibrant paradise, alive with colour and brimming with the energy of a thriving ecosystem. Palm trees sway gently in a warm breeze that simply defies physics. The air is heavy with the sweet scent of ripe fruit and fragrant blossoms, which only serves to heighten my senses.

As I race towards the jewel, my feet kick up fine sand that sparkles like gold in the sunlight. Lush ferns and exotic flowers line the path, their vivid hues a dazzling display of nature's beauty. Around me, the oasis buzzes with life: brilliantly coloured birds flit from branch to branch, their melodic songs filling the air, whilst small mammals dart playfully in and out of the undergrowth.

The sound of water splashing in the distance beckons me, a promise of respite from the heat and exhaustion. I pass by a series of clear, sparkling pools, each fed by a small waterfall cascading down the face of a moss-covered rock. The water shimmers, reflecting the sunlight and casting a soothing, dappled light across the oasis.

As I draw nearer to the stone table, its ancient, weathered surface comes into focus. The table stands alone in a small clearing, a solemn monument to a forgotten time. Atop the table sits the red jewel, its deep crimson colour almost pulsating with an inner light, as if imbued with a power beyond comprehension.

When I finally reach the stone table, Ulrik is already standing in awe at the treasure that awaits us. The gem seems to call to me, its radiant glow a promise of untold mysteries and hidden secrets waiting to be unlocked. In this lush and exotic oasis, with all its beauty, I can't help but think this is all too good to be true. I do not trust it.

Ulrik's eyes bore into the jewel with such hunger, I wonder if they will start salivating and try to eat the thing. I have never seen a jewel so alluring, so enticing, so beautiful, and I can't even comprehend its value given that the gods have sat it undisturbed in this oasis.

"We found it," I say. "Why is it that I feel there is more to this jewel than you are letting on, Ulrik?"

Ulrik shifts uncomfortably at my probing, sparking my concern.

"What is this treasure called, Ulrik?" My mind is awash with the knowledge of this world, the magic and the treasures that inhabit it. A gift from falling into the fountain in

Treventine, my mind now a codex more valuable than any library.

If I could just know its name . . .

"That's not important right now," Ulrik says dismissively as they retrieve a piece of cloth from the inside of their jacket. They place it down on top of the table, just in front of the jewel.

The jewel dances in the reflection it casts in Ulrik's wide, darkened eyes, the pulsating energy within it drawing a warning from the pits of my stomach that feels heavy enough to compress my insides.

"Tell me its name, Ulrik," I demand, placing my hand next to the cloth. If I could draw on my magic, I would summon a flicker as a warning, but for now, they will have to face the storm of my voice. My concern about my missing magic sits heavy at the back of my mind, a problem to be dealt with later.

Ulrik ignores me. Instead, they stretches out their hands and cup the jewel from underneath, lifting it off the circular plinth it sits within. "It's magnificent," they say.

I slam my hand onto the stone table and fetch my other hand to my dagger. "I swear to the gods, Ulrik, if you do not start being honest with me . . ."

Ulrik examines the jewel carefully as if they cradle a baby in their hands, their dirt-filled face speckled with red light. They place it into the cloth, then fold the corners together before stashing the jewel into a satchel that Darmour passes to them.

They cannot look me in the eyes, and for a fleeting moment, I wonder if Ulrik has confided in Darmour what the jewel is.

"I am not going to let this go, Ulrik." I draw upon my dagger and press the blade against their neck.

The crew are not pleased with this, and they draw their own weapons on me to protect their captain, like they should do.

"You would draw your weapon on me?" Ulrik demands.

"You would continue to lie to me?"

"You don't have the guts," they snarl.

I press the blade harder against them and a small slither of blood drips down from underneath my blade. "Don't test me," I speak through gritted teeth, knowing there is so much more to this treasure than they are letting on. "Now tell me what the fuck this is!"

Ulrik slowly raises their hands to either side of them, being careful not to move their head. "If you insist," they say with a reluctant sigh, as if I am some nagging wife. It is enough to spike further frustration from me and I grip my dagger even tighter.

"This jewel is known as Nareva's Tear." Their words are hushed, as if they do not want me to fully hear them.

My chest heaves with the realisation of what this is, what it is that Ulrik has been hiding from me all this time.

"Ulrik, you can't harness this power! It is not natural."

"It is as natural as the magic that flows through our veins. How else would it exist?"

The power in this jewel was definitely created by the gods. I lower my blade slightly, relieving the pressure. "Ulrik, that's the Resurrection Stone."

34

JORDELL

Over the next few days, the young growlite proves to be good company, and I quickly become fond of her. She observes me curiously as I begin gathering supplies to build a raft, and I watch her out of the corner of my eye, not entirely sure why she chooses to stay with me. I watch her peculiar movements, the noises she makes when she is sad, frustrated, or angry, but I still have much to learn.

Despite the youngling not understanding any of the words that I speak, I still find myself conversing with her like you would a friend or ally. The strange part is, I swear that she listens, for when I talk, she settles down and cocks her head. Her appetite is at times insatiable, but given that she is just a youngling, I imagine her bones are growing at an accelerated rate. Foraging for the both of us proves difficult with her devouring any mushrooms or vegetation that I find in a matter of seconds, meaning I am having to spend more time looking for things to eat.

Still, I am still grateful that she chose to follow me,

although how long she will follow me for remains to be seen.

"Come now, Elara," I say, having given her a name. Vines are wrapped around my shoulder as we walk down the sandy embankment. A rumble comes from her throat as she sniffs at a nearby bush. With her wings tucked tightly behind her, she pads ahead of me and rakes the ground with her claws. "Careful around that bush," I chuckle. "You know what happened last time."

She scraps at the ground a few more times before a tiny shrew bolts out, making a bid for freedom. Elara shrieks with delight and scurries after the vole at speed, using her wings to propel her forward. Her claws wrap around the vole and the poor thing does not stand a chance. Elara tightens her claws until the creature no longer moves, then tosses it on the ground and scoops it up with her jaws. Tilting her head back, she swallows the thing in one, and then starts padding the ground in happiness.

"Happy now?" I say, turning to continue my walk to the raft I have been making. When I reach it, I toss the gathered vines on the sand by my feet and start lashing them around the pieces of wood that I have found to bind it together. I have had to hold patience and I am not as strong as I used to be, the majority of my bulk now withered away.

When I am done, I step back from the raft to admire my work. It is ramshackle at best and useless at worse. Still, it is big enough for Elara and myself. The question is, will it get us across the water?

"I think it is time for a test," I say with conviction as I pick up the front of the raft and drag it to the water's edge. "Come on, you hop on first."

To my surprise, Elara skips ahead and hops onto the raft, moving to the front. I push the raft forward until it floats independently, and then I climb aboard, kneeling on the uneven surface. To my relief, it floats, and I grab hold of the makeshift oar I have fashioned and placed in the centre. It is heavier than I would have liked, but beggars cannot be choosers.

I move us further out into the water. The air tastes salty as a light breeze kisses my face, and Elara continues to watch over me from the front as I plunge the oar into the water. Then she does the unimaginable.

"Elara, no!" I say as she starts gnawing on the vines at the front of the raft. I drop the oar and try to stop her, but I am too late. By the time I reach her, her small, jagged teeth have cut through the vines like parchment. The raft starts to pull apart and within seconds I am plunged into the water.

Elara squawks and flaps her wings, taking flight and flying in a circle around me. As frustrated as I am, I can't help but laugh. "It is okay for you," I chuckle, "keeping nice and dry up there." She squawks again and I splash her playfully, something which she does not seem to appreciate as she flies back to the embankment.

When I reach the shore, it dawns on me that perhaps I had been more than naive in thinking that I could fashion a raft so easily and reach the mainland. Still, I would rather pinpoint the flaws of the raft whilst still in the shallows than in the depths of the wider ocean.

I take a moment to look out at the expanse of water between us and the rest of Levanthria, a mist sitting hauntingly across the surface. It is beautiful, but I can't help but think of all the beasties that lie submerged within its darkened depths.

"How are we going to get across?" I ask with a huff, drenched to the bone.

Elara chirps back as if she tells me the greatest of plans. If only I could speak growlite. There would have been safe passage to the north of the keep, but with Codrin attacking me, I can only assume he will have soldiers placed there.

"What now?" I say in frustration. There is not a raft that I could fashion that will safely get us across that water.

I hear a whistling noise from ahead of us, a melodic tune, and I stare into the mist. Through the fog, the form of a person emerges, and then the rest of their small boat comes into sight as it pierces the thick mist.

When our eyes meet, the man looks puzzled, even more so when he sees the growlite perched next to me. He is a middle-aged man, with a thin frame and balding head. His skin hangs from his cheeks and jawline as if once upon a time he was of a plumper build.

"I warn you," he growls, "I have nothing valuable on my boat." The boat is small, it looks like a fishing boat, but I cannot see any fishing equipment on it. A small mast protrudes from the middle with the smallest of cream flags hanging limply from it. It is as though they are made of parchment, torn and flapping aimlessly with the breeze. The man hops out of the boat before grabbing hold of some rope and dragging it to the shore with him.

As he glides slowly towards the bank, I remain away from him and fold my arms behind my back. Elara however, reacts in a more hostile manner. She stretches out her neck and legs before reaching out with her wings, her scaled feathers pointing outwards, giving the appearance of sharpened glass.

"Wh-what is that?" the man says with startled surprise as Elara gives him a warning hiss.

I look down at her once more, surprised myself, but I shouldn't be. She is a wild animal, after all. Perhaps she sees this man as a threat, although she wasn't this hostile to me.

"I think she means to protect me," I say as the boat comes to a stop when it hits the embankment. "What is it that brings you to this point?" I have my own suspicions, though. There is no sign of human activity in these parts, this area of Levanthria long destitute from man.

"Luck," he says, and I notice a tremble in his voice. The man dives from the boat and drops to the ground, scooping sand up in his hand and allowing it to fall through his fingers whilst he studies it with a widening smile. He looks up at me through dark, sunken eyes.

I sense sadness and fear in him, but the relief that covers him is clear to see. "I am no enemy," I assure him. Beside me, Elara settles down and lowers her wings, her scaled feathers returning to their normal position. "Can I be safe in assuming you are not a foe?"

The man looks at me with a puzzled expression as I offer him a hand. Then, tentatively, he accepts it and I help pull him back to his feet. His hand is shaking, and his lips are cracked and broken. The man is malnourished and dehydrated, that much is clear. I walk to my satchel and search for my flask and a piece of derera root that I found earlier. It is a large oval shape, with thick, tangling roots intertwining underneath it, almost rope-like. It has a bitter, sour taste, but it is more substantial than eating mushrooms and this man looks desperately in need of sustenance.

Elara gives him another warning hiss as I pass him the flask with one hand and the derera root with the other. It is a warning that I should heed given my current situation, but I surrender to my biggest flaw, being too trusting. In his weakened state, I do not think that this man is a threat.

He takes the derera root and the flask into his trembling hands, eyeing them as if unsure which to have first. Then he pours the water down his mouth, getting as much in his mouth as he lets cascade down his chin. He sighs and groans with delight as he laps up the water before eventually stopping for air. The man then bites straight into the derera root with a satisfying crunching noise as he takes a huge chunk out of its side.

I simply watch in awe at the man's ravenous demeanour. Just how long has he been out in his boat for?

The man devours the derera fruit, its pulp soaking into his thin, wispy beard and dripping from his chin. When he is finished, he gives his chin a wipe with his torn sleeve before letting out a satisfied sigh.

"I'm sorry," he says, "it's just been days since I last ate or drank." He almost looks ashamed, as if he isn't proud of eating in front of someone this way.

"What happened?" I ask.

"A fog," the man starts, his voice already sounding clearer now that he had a drink and a bite to eat. "There were three of us, Bura, Lena, and I. We are fishermen, we fish for a living, always have done. Just off the coast by Uster Lena warned us, said that something didn't feel right when we set off. If only I had listened to her, she would still be here."

The man looks downcast at the mention of her name, and I wonder if she was more than just a colleague to him. "We set off, and everything started well. We had caught a couple of big fish, nothing major, but enough to feed our families that day. Lena seemed on edge the entire time. She kept looking out at the ocean, saying that she didn't trust the clouds. She has been fishing longer than me too, but me and Bura insisted on carrying on. We just wanted to catch a couple more fish, so that our families would have full bellies, maybe for once have enough to share with some of the villagers too. We were in calm waters, nothing could have prepared us. It came out of nowhere, a fog as thick as smoke. We couldn't see more than an arm's length outside of the boat. Then night fell and the fog was still there. By the time it lifted we could no longer see land, we were lost."

"Where are Bura and Lena now?"

The man gives me another strange look as if he doesn't fully understand my words, which confuses me, so I repeat myself again, this time a little slower, "Bura and Lena, where are they?"

The man looks down at the ground and another wave of fresh grief seems to wash over him like a rising tide. "They are lost to the ocean," he says. "On the third night, we were met by rougher waters. Our boat isn't equipped for that, it is not a ship, it is for fishing, after all. Bura was the first to fall overboard. He was helping us wrap rope around our mast so we could secure ourselves, but he lost his footing."

The man's words seem to stick in his throat as he continues, "He fell before I could do anything. We had been friends for near twenty years and he was gone in an instant. Lena reacted faster, but a wave hit the side of the boat as she reached for him and she went overboard, too. There was nothing that I could do. I called out for them, shouted until my voice was raw, but I could not hear them over the howling winds and the crashing waves. I couldn't see them through the darkness that surrounded me, and all of a sudden I was alone."

He pauses, and I give him a comforting nod, allowing him to compose himself.

"That was at least five days ago," he says. "I had lost all hope when, through the light mist, I heard a commotion, splashing in what sounded like shallow waters. I followed the noise and this is what led me here, to this piece of land, to you. Somehow the gods have willed me to survive." He looks up at the sky in gratitude towards his gods, something that I used to do on a regular basis.

But I lost my faith a long time ago. Yet I find myself in need of a boat, and one just happens to drift in, in the middle of nowhere. Even the most sceptic of people would find that perhaps a little faith could help them in a time of need.

"You have reached the southern isles of Levanthria, Zakron," I explain.

"So far south," the man says with surprise. "I must get back, my children, they must think I have been lost to the sea, too. Please, you must help me. I need to get back or they will be orphaned."

"As it happens, I am in need of passage across the waters. Perhaps we can help each other in these circumstances. We need to restore your boat, first, but could you help me get across the water?"

"What about him?" The man nods at Elara, who in turn hisses at him once again. She is not letting up with her hostilities towards this man.

"She will warm to you, I am sure of it. I think we are east of Zakron's Keep. If we sail northeast of here, we should be able to reach the Isle of Voraz. It should be calmer waters between there and here, and from there, we will be able to set sail for Osar, maybe onboard another ship that may make port there."

"Are you sure?" the man asks. "Seems like an awful lot of guessing."

"Before I was a man of the Great Temple, before I devoted my life to false gods, I spent four years serving aboard a ship of the King's Fleet. I am afraid it is the best way of getting back to your family, to your children. Rest up. I will see what I can do with your sail. Tomorrow we set sail for Voraz. It has been some time since I mapped the ocean, but I am confident that I will be able to map the stars tonight and use the sun, to set us in the right general direction."

"Okay," the man says.

We have a plan, seemingly out of nowhere. It is as if the gods have willed our paths to cross. After all, what are the chances of this situation arising?

I close my eyes and find myself thinking of the lost souls from his boat. I can only hope that they have found solace from this cruel world in the afterlife.

35

MORGANA

There is no true cure for magic addiction only the strength of the human spirit. Magic Wielders will need to show the courage to face life without the crutch of arcane power. It is a daily battle, but one wielders will need to overcome, for the alternative is a slow descent into madness and despair.

-Archyriel Dawnwhisper, Magic, A Truth 112 KR

The night seems to drag on for an eternity as I continue to race towards the Gondoron Pass. It has been quite a length of time since whatever it was that was stalking me vanished.

I have faced so much adversity and cruelty in this life, I have seen and enacted the most heinous acts on other men and women, and fae, for that matter. Nothing in my life has ever forced fear to erupt within my body or my mind.

Despite seeing nothing else for quite a long time, it has not stopped me constantly scouring the shadows on the periphery of my vision, constantly questioning whether there is something still out there, watching me, waiting for me. It is to a point where I question if I have descended into madness myself, for this is the kind of mind trick that I have often played on others using my magic, and despite having good defences, having honed my magic beyond anything that any other person could comprehend, I wonder if another spell-caster has somehow managed to pierce through my mental shields to alter my perception and affect my mind. There is a deadly calmness around me as I gaze at the stars above.

A deafening roar startles me. I have been that focused on the shadowy figures that I have not been focused on the dangers that the Gondoron Pass brings on its own. It is a guttural roar, one which again startles my exhausted horse. Before I even have time to react, an indescribable force crashes into us, sending me flying from the horse and bouncing off the ground. My forearm bone snaps and cracks. I let out a yelp of pain as I try to push myself up from the ground, but I know my arm is broken. It is an agonising pain but I have little time to dwell on my wound when I see what it is that has attacked me.

A wyvern stands about ten feet tall on its hind legs. Its wings stretch out wide, showing off its bony, malnourished body. There is only one thing I can think of worse than meeting a wyvern, and that is coming face to face with a clearly malnourished, starving, and desperate one.

Within seconds, the wyvern strides over to my horse and emits another guttural roar before biting down on its neck. The horse cries out in fear and pain, but soon falls silent as its life fades away, its blood spraying up the wyvern's face. The hungry beast begins to devour my horse's flesh in a frantic and frenzied manner. Ferocious claws tear through the horse's side, shredding its skin like parchment.

I sit frozen on the spot, the pain in my arm excruciating. I did not expect to ever come face to face with a wyvern. They have not been seen here for such a long time, you would have been forgiven for thinking that they had become extinct.

The sound of the beast ripping my horse from limb to limb and feasting on it like a pompous lord would a buffet at a banquet snaps me out of my shocked stupor. With the wyvern distracted, I try to sneak away, to get as much distance as I can.

As soon as I try to move away, the wyvern raises its head to look at me, and its large, frosted eyes widen as it sniffs the air. That's when I realise that this wyvern has either no vision, or very little, and given its withered frame, I question if it is at the end stages of its life.

Blind or not, I'm not going to be able to outrun it. If I am to survive this fight, I'm going to have to find a way to kill this creature, and I'm going to have to do it quickly. I am already exhausted, and with my horse being dead, I have nothing to syphon my magic through.

The wyvern roars once again, then rushes towards me. With no other options, I begin to channel as much power as I can through my own body and down my good arm to the palm of my hand. When I feel the connection, I let it pull from my core towards the creature to syphon its life in an attempt to replenish myself from my broken arm.

To my horror, my magic does not work, and I realise my powers might be worthless against the magical properties that wyverns themselves have. The wyvern is at me in no time, crashing its head into my body and sending me sprawling once more. It rushes at me again, jumping and flapping its wings to hover above the ground. I draw my power once more, unleashing a flash of green light that does not seem to deter the creature at all. This confirms to me that the creature is blind. As it tries to land on top of me, I frantically roll to my side, barely moving out of the way as the beast crashes into the ground, covering me in the dirt it frantically claws against.

I shuffle backwards again, trying to get as much distance as I can between me and the wyvern. Shocking pain erupts in my broken arm when I press down on it and as I cry out in agony, the wyvern snaps its head to its left, clearly following the sounds. It begins to move in my general direction once again. I allow my power to flow through me, channelling my magic and bringing my arm across in front of me. This time, I cast a degenerative spell, focusing as much energy as I can into the creature's wings.

It is the wyvern's turn to cry out in pain, and it lets out an almighty roar as I watch one of its wings snap like a falling branch from a tree. Then I aim my hand at the other wing, tightening my fist is if I hold the beast's bones in my own hand. As I twist, the creature's other wing snaps, and when I pull my arm down, a green energy drags on the wyvern, pulling it into the ground. A tsunami of earth flies through the air and I feel a stone slam into my shoulder above my broken arm. I drop to my knees.

I try to stand up again, but I have already drawn on a high amount of power with that one spell. Normally it would be syphoned from another, but now my magic is eating away at my own body. I look down at my arms to see my veins protruding so violently from my skin, it is as though they're trying to rip themselves free. A horrendous cramping sensation tightens my muscles all over my body as if an unseen force squeezes me in their palms. I cry out in agony, screaming at the wyvern in frustration, in anger and pain.

I will not be ended in this way. I will not become a meal for this creature and simply forgotten in history books, the queen that vanished. I will find my sister. I will ensure my niece's safety.

I use every ounce of my need to find them as strength to push myself up from the ground. Despite the pain, despite the agony, I push through the pain barrier and heave myself to my feet. Even with my buckling legs, I stand tall.

The wyvern tries to push itself up with its wings, but with another sickening crunch, they collapse underneath and its chest slams onto the ground in front of me. I stretch out my good arm and focus my magic once again until my entire forearm and hand emit dark green energy that is linked to my necromancy. With a scream that I can only imagine would scare off any other creature in the vicinity, I focus my magic and press it towards the wyvern's face. it begins to shake its head as if trying to escape whatever it is that's inside it.

The wyvern lets out its own roar of pain as I continue to channel my magic, forcing it as much as I can into the creature's skull, hammering against it, increasing the pressure as the creature's eyes begin to weep with blood. My legs tremble as my power erupts around me. I continue to scream out at the dragon, and when I snap my fists closed, a strange squelching noise followed by a pop leaves the beast. The creature's neck falls limp straight away and its head slams into the ground. Blood and pulp begin to ooze from its eyes, nose, and mouth.

If I thought the pain of my broken arm was bad, it pales in comparison to what greets me now as what feels like ice breaks up my arm and throughout my body.

The wyvern might be dead, but how am I meant to get to Yaelor and Gillam in this sorry condition? I so desperately need rest. I could just make a fire, have done with tonight, and continue my journey in the morning, but even then, that would be so much time wasted. That could put me even farther away from my sister and niece.

I just want to curl up and cry as the affliction from magic use begins to ravage my body, but I refuse to let it control me. I take an agonising step forward, followed by another, and another, and another. My progress is slow, but I keep moving. I have to find them. I cannot stop and I will not stop. I do not care what happens to me as long as I know they're safe.

I continue to stagger on my path, leaving the wyvern and my dead horse behind me. I clutch my broken arm as tears stream down my face.

And then, from the shadows, figures move towards me. The light in their eyes is what alerts me to their presence first.

There is a lot more than three of them this time.

"What do you want from me!" I cry out as they move slowly towards me. I am in no state to outrun them, nor could I push through them. Whoever they are and whatever they want, I am about to find out, because I am too exhausted to do anything about it.

Nothing can prepare me for what greets me when they move out from the darkness and into the light that the moon casts hauntingly from above. It is not men that stalk me.

These are spectres. The one at the front bears no resemblance to anything that I have ever seen. It moves slowly, quite clearly not of this world. Its skin is decaying, and there are gaps in its flesh where bone and sinew can be seen. You would be forgiven for mistaking these as undead, but it is the soft glow around them and the light that emits from their eyes that makes it clear they are spectres.

"Who are you?" I demand.

The spectre at the front opens its mouth and I expect the haunting, croaking noise once more. Instead, a pained voice speaks. "We are neither living or dead," the voice rasps, as if gasping for breath. They continue to step towards me. "We have not been able to pass through to the afterlife."

"What is it you want from me?" I ask desperately as they draw closer. The air around me feels colder and colder, and I don't know whether this is the aftereffects of my magic use or if it's caused by these spectres.

The spectre in front of me is expressionless as he continues to step towards me, the others following close behind. "We are consequences of you," he rasps, his voice becoming deeper, more menacing. "We are not of this earth because of you, because you stole our lives, because you devoured our souls. This has caused an imbalance that has prevented us from passing over to the afterlife. You will pay for what you have done to us."

"No – no, this can't be," I stammer as they step into my personal space.

One by one, they claw at me, yet my skin remains as their translucent arms shred through my body. A nauseating sensation grips me and I feel as though I can't breathe as I am mauled by the horde of spectral ravagers.

I cry out, but no noise leaves my throat. Then the spectres all open their mouths, and I'm surrounded by the deafening croaking noise that I was greeted with earlier. With every strike, I can feel their anger, their pain flooding through me, the fear that they faced in their final moments, all caused by me. They continue their onslaught for what feels like an eternity as wave upon wave lets their arms and bodies pass through me. The sensation feels as though my insides are being moved around despite no apparent injury being caused.

Then, just when I feel on the edge of collapse, they stop, vanishing just as quickly as they appeared. Nothing but a wisp of spectral trace remains in the air as I am left alone.

I collapse onto my knees and rub my hands over my body, checking myself for wounds and injuries, but there is nothing. I don't feel right though. Something has changed, they have done something to me. Whatever it is, I don't like how I feel. It is as though I am empty.

I raise my hand and try to channel just the smallest amount of magic. After all, if I can endure this much pain, what would a little more be?

Nothing happens. Panic overcomes me. I look at my hand and try once again to channel my magic, and once again, it does not work.

"This can't be," I say through hushed breath as I stare down at my hands in expectation that my magic will manifest, that it will let me know that it is still there.

But my magic is gone.

36

YAELOR

The gods of Levanthria and beyond are immensely powerful beings who shape reality itself. Each deity commands vast domains and legions of followers. They grant boons to those who curry their favor, but their blessings are often double-edged, for the gods are capricious and their motives inscrutable. Woe betide those who fall on the wrong side of them and their curses.

-Thalia Silverleaf, On the Nature of the Gods, 128 KR

Dim light creeps in through the cracks above in between the cliff edges. My eyes sting and there is a ringing in my ears that causes me to wince. My head feels as though it has been smashed against a tree. Instinctively I try to raise my hands to my head but find them bound tightly together. When I drag my gaze down to my wrist, I see a thick, coarse rope leaving friction marks against my skin.

"Gillam," I call out groggily. My heart sinks as fear

consumes me at the thought of these monsters getting their hands on her. "Where is my daughter?" I demand, coming to slightly more with fierce tenacity in my words. "If you have harmed one hair on her head, I'll –"

I'm greeted with a strike across the face that forces my head to the side. A rough, firm hand grips my chin and pulls my face forward again. My vision is blurred but I can just about see the details of my captor. Thick, unkempt white eyebrows accompany furious deep brown eyes. The skin around them is cracked and aged, and a weathered, messy beard hides the majority of his face.

"You killed one of my men," he growls as he tilts my chin up to meet his eyes. His rancid breath is understandable given the stained and blackened teeth in his mouth.

My eyes meet his and I give him nothing but a stare of defiance. I do not care what this man does to me. After everything I've been through, there is no way that he could ever break me. Unless . . .

Gillam's beautiful green eyes come to the forefront of my mind.

I continue to stare for a moment before finally moving my eyes from his, searching my surroundings for my daughter. She is as fiery as I am, and I have no doubt that, had they captured her, I would be able to hear her fighting. The last thing I saw before I blacked out was her riding off on my horse, and again my heart sinks, feeling as if it is falling into a black void.

She is but a child. How is she to know how to fend off the dangers of this world? Where will she go? She has escaped these bandits, but for how long will she remain safe without anyone to protect her? She needs me. I must find a way to get to her, and I will do whatever it takes.

The bandit slams another blunt fist into my jaw, snapping my head to the side once again. I turn my head slowly to face him, then hold his gaze as I spit blood at his feet. It splashes over his boots and mixes with the dirt and sand on the ground. Just where have they taken me?

"This one's got some fight in her," he sneers through a gritted smile that puts all his disgusting teeth on full show. His breath lingers against my skin.

The group of men that surround me cackle like wildlings as I search for each one of them in the room. I count at least six figures of varying sizes and ages, from relatively young all the way to the oldest man that stands in front of me. My vision now returning offers me an opportunity to weigh up my surroundings as I try to figure out just where I am. The room looks primitive and ramshackle, with no apparent order to their den of evil. Wooden slabs sit on top of barrels, serving as hastily put-together tables. Lanterns are scattered around, some on the ground, some atop the tables, and some on top of what look like crates. A couple of them are lit, causing large shadows to form on the walls around the stone, shadows that give these men the appearance of the monsters that they are.

The chorus of cheers eventually dies down as the man in front of me eyes me up like I am a prized steak. I have no doubt what is on his mind, what he intends to do with me.

A loud cry catches my attention, a wail, one of unmistakable heartache and pain. To the far side of the room, another woman is shackled inside a cage like a wild animal had been captured on the plains, ready to be traded. To her side, a child grips her in sheer desperation, and it breaks my heart to even think about the deplorable things that they must have already endured before I arrived.

"Please, let us go," the woman pleads her, voice broken

just as much as her soul. Even from across the room, I can see the emptiness in her eyes.

"Shut up," the man by the cage demands, slamming a metal tankard against the bars. The sound echoes out, causing the two inside to flinch. Beside the cage, I see another, but the men in from of me obscure it from view so I cannot see who is inside.

The woman flinches and the child with her instantly starts to cry. Their skin is dirty and their faces are bloodied from whatever torture these vile creatures have inflicted on them.

"See, what we've done to them, we're going to do to you," the older man tells me. His lecherous face reaches my cheek and he breathes in my scent as though savouring every single moment. If only he knew what he was dealing with. I am not some damsel in distress that will plead for them to stop, for them to go easy on me. I would not allow them to think for one second that I am scared of any of them. If only they knew the things I would do to them if my hands were not bound.

"I reckon this one will fetch a pretty price," the man says, licking the side of my face. My blood runs cold with anger. Who do these bastards think they are?

Instinctively I throw my head forward and enjoy the sound of his crunching nose as it shatters upon the impact.

The others cackle with laughter as the man in front of me howls like a banshee, clasping his hands around his face as blood oozes between the gaps of his fingers.

"Fucking bitch!" he says, his words masked by the hands clasped around his nose and mouth. Rage fills his eyes as he pulls his arm back and throws another punch into my jaw, and I feel the skin of my lip tear as my own blood begins to pour down from my mouth.

It was worth it.

"I'll teach you. We will all teach you, one by one." He reaches out expectantly as another man passes him some cloth which he then presses against his face to stem the bleeding.

"I would like to see you try," I say.

The next few moments pass in a blur as the men circle around me and begin beating me over and over. It's surprising how quickly the pain seems to dampen instead of worsening with each blow. As the room starts to darken again, I am just grateful that my daughter is not here to see this happen to me.

But mark my words, as soon as my hands are unbound, these men will meet their end.

It is only a matter of time.

37

ORJAN

"How are you feeling, old man?" Rior teases me as we continue our journey home to Eltera. We decided against travelling across the Biterian Plains, as the weather conditions are simply too harsh this time of year.

"Less of the old man," I warn him. "I may not have the strength of the lizard man anymore, but I am still as skilled with my mace. Do not tempt me to use it on you, Rior." I give him a menacing smile with only the slightest hint that I may be joking.

"You're forgetting that I can actually see your appearance. You are a lot greyer than I thought you would be. I suppose you aged much better when you had the skin of a lizard. Now your skin just looks like worn leather." He laughs, and the temptation to kick him from his horse is overwhelming, but I avoid that temptation and instead choose to ignore him. I would rather have the appearance of the ageing man that I am than be burdened with that curse another day.

The air we breathe feels crisper and fresher than it ever

has before, and with this being the first day that I find myself free from my curse, I think it is apt to think of this as the best day of my life.

"We should have passed through the plains," Rior moans with a sigh.

"Have I not taught you anything over these years?" I call to him over my shoulder. "The plains would have been far too harsh. Yes, heading east takes longer to get back to Eltera, but I would rather do so in one piece. If a stand storm was to set upon us, we could find ourselves lost in an instant, or worse still, end up as dinner for the wild grouveres who call those lands home."

"You could argue that if we travel a little closer to the Gondoron Pass, we would be in danger as well, so the question is, which path would have been safer?" he fires back in a cocksure manner. That tongue of his will get him into trouble one day. I'm surprised he's not already made more enemies.

He's half right in what he says; there are far too many bandits that now frequent the Gondoron Pass. It wouldn't be safe for the two of us to travel through alone. "We will miss the pass," I say "that's why we head on this route, to the east. Then we'll travel north and get back on track to the main path into Eltera."

"What's that?" Rior nods ahead of us and I follow his gaze.

There is a horse galloping towards us at speed. At first it looks as though its rider has been dismounted, but then I see what looks like a child clinging on for dear life.

"Come," I say as I run towards the horse. Rior follows me, riding by my side. When we reach the horse, I positions myself in front to try and get it to stop. "Woah," I call out, and the horse bucks, then kicks out, skittish in behaviour.

"Get back," the voice of a young girl full of venom threatens us. "I swear to the gods I will end you!"

"She's got spunk," Rior laughs.

"I assure you, child, we mean you no harm," I say, raising my hands to show that I am unarmed. I cast Rior a scowl and he follows suit, raising his hands into the air as well.

The girl has panic and fear etched all over her face. The way her long blond hair is braided tightly against her head reminds of a common Barbaraq hairstyle, which I find peculiar given her accent does not match. Her face is peppered with freckles, and judging by her slender frame, I would put her at about seven or eight years of age.

"They have my mama," she says. "I don't know who they are, but they attacked us. I need to go back, I need to save her! We were in the mountains, I was counting the birds. Something happened and she fell from the horse. They have her!" She speaks quickly and frantically.

"How do we know this is not a trap?" Rior asks. Perhaps he has been listening to me all these years, because part of me fears that this may be a trap, too. However, there is something about this girl that draws me in, and for some reason, I believe her.

"When did this happen? How long have you been running?" I ask her.

"Not long," she says, tears streaming down her face. "I have to go back!"

"And do what, child? We will go with you. Can you remember where this happened?" I ask.

Rior sighs an almighty sigh of disagreement. "Orjan, are you sure this is the right choice? That pass is riddled with slave traders. Think too of our own urgency."

"It is a risk that I am willing to take. You do not need to

follow me into the pass. Although it wasn't that long ago that I remember seeing a child on the streets of Eltera that needed aid."

"You had to go there," Rior retorts.

"Tell me, child, what is your name?" I offer my hand and pull her across to my horse. The one she is riding does not look in a good state. The child doesn't attempt to fight me off, and voluntarily climbs across onto my horse, sitting in front of me.

"Gillam, my name is Gillam," she says as she nestles in front of me.

Without any hesitation, we set off at pace towards the very path that I hoped we would avoid.

Once we are inside the pass, something about the air makes me feel uneasy. It is quiet, far too quiet. We haven't been running too long, but we're far enough in for me to know that we could be walking straight into a trap. The cliff faces on either side of us would be perfect vantage points for any would-be attackers.

"It was around over there," Gillam says, motioning towards a tree in the distance. "I recognise that tree, that's where the attacks came from."

No sooner does she point it out, I notice the blood stain on the floor and I slow my horse down, then hop off and kneel to inspect it. I rub my fingers through it to find that it is still wet, although thickening. Then, further ahead, I see a body on the floor, surrounded by large birds. Thinking this is Gillam's mother, I rush towards it.

"Orjan!" Rior calls after me. I hear him cursing to himself, but I am unsure what it is that he says under his breath.

When I reach the body, the flock of birds scatters, abandoning the carcass they have been pecking at. As I draw closer, I realise that this is not the body of a woman, but the body of a trader. A hatchet is burrowed into his chest. He lies in a pool of his own blood, a fate he no doubt deserved. Fucking slavers are the scum of this world.

"They must be close," I say as Gillam approaches me hurriedly.

"Over here," Rior calls. "There's more blood here." He's right; a trail of blood continues all the way to the cliff's edge. With little else to go on, we follow it until we reach the rock face, then I see some footprints in the dirt from their horses. I count two or three horses at most as we continue to walk along the wall, hopefully keeping out of sight from any prying eyes.

I reach for my morning star and ready myself for a fight. Only the gods know how many of them are here, although after the Barbaraq incursion on Eltera, I have little reason to fear these people. That either makes me arrogant or foolish. Probably both, but I will sleep at night knowing that on this occasion, I've chosen to do the right thing.

When the tracks stop, I know that we are close to their hiding spot. The gust of air that comes from my left draws my attention to a crack in the rocks. This must be where they have made their base. The crack forms all the way up the rock face, splintering towards the top and leaving it open, like a cave.

"Ready?" I ask.

Rior unsheathes his two swords and nods.

"We won't take any chances inside. Gillam, stay by my side at all times. That is the only way I can guarantee your safety. Once inside, if there is an opportunity for you to hide, take it. We will do what we must to try and ensure your mother's safety."

Part of me fears for what we're about to walk into.

Slavers behave like nothing other than savages, and in some sense, perhaps death would be more of a kindness for the girl's mother.

I lead the way, gripping my morning star with both hands, ready to swing at anyone who might jump out and surprise us. The crack in the wall is claustrophobic and confined, barely big enough for a horse to walk though. Ahead of us, I can hear the echoed voices of the people we trail.

A group of men talk to one another with raucous laughter and jeering, but their words are not clear enough for me to decipher. Luckily the wall opens up, allowing us more space to move freely, and I see why this space is perfect for a band of men – if you can call them that – to create a base.

I raise my hand to tell the others to stop as I lean forward and take in the surroundings. This place is not too dissimilar to a tavern like one you would find on the Isle of Voraz. Tables fashioned from barrels are scattered around the room. Crates are stacked up on top of each other, two to three aplenty at the far side of the room. Beside them, cages – some with people in them, some with animals – lend to the noise with the wailings of the people that they have captured and the roars and whimpering of the animals too. Across the top of the walls, rows and rows of leather hides sit in stacks, and a weapons rack is filled to the brim with swords, shields, pikes, bows, crossbows, and other items of different makes and sizes.

A burly man walks up to one of the cages where two women and a child are housed. He has a thick coat, long grey hair, and a short, grey beard adorning his face. Quite frankly, he is an ugly bastard, with a face covered in scars.

"Shut up," he growls, slamming a metal tankard against

the bars. The people inside cower and whimper, then scramble to the other side of the cage. It is clear they are terrified of him. "Unless you want my men to have their fun with you again," he sneers. "Except you, you will fetch a better price if you are fresh." His eyes widen as he addresses the child, who cannot be much older than Gillam.

I feel my anger rising and my knuckles crack as I squeeze the hilt of my morning star. If one thing is for sure, it is that on this day, my morning star will taste the blood of that man.

"Do you see your mother?" Rior asks under hushed breath.

A moment's silence greets us as I continue to survey room. I count at least seven in this band of slave traders.

"Bring the new one here," the burly man demands. His nose is bloodied and swollen. A woman is dragged by two other men into view, her feet trailing behind her. She does not look in a good way; her right-hand side is covered in blood and her blond braided hair is splattered crimson. I can tell by the style of the braid that this is Gillam's mother.

The burly man slaps her across the face, trying to pull her back from unconsciousness. She raises her head and spits in the man's face as he draws level with her. I can already tell I like her; the woman has fight.

"You killed one of my men," he snarls as he gets right into her face. "I think it's only fair that I let the rest of my men do what they want with you."

Sinister jeers echo around us as they plot what they are to do with her. I know we must act quickly if we are to succeed in her rescue.

"Mama!" Gillam cries out loudly as she pushes her way past me.

"Fuck!" I curse to myself. I did not expect the child to do

that. The burly man's gaze meets my own, and his face a picture of surprise and anger.

I rush into the room and try to grab hold of Gillam, but she's just outside my grasp. She ducks under the arm of the nearest slave trader and rushes to her mother's side.

For a moment, the burly man and I stare at one another whilst his men look on in confusion by our sudden arrival.

"Who the fuck are you?" one of the slave traders asks.

"Vengeance," I growl. He has little time to react. The second I reach him, I slam my morning star into the side of his face. With a sickening crunch, his cheek implodes and his blood sprays across the room.

"Get them!" the burly man demands.

Two of the men head in my direction whilst one lunges at Rior. This leaves the two men holding Gillam's mother and the burly man that is clearly their leader.

Rior does not waste any time. He parries away his attacker's blow with ease before driving one sword into his shoulder, then quickly follows up with his second blade, which he runs into the man's stomach. Blood pools in the man's mouth and billows down his chin. Rior quickly remove his blade and kicks the man so that he lies in a heap on the floor. Even I am impressed by the speed with which Rior moves and the skill that he shows with his blades.

My two opponents approach me in tandem, deciding to attack me at the same time. Both lunge for me with their blades, and I use my morning star to parry the first blade away before backhanding the second man across the face with my weapon. He falls to the floor instantly. I may not hold the strength of a lizard man any longer, but I am still strong, and no one can bear that force. Using my momentum, I swing my morning star back into the second man's stomach whilst using my free hand to grab his wrist and prevent him from slicing me open. The spikes of my weapon embed into his stomach and he howls in pain. I pull back my weapon and hit him a second time, then a third in the same spot. On the fourth strike, I drag the morning star across his stomach, spilling his guts where he stands.

"Ooof," the burly man cries out, and when I look up, it is to see that Gillam's mother has kicked him in the chest even as two guards attempt to restrain her. The momentum causes the guards to release her arms and she drops to the floor with the thud, groaning loudly and gasping for air.

Rior and I exchange glances in silent communication, and then we both run at speed towards the men. He dives into the fold, raising both swords above him and then bringing them down into the back of the slaver to the woman's left. With a roar, I swing my morning star down with as much force as I can muster into the centre of the other man's head. I feel his skull collapse under the force, and both men drop to the floor at the same time.

The leader of the group scrambles on the floor like a rat, trying to get away from us as fast as he can.

"You – you can't do this!" he says through hurried breaths. "You have no idea who you are messing with! Do you know who I am?"

But there is nothing he can say that is going to save him. I couldn't give a shit whose bed he lies in.

"You are a coward," I snarl, spittle leaving my mouth like venom.

The burly man continues to scramble backwards away from me until he is stopped by the bars of the cage. No sooner does his back hit the bars, a withered arm reaches out from behind him and wraps around his neck, pulling him tightly against the enclosure.

"I think it is clear that the gods do not favour you, friend," Rior teases the man, but I can tell by his tone that he is as angry with these men as I am. "You are no better than the men that slaughtered my parents. In fact, I'd go as far as saying that you are worse. You are scum."

I glance at Rior, surprised by the mention of his parents. Sometimes his good nature makes me forget the hardships he has been through.

"Please, let me go," the man begs, placing his hands together in front of him as if praying to us like we are his gods.

"We are not going to let you go," I tell him, and I can't help but laugh as I speak. He has just seen us slaughter his men in a matter of seconds with little to no effort. Why would we let him go when he is the reason that they were there? If not for his actions, this situation would not have arisen. The blood that has been spilled is down to him, and no one else.

He has to pay for that.

"I'll let these women decide what to do with you," I tell him, and a look of hope flashes in his eyes, as if he thinks they might spare him. Foolish man.

I help Gillam's mother to her feet, then fetch a dagger from my belt and place it into her hands. "Show no mercy. He does not deserve it," I say.

More hands reach out from within the cage and grab hold of the man as he frantically tries to escape. Gillam's mother steps towards him, slowly and with murderous intent in her eyes.

"This is for these women." She smiles as she buries the dagger into his stomach, then pulls the blade out again. "And this is for me." There is a real venom on her tongue as she plunges the dagger into his groin. He yelps like a dog as she drags the knife upwards, through his groin and into his stomach. His body starts to convulse with shock as his blood pours out around him. And through his panicked eyes the light within them fades, his fate sealed.

Gillam's mother searches the man and fishes the keys from his pockets before unlocking the cage. Then she looks down at the man, stands tall, and spits on him.

"Thank you," she says, turning to face me.

I step back in shock. Hers is a face that I recognise, even though it is one that I have not seen for eight years.

I have seen her before. I saw this woman standing side by side with Laith during the Battle of Opiya, before Rhagor possessed his body. It is clear she doesn't recognise me, and why would she? The last time she saw me, I was covered in scales.

What game are the gods playing?

38

ULRIK

Zerina's face is exactly how I imagined it would look when she learned of what powers this treasure possesses. Her expression is that of concern and horror as she lowers the blade that she had the audacity to press against my throat.

"Ulrik, I know what you intend to do with this. You can't."

"But I can. Look at what we have done, look at what we have achieved. No one of this world has ever believed that this stone exists, but we have proved that it does. Our names will be enshrined in lore for millennia for the things we have found, for the things that we are still yet to do." I cast her a smile, my blood coursing quickly through my veins, in part from the excitement of finding the jewel that I have spent so long searching far, and part from wondering whether Zerina has it in her to slit my throat. For a second, it did cross my mind that she actually might, but now she has lowered her guard.

"This stone, Ulrik . . . If the power it is said to possess is true, then you cannot use it, you cannot bring him back. To do so would upset the balance of nature itself," she protests as she tries to appeal to my rational side. She should know by now that I no longer have a rational side. That part of me died when my brother passed to the afterlife. A place from which I plan on bringing him back. It is the only way I am going to be free of the grief that has consumed me for so long, forced me down a path where I have done unforgivable things, where my heart has become encased in stone.

"Why can't I?" I growl, the heated words pouring out of my mouth like ash from a volcano. "I have lost everything. Why can't I use this treasure to bring me happiness? Why else would such a treasure exist, if not to be used?" I stare into Zerina's large eyes and they quiver at the mere thought of my plan.

"I will do what I must, Ulrik. You can't use that stone. The consequences will be far greater than you can ever understand." With a trembling hand, she raises her dagger again.

Anticipating this, I quickly grab hold of her arm and slam it into the stone table, causing her to drop the blade she seeks to threaten me with. "And I have just about had enough of your mutinous threats," I snarl as I draw her face closer to my own. "It is something that I would not let any other member of this crew get away with, so tell me, Zerina, why should I let you?"

When she raises her other hand to strike me, anger ripples through me at her insolence. Why is it that she does not heed my warnings? I cannot and will not allow her to undermine me like she does. For years she has watched out for me, and in another life I would have seen her as a sister. But in this life, she is insistent on being the thing in between me being reunited with my brother, and that cannot continue. I will not allow her to continue to be a jagged thorn in my side.

Grabbing hold of her striking arm, I hold her firmly in my grasp. "You will not stop me, Zerina. I will not let you get in my way." I squeeze my fingers into her arms and in an instant I know she is weakened. For some reason the gods have stripped her of her magic. If they hadn't, she would be turning my hands into nothing but ash and embers.

"Ulrik, you are hurting me."

"What did you expect? That I would allow you to continue to make threats on my life, to draw blood from me? All you had to do was follow me. Support me." My throat grows hoarse from her betrayal, but it is a pain that I will not allow the rest of the crew to see. "Bind her," I say reluctantly. It is not the path I wanted to take, but she has given me little option.

"Captain, are you sure that is the right thing to do?" Darmour says in a vain attempt to negotiate a truce between us. "Perhaps a bit of space and calm will aid the situation."

I glower at him and something ignites in my mind, that darkened sinister side of me that people insist on pushing me to be. "You do it," I say. "You bind her. I warned you that you will need to make a choice at some point. Here is that moment. Bind her like the mutinous coward that she is, or you will join her, Darmour." I throw Zerina's arms away from her and she looks at me with hurt and anguish.

I feel nothing other than anger in this moment.

"DO IT!" I demand. "Or I swear to the gods, I will strike down each and every one of you. Do you not remember what happened in that last chamber? Not even a stone golem could stop me!"

Zerina shakes as I roar, my voice forcing the birds to flee from the trees above us. She turns to Darmour and raises her arms in front of her. "It's okay, Darmour," she says, "I promised you I would not make you choose."

"Captain, please," Darmour begs.

"Do not make me ask again," I growl.

Reluctantly, Darmour turns to face the crew. "Lerent, fetch me some irons."

A thickly built man grabs the irons from his belt and places them over Darmour's outstretched hook.

Darmour takes Zerina's hand, looking at her tenderly. "I am sorry," he says.

Zerina's head is bowed, but it is what I must do. It is either this, or I end her life here and now, and that is not a depth I am willing to sink to. Perhaps I do possess a soul after all, despite her accusations. Provided that she does not get in my way, it will stay this way. She will remain my prisoner until I have finished with my plan. When my brother walks the sands of this world once more, I will free her, but only then.

Every day, I wake up with a void in my chest, a black hole where my heart used to be. It's been years since I lost my brother, but the pain hasn't lessened; if anything, it's grown, festering and gnawing at me from the inside. Time, they say, heals all wounds, but the passing days only seem to deepen the chasm that his absence has left behind.

For years I have tried to hold on to the memories of him, the sound of his laughter and the warmth of his smile, but those memories of him are slipping through my fingers like grains of sand as time passes, and I'm left grasping at shadows. It's as if the gods are slowly erasing him from my life, and I'm powerless to stop it. I'm haunted by the moments I took for granted, the times I didn't heed his advice, and the petty arguments that now seem so insignificant. How could I have known that one day he'd be gone, leaving me with a lifetime of regret?

The world around us goes on, indifferent to my loss, and it leaves a bitter taste in my mouth. I watch as people laugh and love, enjoying their lives as best they can, oblivious to the darkness that has swallowed me whole. It's an isolating feeling, this grief, as if I'm trapped beneath the surface of a frozen lake, pounding my fists against the ice, desperate to break free but unable to find the strength.

My dreams are haunted by his presence, a cruel reminder of what I've lost. Sometimes, in the moments between sleep and wakefulness, I can almost feel him beside me, as if he's reaching out from beyond the veil, trying to offer me comfort. But then reality comes crashing down, and I'm left with the cold, empty truth: he's gone, and he's never coming back.

Until now.

Now that I have the Resurrection Stone, I can bring him back, and through his resurrection I will finally find a way to heal, to fill the void that has consumed my life. I have been lost, stumbling through the darkness with no map to guide me, and I can't help but think that once he has returned, we can make new memories. Ones that will bring me solace instead of sorrow.

"Come," I say, "we must make our way back to *Esara's Revenge*. We have a long voyage ahead of us."

"Where is it we set a course to, Captain?" Darmour asks reluctantly. His hook is placed around the chains of the irons that bind Zerina. He is downcast, his morale ripped from him.

"Levanthria," I say. "We set sail to Levanthria."

The rest of the crew's faces light up with news that we

are returning to the land we have not visited since before I assassinated King Athos Almerion, years past. I have no clue what state we will find Levanthria in. We last stepped foot on those tarnished lands when Zerina insisted on visiting her family home and making a grave for her sisters.

Thanks to the witch trials, we have no remains of her sisters or my mother, otherwise, with this stone, I would be able to bring them back from the afterlife too. I do, however, have the remains of my brother, having buried him in the village of Osar.

It is here where I will use this stone to bring him back, where I will at last be reunited with him.

"Ulrik, please think on this," Zerina pleads with me, but her words fall on deaf ears. I have no interest in listening to her pleas. This plan has been set in motion for too long, I have worked too hard to get to this point and not go through with it.

"If you are not with me, then you are against me," I say.

It will take us time to travel, but it is a voyage that fills me with excitement like no other has since we first set off in search of the Fountain of Youth when I was just a child.

For the first time since I was that child, I feel alive and find the corners of my cheeks forming a joyous yet wicked smile.

39
VIREO

In the misty valleys of the Grimholt Mountains, the Fachan is whispered to roam - a malformed creature with a single eye, arm, and leg centered in the middle of its twisted body. This abomination is said to possess incredible strength and mobility and harbours a grim taste for human flesh.

- Gregor Yerald, Myths And Monsters, 187KR

"Are you sure that I can count on you?" I ask as Gregor and Leandra ready to leave. Both of them are standing on Gregor's sleigh, Gregor at the front with Leandra behind him, holding onto the sides. "I do not know when my plan will escalate. There is still much to do."

"Know that when the time comes, you will have the aid of my blade," Gregor says. "However, I cannot speak for Leandra," he adds as he unhooks the reins and gives them a tight squeeze. The mist has left us and it looks as though it will be a clear day today, with not a cloud in sight.

"I will also lend aid, although I do not know how effective I will be against a being as powerful as this Rhagor, given that I am now in my human form," Leandra replies.

I grin. "After witnessing your skill with a hatchet, I have no doubt you will play a key part in the coming battle. Are you sure this thing will work?" I look down at the wooden, tooth-shaped pendant hanging from my neck. When I squeeze it gently, I swear I can feel a latent energy pulsating within.

"I assure you, it will work," Gregor laughs. "It is imbued with my power. To activate it, just focus your mind and search for me. It will allow me to trace your location. I can't explain it, but it is a power I have harnessed over the many years."

Gregor pulls on the reins, and as his twelve yakulas stand tall, I take a moment to appreciate their size, strength, and sheer presence. Their huge antlers are of varying shapes, twisting and turning upwards, giving each yakula their own spark of personality. I would certainly not like to get on the wrong side of one of them as they buck and wail loudly. The sheer noise of them crying out together in tandem hits me like thunder in my heart, and I am blown away by these majestic creatures' almost ethereal appearance.

"Where will you go now?" I call over the noise.

"To the mountains. Leandra's clan was wiped out in the battle prior to her curse."

Leandra nods. "My clan's land lies to the north of the Loch in the Ferevour Mountains. Although they may no longer exist, Gregor is going to help me consecrate the grounds, and in doing so, I may find closure. If such a thing exists. Thank you for your help in freeing me from my curse."

"Until we meet again, Vireo," Gregor says, snapping at the reins. "Yah!"

The yakulas heave and set off at once at an alarming speed, and I watch on as Gregor and Leandra head off into the distance, the backdrop of the mountains giving a mesmerising view.

After a short while, I am also packed and ready to leave. Rather than following them to the mountains, my plan is to head into the mainland in search of more people to join my quest. I ready my horse and mount her before surveying the area one final time. I mean the area no disrespect, but I plan on this being the last time I frequent these parts.

I spend the rest of the day riding north. For some reason I feel calmer than usual, my spirits lifted from recruiting Gregor and Leandra to our cause. But we have much more to achieve before we will be ready to face Rhagor.

Towards the end of the day, my lower back is starting to ache, which I take as a sign that I need to rest. After I hop down from my horse, I give her a gentle rub before reaching into my satchel and passing her an apple. She snaffles the apple without hesitation and I walk with her on the path, looking for a shaded area for us to rest. We travel to the pass that is south of Askela. From there, my plan is to head east across the shoreline. Perhaps when I reach Osar, I will visit Yaelor and Gillam. I will not see them in person, but perhaps I can watch from the shadows to see that they are both okay. It has been three years since I last visited, not that either of them know. We agreed that it was not safe for us to be seen together, not after everything we went through to find Yaelor somewhere safe to live.

After the Barbaraq attacks on Eltera and Uster, we needed to find a town that would not only forgive but also forget, somewhere where Yaelor's Barbaraq upbringing would not betray her to the locals. We provided her with enough coin to enable her housing and to start her new life.

Across the pathway, I see a heavily shaded area where we will be able to rest for an hour or two. I want to get another couple of hours of riding in before I make camp, and this open path is not ideal. I would be a sitting duck for a bandit attack.

When I reach the shaded area, I tie my horse's reins around a tree that stands beside a small rock formation where I make myself comfortable. Leaning back, I rest my eyes for a moment and find myself lost in thought as the gentle downwind from the pass hits me. I take a few moments to think over everything I have been through since leaving Askela, everyone I have met and lost, everyone I have affected.

The air tastes bare here, most likely because of the lack of plant life in these parts. I have lived in the forest for so long, I have become used to the earthy smells as well as the scent of wildflowers and vibrant trees. This is the longest I have ever been away from the forest.

I miss it.

With my eyes closed, I can see the campsite, hear the laughter of the children and banter from the men and women who have made the forest their home.

The sound of a horse and cart forces me to snap my eyes open. From where I am sitting, I can make out two people perched at the front of the carriage. I quickly scan them for Askelan colours, but to my relief, this does not appear to be a caravan. Still, I must keep my wits about me.

The cart has seen better days. Its large wooden wheels are cracked with spokes missing, and it wobbles precariously as a woman steers the cart down the hill.

As they draw close, I step out and raise my hand. I don't

know if they have seen the wheel, especially the one closer to me, but it looks ready to fall off.

"Woah," I say, lowering my hood; I do not want these people to think that I am a bandit.

The woman pulls on the reins tightly and the two horses buck, causing the cart to skid to a halt with its wheel sitting at an odd angle.

"What in the gods!" the woman says in a northern accent. She has long, wavy brown hair that sits on her shoulders. Her face is malnourished, with patches of dirt speckled across her skin. Her clothes are tattered and torn, and her dress is a diminished, pale blue. To her right sits a girl who looks to be around five years old. Her hair is cut short and the colour matches that of who I presume is her mother. She looks panicked to see me, and I wonder why a woman and child would be travelling alone this far south, so far from any settlements.

"I can only apologise," I start with a smile. "You see, I notice your wheels are not sat well on your cart, and I fear that if you are to carry on much further, you risk one if not both of them being damaged beyond repair. Take it from me, you do not wish to remain in this area for long. It is rife with bandits." I give a look behind me and shrug my shoulders. "Although I have not come across any on my travels."

The woman leans back and looks over her shoulder at the wheel. It is leaning inwards, towards the body of the cart. "Fuck!" she says, before looking at her daughter. "Sorry," she says. She turns her attention back to me. "Don't try anything fishy."

I raise my hands in the air and say, "I can assure you that I mean you no harm." I laugh to myself. The number of times I have had to say this line over the years when we robbed caravans of their wares gives me a sense of irony.

"Something funny?" the woman says, stony-faced and untrusting. I do not blame her, I could just as easily be the very bandit that I am warning her of.

"Listen, I am travelling north," I tell her. "I have merely stopped to allow my horse to rest." I point at my horse which remains tethered to the small tree, grazing on the short, dried grass. "If you wish, I can see if I can help repair your wheels and send you on your way. It will be dark in just a few hours, and I would not like to see you stuck out here."

The woman continues to eye me up suspiciously, and her daughter clings tightly to a doll that sits on her lap.

"My name is Vi –" I stop myself. My name is well known across Levanthria, and I do not know this woman. "Vincent. My name is Vincent."

"Hmm," the woman murmurs. "And you have the means to fix my wheels?"

"Well, I only have these," I say as I show her my hands. "Do you perhaps have any tools that I can use?"

"Should be some in the back of the cart," she says, gesturing to the empty crates.

"Then I shall get to work. The sooner I can fix them, the sooner you can be on your way," I say.

I have completely lost track of time by the time I finish with the second of the damaged wheels. They still remain in poor condition, but at least now they do not sit so loosely.

"That should about do it," I say as I walk to the front of the cart where the woman and her daughter sit. "Make sure you take it easy though. If you hit any rocks, those wheels may not hold up. They will need to be repaired properly when you reach wherever you are going."

"That would assume we have some coin to barter with,"

the woman says hastily. "There is not exactly plenty going around."

Her daughter shivers and the woman takes her shrug from her shoulders and wraps it around the girl.

"Where is it you are travelling? There is nothing in this direction for you."

"Except there is," she says. "I've seen a ship, making berth in the cove beyond the woodlands to the southeast of here. My husband, Hugo – gods rest his soul – normally trades with them. It has been so many years though since the ship was last seen, I thought it had been lost to the depths of the ocean."

"I am sorry for your loss," I say, bowing my head as a mark of respect.

"Nothing to apologise for," she says. "It's not like it's your fault Levanthria is in the state that it is in."

"If you don't mind me asking, what happened to your husband?"

"He was a trader. We didn't live a plush life, but we were able to get by. He used to travel down these parts. He had made contact with the ship's captain, and he would give them coin for wares that he could fetch and sell at a profit."

"Why make port there?" I ask, but then it dawns on me. There is only one reason that they would trade from a hidden cove and keep away from the main ports in Levanthria. "Pirates," I say.

The woman lowers her eyes, then raises them defiantly. "You can't judge us. There is no money, no riches, only poverty in these lands. My husband Hugo did what he needed to keep us fed and a roof over our heads."

"I do not judge," I say with a smile as I continue to listen to the woman. "Why is it you put yourselves in danger travelling this path?"

"I have no choice," she says, "they came, they took Hugo away. That monster Codrin, he had him flayed and paraded around like he was a murderer when all he had done was trade some trinkets and artefacts that he had sourced from his contact." The woman's eyes well with tears as she relives her pain. I understand the loss of loving someone so close to the heart and it brings back haunting memories of my own.

"The pirate ship you are going to see? Is this a risk worth taking?" I ask. "If it cost your husband his life, then why risk that of yours and your child?" Something seems odd. Why would Codrin react this way, why would he concern himself with the actions of a trader, even if it did involve pirates? This is not something he would usually involve himself in.

"I have no choice, we need coin for food, our house is crumbling, and I fear that we will not survive the coming months. I need to take this opportunity. If *Esara's Revenge* is going to make berth more regularly, I can offer to sell their wares and keep some of the gold for our troubles. This is how my husband always worked. The captain is an angry bastard, but his first mate understands how to run this side of things. I think his name is Darmour."

"*Esara's Revenge?*" I repeat, the hairs on my arm spiking. I have heard of the ship from the stories that reach me in the forest. I also heard about the fierce Captain Ulrik and the witch that accompanies him, Zerina, firsthand from Jordell. He told me that she was the most powerful witch that he had come across, that she had found a way to unlock her full potential and that somehow the use of magic did not affect her the same as it did anyone else who could wield the latent power. This must be a sign. If they are not far from here, I could perhaps speak with Zerina and ask for her assistance. As pirates, I can only assume they are opposed to the king. With Zerina's help, it would compensate for the loss of Jordell. I have heard about the king's keep, deep in the heart of Zarubia, how she single-handedly brought destruction down on the advancing Zarubian forces. The same battle that saw King Athos Almerion perish. That is a power that would certainly help against Rhagor.

"I can't allow you to put yourself or your child at risk, however I am in need of a guide to the cove where this ship makes berth." I reach into my tunic and pull out a bag of coins. I have more in my satchel but it would be foolish of me to give them all away. "How does thirty gold coins sound?"

The woman's eyes light up with a ravenous hunger.

"You take me to the ship, then you head home with your daughter. This should be more than enough to keep you both well fed and have your house repaired."

"With thirty gold we wouldn't need to return to Askela. We would be able to make a new home for ourselves somewhere else, somewhere as far away from those bastards Codrin, Morgana, and Rhagor." She spits on the ground at the very mention of their names.

I toss the bag to her and she catches it with open arms before opening the bag and pulling out one of the coins. She bites onto it as if they are made of wood.

"You offer us a kindness, sir, one that I no longer expect to see in Levanthria."

"Come, I will ride beside you on my horse. If you could just show me the location of this ship and then be on your way. As I said, the sooner you leave this place, the better.

How far do we have to travel?" We do not have too much time before the sun will begin to set.

"Oh not far from this point, no more than an afternoon's ride, I think."

The last few days have proven fruitful. I can only hope that Zerina and Ulrik will be willing to join my cause.

For the first time in a long time, I start to feel a spark of hope.

40

RHAGOR

In Levanthria and beyond, the gods are powerful beings who shape reality. They command vast domains and legions of followers, granting boons to those who curry their favor. However, their blessings are often double-edged, as the gods are capricious and their motives inscrutable.

-Woranspine Silverleaf, On the Nature of the Gods, 128 KR

My heart races, a tremor surging around my body. Is this nervousness or excitement? I am not sure, but one thing I do know is that this next part is going to be fun.

I close my eyes and take a deep inhale through my nose, savouring the scent of the trees that line the outer perimeter of the Forest of Opiya. A fresh breeze blows against my face. Above, the setting sun leaves a haunting, purple hue in the night sky. My shadow stretches far ahead of me, reaching into the grounds that I have avoided for the last eight years, until now.

For so many years, this forest was the home of my prison. All the time that passed whilst I was frozen did not mean that I was unaware of that time passing. I take another deep breath, then step into the trees on the way from the setting sun. I have bided my time until this moment, and it angers me that my plan has been hastened because of Morgana's scheming. I was going to wait until I had that amulet in my possession, but needs must.

When I enter the forest, the first thing I notice is the smell. Sweet and floral, a hint of honey, perhaps, mixed with the cedar of the trees. Most would find it quite warming, almost welcoming, but I find it a reminder of everything that is wrong with this world. I spit on the floor, then continue my journey. I hasten my footsteps, wanting to be here for as little time as possible.

For hours I walk with nothing more than my darkened thoughts for company. I stew on the memories that brought me to this moment, on all the ways that I have been mistreated, how I was imprisoned, disregarded like I was nothing more than the shit that lines the streets of Askela. Time seems to pass slowly in this place, something that I'm all too familiar with.

At long last, the Elder Tree stands before me. It is far greater, far taller than one could ever truly describe, reaching high into the clouds. It is as though its branches are a ladder to the gods. The bark is cracked and aged. It has witnessed the very growth, the very birth of this landscape, and I fume as I stare deep into its cracks and crevices. Despite the tree's age, its branches stretch out far and wide and high, still decorated with luscious green leaves larger than a man, with flowers larger than a goat.

I walk towards the tree and place my hand against the rough bark. It grounds me more than I thought it would. I can feel the energy pulsating from deep within it, I can sense the magic that extends deep into the ground through its roots. This tree is the centre of everything. It is the lifeblood of the magic that runs through these lands.

"I was wondering how long it would take you to visit," a well-spoken, soft accent greets me from behind. I do not need to turn around to know who it is. "What is it that draws you here?"

"Hello, sister," I say with sarcasm. "I would say it's great to see you, but we both know that would be a lie." I turn to see the pale blue skin of the fae queen herself. "Zariah," I say, "you haven't aged a day." A smile erupts on my face as I raise my arms out wide as if expecting her to embrace me.

Zariah stands firm, her green eyes fixed on me. Her pointed ears remind me of my former body, my true form. Her hair is a dark, pristinely woven tapestry that falls far down her back. A crown made of branches adorns her head. She remains unmoved, almost stern in her demeanour, but she has not changed at all from what I remember. She was fierce then, and I imagine she is still fierce now.

Zariah tilts her head slowly from one side to the other as if examining my face for every detail. She remains silent, with nothing but the rustling leaves disrupting the tension between us.

"Your face may have changed, brother, but I would recognise your essence anywhere," she says.

My arms still outstretched, I ask, "Now Zariah, are you not going to give your dear brother a hug? After all, it's been so long."

Zariah does not move. "I will repeat the question, *dear* brother."

"Zariah, Zariah, Zariah, is there such a need to treat your brother with such hostility?" I ask with a jovial tone. "After all, it has been so long, there was me thinking that you would be happy to see me."

She continues to stare me down like a sworn enemy whom she would not trust with any morsel of her being. "If it was not the fact that you are my brother, you would already be dead for the chaos that you have caused in this world." Her soft tone is like ice.

I turn to face the Elder Tree once again and rub my hand slowly down the bark. "Isn't she a thing of beauty? I often wondered how this tree's powers worked. Why our mother planted it in the first place. You should hear the stories that they tell in Levanthria. The scribes believe that mother planted it when I killed you. If only they knew the truth." I cast her a smile that is both sinister and dark.

"What do you want, Rhagor? Why are you here?" Her eyes remained fixed firmly on me. "You know it is considered amongst my people to be a crime to show the Elder Tree such disrespect."

I give her a feigned look of concern, but I step away from the tree. "And some would consider it blasphemous to imprison their own blood in stone for two millennia." My voice grumbles and the earth beneath me shudders as I talk.

"You were out of control. You were –" she pauses for a moment, then corrects herself – "you are a monster. You thrive off the pain and suffering of others. You are the opposite of everything that I stand for in this life, in this world."

"My sweet, innocent sister," I laugh, "what is it that you expect from the God of Chaos?"

"The last time I checked, you were not a god any longer, Rhagor."

Anger surges through me from the manner in which she dares speak to me, and I slam my fist into the Elder Tree, causing pieces of the bark to fall from it. "I am in this form because of you," I hiss, "because of what you and our mother did to me."

"What would you expect our mother to do when she found you standing over my dead body?"

"Yet here you stand. I must admit, sister, it took me a long time to realise that you still walked these lands, that you had returned to this world despite me using this very sword to cut out your heart."

I look up at the Elder Tree, my gaze raking across its thick bark, following it to the base of the trunk and the ginormous roots that bury themselves into the ground. Then I meet my sister's eyes.

It took me a long time to piece it all together. I've had plenty of time to read the literature that the world has to offer. And through the stories that have passed down from one generation to the next, from one scribe to another, as codex upon codex was formed documenting the history of the world over the last two millennia, I slowly started to piece it together.

"For two thousand years, our mother thought it fit to leave me encased in stone, despite it being you who threw the first punch. You who was the one that tried to end me. Tell me, Zariah does she know that, did you ever tell her?" It is impossible to hide my disdain as I speak, and I slam my fist into the bark of the Elder Tree once again.

"I did what I had to do. I had to try and stop you. You did not listen, you are incapable of negotiation. I will do what I must to ensure that balance remains in this world."

With this, she lowers her hand and rests it on the hilt of the blade that sits on her waistline.

I can't help but muster a laugh. "This did not end well for you last time," I tell her. I look around the forest, making a show of searching for something. "Mother didn't stop me from cutting out your heart then, and I don't see her around now. She may have found a way to resurrect you, but I assure you, I know what magic she wields. I know the lifeblood that courses through you, and I know how to stop your resurrection from happening ever again."

I look at the Elder Tree once again, then reach for my sword which is strapped to my back. "Your move, I guess."

Zariah does not hesitate. She sprints towards me at alarming speed, catching me off guard. There is no sign of anger in her eyes, no amount of malice etched into her expression. In her eyes, she is merely doing what she must.

Unfortunately for her, so am I.

In a flash, she draws on her blade and takes a wild swipe towards me. I barely have a chance to step out of the way as her blade flies past me, closer than I would have liked. Before I have a chance to do anything, she's already spun on the spot and is taking another swipe, this time trying to cleave my head from my body. Apparently she wants a quick and swift end to this fight.

I, however, want to draw this out. I want it to last as long as possible so that I can savour her last breaths. It is no less than what she deserves. Twice now she has made the mistake of trying to land the first blow. Her spin continues and she tries to detach my head once more, but I draw my weapon and bring it down in front of me, blocking the strike. Sparks fly between us as we come face to face for the first time.

She is stronger than I remember, but then again, she

has had two millennia to practise, and I wonder if she spent all this time in preparation for my return, waiting for this moment.

I push her back before I raise my sword high above my head and bring it down towards her. This time it is her turn to block, and I let out a roar as I bring my sword down again and again and again, each time increasing the power that I choose to exert.

She blocks each blow and sparks continue to splash at our feet as a grimace of strain falls on her face. She may be strong, but she is not as strong as me, and she knows it. If she is to win this game, she's going to have to find another way to outsmart me, to beat me.

Out of nowhere, she flips backwards, kicking my blade up into the sky above us and I lose my grip on the hilt. As her first foot kicks the blade, her second foot hits me square in the chin, sending me backwards into the trunk of the Elder Tree. She moves like a dancer as she holds the hilt of her weapon against her forearm. With the blade tracing her arm to her elbow, she crouches, placing her free hand onto the ground, waiting for my next move.

My sword lands with a thud in the ground a few feet away from me.

I raise the back of my hand towards my lip to see that blood has been drawn. The taste of iron spills into my mouth, and the moment she sees blood, my sister's face lights up with anticipation.

"You are mortal," she says.

"Don't let that fool you into thinking that you can beat me," I growl, my anger continuing to surge. I don't have a weapon, and so I know it would be foolish to lose my temper and rush Zariah. Instead, I lift both hands in anticipation of her next move. It would appear that her drawing first blood has also caused her to drop her guard. She would be a fool to think I am the one at a disadvantage.

Zariah approaches me at speed once more, apparently thinking she has the upper hand. She lets out a roar of anger as she swipes her blade at me, but this time I am quick to it. Rather than waiting for her to reach me, I take a step forward and grab hold of her hand holding the blade, anticipating a frustrated strike from her free hand. I am right, and she tries to strike me across the face, but I use my other hand to grab her fist and squeeze it tightly. We stand rooted to the spot, desperately trying to outmanoeuvre the other, but both of us stand as firm and resolute as the Elder Tree behind me. I continue to squeeze her clenched fist tightly until eventually I feel the crack of a bone underneath my grasp. My sister lets out a groan of pain.

Sensing the opportunity, I quickly snap her wrist, forcing her to let go of her weapon, and then I slam a full fist straight into her jaw, flinging her straight into the earth. Stepping onto the hand that holds the blade, I press down heavily, and Zariah lets out another groan of pain as she releases her grip on her sword.

"Now, now, sister, I must say I'm a little disappointed," I goad her with a wide grin on my face, my eyes wide at the spectacle. "Imagine training all that time to be bested so easily by your unarmed, mortal brother." I press down even harder on her hand with my boots. She cries out in pain, and I hear more bones crunch under my strength. I may be mortal, but I am far stronger than any man across Levanthria.

"You cannot kill me. You can strike me down as many times as you wish, you can bury me as deep as you want, but nothing will stop me from rising up from the ground once again, just as I have done the last time you murdered me." Tears of frustration well in her eyes and they sparkle under the luminous lights that this enchanted forest brings.

I let up off her wrist and hear her sigh a breath of relief. I look around for where my sword landed. It is embedded into the dirt, its golden hilt glistening as if it calls to me.

"That's interesting that you should say that. You see, I've developed a theory, and in truth, that is why I am here." Reaching down, I grab Zariah's blade and toss it from one hand to the next. The metal of the hilt is cold, and the blade itself is remarkably light, the blade twisting as it rises to cause maximum damage to anyone it pierces. Without hesitation, I raise the blade high into the air, then slam it into my sister's back, skewering her to the ground until the hilt of the blade reaches her skin.

Zariah lets out an agonising scream of pain. She may have immortality for now, but she is not invulnerable.

"Seems like I'm not the only one that can bleed. Be a darling and stay there." I clap my hands together slowly, as if brushing dust from the palms of my hands. Then I walk over to my sword and grab its hilt, feeling its power surge through me, energising me. The throbbing in my lip fades in an instant. I look at my sister writhing on the ground as she claws desperately and pathetically in vain at the hilt that protrudes from her back. Deep, purple-like crimson blood pools around her. My gaze wanders from her to the Elder Tree, then back to her, where I meet her eyes and give her a sickening smile of satisfaction.

Even through her pain, she tries to smirk at me with triumph. "I've already told you. If you kill me, I will just rise again."

"Oh yes, my theory." It is as if I've forgotten my thoughts. "Well, it's funny you should mention this resurrection that you seem capable of, because my understanding is that when a god kills a god, there is no such thing as an afterlife. They simply disappear, yet here you are. And the funny thing is, the only thing that has changed in this forest since I killed you last time is this tree."

I look at the old bark. It must be two thousand years old, which would be precisely how long I was held captive in my stone prison. I channel my anger into my blade and it ignites into flames. The heat is ferocious and fierce as I feel the power surging all around me as though I am in the midst of a storm.

"No," Zariah pleads as realisation seems to dawn on her. "You can't do this, brother. I beg you. To do so would risk changing the face of magic across this land, including the protection it offers from the outside world."

I cast her another smile. "Dear sister, that is what I'm hoping for."

With this, I slam my sword into the base of the Elder Tree with as much force as I can muster. The blade buries deep into the trunk, and as I channel my magic, a blast of flames erupts into the tree.

My sister shrieks in agony behind me and I know in an instant that my theory is true. Her life essence is linked to this tree. In killing the tree, I will indeed kill her.

"Please stop!" Zariah begs, but I have no interest in her pleas. Because of her, our mother trapped me, and in that our mother let me know that Zariah was her favourite. And that is why she will be the first to die. Mother will feel the pain of losing her dear daughter.

Ignoring my sister, I pull out the blade, then take another wild swing at the tree, this time bedding it even deeper. I repeat this again and again and again, until the trunk of the tree is fully aflame and the smoke is rising into the night sky.

"What have you done?" my sister screams as the flames climb higher and higher, the tree squealing as if it too feels agonising pain.

"Don't you see, Zariah? This is the beginning of the end."

My plan is now in motion.

I walk past my flailing sister, my surroundings lit up by the burning tree, and begin to make my way back to Askela.

All I need now is for Codrin to find that blasted amulet. And then I will be able to exact the revenge I have desired for so long.

PRE-ORDER

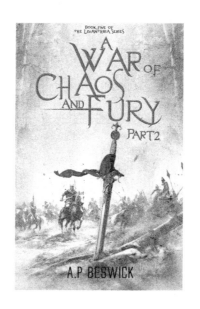

Get Ready For The Epic Conclusion
September 2024
Pre-Order HERE

You can also buy from
www.apbeswickpublications.com
www.Amazon.com

JOIN MY NEWSLETTER

Join my newsletter and keep unto date on all my upcoming projects as well as behind the scenes updates direct from me.

You can join HERE